The Cue for Passion

The Cue for Passion

GRIEF AND ITS POLITICAL USES

Gail Holst-Warhaft

HARVARD UNIVERSITY PRESS

Cambridge, Massachusetts
London, England   2000

Library of Congress Cataloging-in-Publication Data

Holst-Warhaft, Gail, 1941–
    The cue for passion : grief and its political uses / Gail Holst-Warhaft.
       p.   cm.
    Includes bibliographical references and index.
    ISBN 0-674-00224-5 (alk. paper)
      1. Mourning customs—Political aspects.   2. Grief—Political aspects.
    I. Title.
GT3390 .H65   2000
393′.9—dc21   00-021841

For Zoe and Simon

Acknowledgments

I owe thanks to many people who have read this book in its various earlier incarnations and offered advice and encouragement. In particular I thank Margaret Alexiou, Cynthia Chase, David Curzon, Gregory Dobrov, Michael Fishbane, Sander Gilman, Elliot Ginsburg, Lorraine Helms, Michael Herzfeld, Iakovos Kambanellis, Chana Kronfeld, David McCann, Sarah McKibben, Paul Muldoon, Spyros Orfanos, Carlos Rodríguez Matos, Keith Taylor, Sidney Tarrow, Susan Tarrow, James Winn, James Young, and the Institute for the Humanities at the University of Michigan, which invited me to present a paper based on some of the material in Chapter 2.

Research for this book began while I was a fellow at the Society for the Humanities at Cornell University. I thank its director, Dominick LaCapra, and the fellows of the year 1996–97 for their stimulating discussions. I thank Daniel Fireside for interpreting and facilitating my discussions with two of the mothers of the "disappeared" of Argentina, Elsa Santí de Manzoti and Evel Aztarbe Petrini, and with members of the Guatemalan "Organization of Widows." I also wish to thank Georgette King and Angel Sierra, of AIDSWORK, for information about the Ithaca community, and Caroline Spicer, reference librarian at Cornell's Olin Library, for her invaluable help.

Lastly, I thank my dear, demanding reader, Zellman.

Contents

The Cue for Passion

Introduction: The Theater of Mourning

O, what a rogue and peasant slave am I!
Is it not monstrous that this player here,
But in a fiction, in a dream of passion,
Could force his soul so to his own conceit
That from her working all his visage wann'd,
Tears in his eyes, distraction in his aspect,
A broken voice, and his whole function suiting
With forms to his conceit? And all for nothing!
For Hecuba!
What's Hecuba to him, or he to Hecuba,
That he should weep for her? What would he do,
Had he the motive and cue for passion
That I have? He would drown the stage with tears
And cleave the general ear with horrid speech,
Make mad the guilty and appall the free,
Confound the ignorant, and amaze indeed
The very faculties of eyes and ears.

Hamlet, II.ii.550–566

*H*AMLET, LIKE MOST TRAGEDIES, is an exploration of death, grief, and mourning. Mourning is, of its nature, theatrical. Grief is an emotional state most of us experience at some point in our lives. How we display that grief, how we act it out in public, or how others act it out for us is what mourning and its rituals are about. Hamlet's problem is not a dilemma; his rhetorical questions are a bid for time. His failure to translate his "motive and cue for passion" into some outward display, so that the "forms" and "function" of grief match, is what appalls him. It is clear to the prince, seeing an actor lose himself in imagining the crazed grief of Hecuba, that his own performance of grief is incommensurate with the injury he has suffered. The only gesture of mourning that fits his "cue for passion" is violent action.

As he watches the actor "in a dream of passion," Hamlet is not only moved; he is jealous. He is the one who should be able to weep, but something prevents him. The mourning that should have followed his father's death is tainted, the state of Denmark is "rotten," his mother "stewed in corruption," his uncle a "mildewed ear." While the king's murderer holds on to the spoils of his crime, while he sits on the throne beside Hamlet's mother and sleeps in her bed, how can mourning be performed? Hamlet's own grief is tainted by his imagination, his dreaming that strays from grief to disgust and self-loathing. But in his vacillating and unstable state he is recognized as a dangerous creature, something to be removed from society, destroyed before his smoldering passion ignites.

The passion of grief is volatile. The rites of mourning, whether generated from within or imposed from above, are a society's means of performing and containing it. If there is a reason not to contain grief—if rage serves some purpose, becomes political *outrage*—then it may be translated into violence. Revolutions and riots often begin with a funeral. In our time we have witnessed such eruptions at the the funerals of IRA supporters, *Intifada* fighters, the Ayatollah Khomeini. Kings, governments, and political activists have all understood the danger and political potential of extreme grief and have sought to control or channel it. The manipulation and management of grief through mourning rituals are both the essence of tragedy and a theatrical exercise.

The thin line that divided funerals from tragedy was graphically represented in the Elizabethan theater. When a tragedy was performed, the canopy that projected over the stage was traditionally draped in black in imitation of the draperies that decorated churches during heraldic funerals.[1] The doubling of funeral and theatrical representation of funeral is hinted at in the opening lines of the *Henry VI* trilogy when Bedford speaks at the funeral of Henry V (I.i.1): "Hung be the heavens with black, yield day to night!"

During the Elizabethan age, the heraldic funeral came increasingly under state control through the offices of the College of Arms: "Its costly furnishings were regularly imposed from above upon an increasingly truculent aristocracy . . . for the heraldic funeral served the crown's purposes. In presenting the arms and achievements of the deceased to his legitimate heir, the heralds affirmed stratification and stability."[2] In the egalitarian oligarchy of the early Greek city-states, there was a similar attempt to bring mourning under state control. Again, the purpose was to contain mourning, but the means were different. By limiting the expenditure at funerals and preventing noisy public displays of grief by women mourners, Athens and other democratic cities tried to prevent the violence that had led to blood feuds in their recent past, and to minimize the display of difference between citizens. In Athens as in Elizabethan England, the boundary between the tragic theater and the funeral's staging of mourning was often blurred.

The tragic heroines who dominate ancient tragedy are object lessons in the violent power of grief. Electra, Antigone, and, above all, Medea remind an audience that the very foundations of society may crumble if grief is unappeased. As she watches her mother, Clytemnestra, and her mother's lover, Aegisthus, rule Mycenae, Electra, like Hamlet, is tormented by grief but has no satisfactory way to mourn. Clytemnestra's nightmare that she is suckling a snake prompts her to send Electra to her father's tomb with offerings in an attempt to appease the spirit of the man she and her lover have slaughtered in his bath. Electra is well aware that the libations she pours are an abominable travesty of mourning rituals:

> What shall I say as I pour out these outpourings
> of sorrow? How say the good word, how make my prayer
> to my father? Shall I say I bring it to the man
> beloved, from a loving wife, and mean my mother? I
> have not the daring to say this, nor know what else
> to say, as I pour this liquid on my father's tomb.
> Shall I say this sentence, regular in human use:
> "Grant good return to those who send you these flowers
> of honor: gifts to match the . . . evil they have done."
> Or, quiet and dishonored, as my father died
> shall I pour out this offering for the ground to drink,
> and go, like one who empties garbage out of doors,
> and turn my eyes and throw the vessel far away.
>   (*Libation Bearers* 87–99, trans. Lattimore)

The title of Aeschylus' play, the earliest of the three classical treatments of Electra's story, reminds us what lies at the heart of his tragedy. *The Libation Bearers* is a play about mourning rituals, laments for the dead, and their capacity to incite revenge. In Greek tragedy we are presented with a series of spectacles that warn us of the dangers of unappeased grief, but the very nature of the performance, confined as it is in time and space, distanced by its mythical setting in an age as remote to the Greeks as Elsinore to the Elizabethans, sets a limit on our vicarious emotional response. The rituals of mourning themselves have less distance. They are theatrical in the sense that they perform grief for an audience, turning formless tears into artful song, choreographing movement and gesture, designing costume. They may be thought of as a sort of prototheater, where the chorus surrounds and contains the protagonists, interpreting their inarticulate grief.

The almost universal art of mourning is usually performed by women. It can be argued that ritual and art are two very different things, that, say, the laments of modern Greek villagers and the laments of the chorus in Aeschylus have little in common. When Aeschylus creates a scene of mourning, he may employ some of the language and gestures of women's mourning to affect the audience, but he is using his art to "play" with the audience's emotions. Laments, by contrast, are part of the rituals of death. They are an expression of genuine grief. Still, they are artful and manipulative. The women who sing laments today in some parts of the world, like those who once performed them in many parts of Europe, are frequently not the immediately bereaved. The use of professional mourners who beat their breasts, wept, and tore their hair out at funerals was so widespread in Europe and the Middle East, so frequently condemned and yet persistent, that it must have filled an important social need to see grief performed.

The passionate, theatrical expression of grief in lament has always been measured in the same sense that an actor's performance is measured. Hamlet, envying the player king his "passion," knows that even the mimesis of it can be overdone: "For in the very torrent, tempest, and, as I may say, whirlwind of your passion, you must acquire and beget a temperance that may give it smoothness" (III.ii.6–8).

Just as the actor must temper passion if he is to convey it, so the blues singer, the dancer of flamenco, the elegist, the singer of laments, and all the other artists who interpret grief and pain must exercise control even while arousing a passionate response. Similarly, within the theatrical space of the funeral, a certain order must be maintained so that mourning rituals can be performed to their full effect. Funeral ritual or theater, the lines must be heard, the action choreographed. The emotional spectacle is always enacted for an audience.

The Political Uses of Grief

Because it arouses passion, grief can always be manipulated for political ends. It may be positively harnessed as a means to effect political change, and it may be callously prolonged and exacerbated. Institutions, secular and religious, have periodically sought to control the rituals of death and mourning for their political purposes. In our own age we have seen an increasing manipulation of grief by the media, by professional counselors of the bereaved, by the creators of a spate of monuments and museums designed as sites for communal mourning, and by the funeral industry. What effect has this had on the way people mourn? Are there modern rituals of mourning that have replaced older, traditional ways of expressing grief and "working through" it? Have we renounced any agency in dealing with mourning, or are there ways we can individually or collectively respond to the death of relatives and friends?

The modern psychoanalytic literature of grief and mourning, beginning with Freud and continuing through Lacan and others, has paid relatively little attention to traditional practices surrounding death and mourning in pre-industrial society, practices that demonstrate surprisingly little variety across cultures.[3] The insistence on individual psychological processes of coping with mourning, institutionally supported but not collective, may be an unavoidable concomitant of our modern urban condition, but it does not preclude an examination of older, more universal approaches to mourning that appear to have achieved a communal as well as a personal resolution of grief. It would be naive to think that such an inquiry could result in a "theory" of grief or encourage some return to earlier forms of expressing the pain of death. The most one can hope for, in such an inquiry, is that it may throw some light on the way grief is managed in our times, on how the performance of mourning is controlled and manipulated by others.

Freud (1957) believed that if the "work" of mourning was to be successful, the boundary between the self and the other had to be clearly drawn from infancy. The absence of the ones we love could then be tolerated and a substitution eventually made. If the boundary was not clearly drawn, the grief of separation could never be fully accepted. The result would be an unhealthy avoidance of mourning and a lingering state of depression or melancholia. The traditional rituals that performed mourning may well have had the effect on the bereaved of "working through" their grief. At funerals in numerous societies, women's tearful songs or laments for the dead were followed by feasting, games, and dancing. The same people who were tearing their hair and scratching their faces in grief were expected to sit and eat their fill when their songs of mourning had ended. To this day in many societies, the practice of exhuming the bones of the dead and reburying them in an ossuary or urn marks the end of a period of grieving and the beginning of a new acceptance of death. Sometimes grief is held onto for a particular reason. In the death of an elderly person there is nothing unexpected to complicate grief, and open displays of grief by the mourners are followed by a process of reintegration into society. But when a man is murdered, or a girl dies shortly before marriage, or when a man disappears in war and his bones cannot be found, grief may be prolonged indefinitely.

Prolonged Grief: A Threat to Social Order

Most societies have developed customs or "markers" to indicate the special nature of the period of mourning. Other markers and ceremonies inform the bereaved and the rest of the community that the temporary isolation of mourning is over. The emotional state of the bereaved is regarded as potentially dangerous; they are considered in need of special care and restraint. If care is not taken, if grief is artificially inflamed or prolonged, or if the expected conclusion is never satisfactorily achieved, the temporary chaos of death and mourning can spill over into the society at large and threaten its stability. A very few societies based on the deliberate inflammation of grief have managed to survive. The headhunters of the New Guinea Highlands and the vendetta societies of rural Sicily, Corsica, and Mani (the central prong of the southern Peloponnese) are groups that have translated grief into cycles of violent retribution. For most of our own century, the Italian government has tried unsuccessfully to put an end to the violence of the mafia, which has carried the laws of vendetta into the international arena of business and crime and frequently threatened the stability of Italian society. For such groups a funeral is always a central event. The intensity of emotion displayed by the mourners is a resource to be drawn on, a weapon that may be used by the bereaved themselves or by political opportunists to keep the cycle of violence in motion.

In larger social units, the destructive potential of clan or family blood feuds has been recognized and generally controlled by law. The blood feuding of rival clans in sixth-century B.C.E. Athens was one of the motivations behind Solon's legislation restricting women's laments at funerals.[4] Recognizing the funeral as the occasion most likely to inflame grief and transform it into violence, Solon aimed to put an end to the cycle of murders that threatened the existence of the newly formed state of Athens. Aeschylus, Sophocles, and Euripides were all attracted by mythical subjects that dealt with the dangers of excessive mourning, particularly of mourning women. Clytemnestra, Electra, Antigone, and Medea are all women who carried mourning too far, so far that it darkened their minds and drew them into the realm of madness and death. Women whose grief drives them to violence are portrayed, in tragedy, as sister spirits of the Erinyes, or Furies, daughters of Night. Repulsive and implacable, the Furies never lost their fascination for a society proud of its new political and legal institutions but still in touch with an older world of superstition and magic.

The theater has always been a relatively safe place to unleash excess. Within its physical and artistic confines, madness and violence can be feigned without fear of contagion. Even so, the performance of a trilogy of tragedies was followed, in Athens, by a satyr play that must have quickly dispersed the gravity of the long winter afternoon. Taking the mythical themes they had used in their serious plays, the authors turned the same material into farcical comedies, full of coarse sexual jests and horseplay. Most of the plays have disappeared, and the idea of tacking such a piece onto the *Oresteia* now seems downright blasphemous. Still, we must presume that the satyr plays were added to a trilogy for some reason. Was it simply to ensure that the audience left the theater laughing and not weeping? Or did it mimic the progression from tearful laments to laughter in the funeral itself?

Sexual Games

Feasting, mirth, and sexual exuberance seem once to have been the sequel to laments and a means of putting an end to the tears they induced. Like laments, the wake games that once followed them in many parts of Europe offered an unusual license to women, who joined in the festivities on an equal footing with men, sometimes exchanging sexual roles with them for the duration of the wake. Like laments, the wake games were the target of attacks from the state and the established church. The opposition of the Christian church to the wake games was even stronger than to laments, and by the end of the nineteenth century they had almost disappeared from Europe. A few accounts from Ireland and the Balkans, together with official proclamations against them, give us some idea of the nature of these strange rituals that followed the tears and sad songs of the funeral and occupied an equally important part in the theater of mourning. It seems that the opposition to wake games centered on their sexually explicit and "blasphemous" aspects. Whether they contained elements of pre-Christian religious beliefs or were deliberate parodies of church teaching, they were, like the carnival, occasions for mockery and parody, for debunking and sexual play.

From the surviving accounts of Irish wake games by English observers, we discover that they included elaborate "plays" that were performed in the presence of the corpse as well as the community of mourners. It was at the wake that Irish women traditionally met their mates. Love and Death, Eros and Thanatos, have a long history as twins. Both the pangs of erotic love and the fear and grief surrounding death are paradoxical forces. They transform, provoking emotions so strong they border on madness. In this madness, though, there is something of the divine, something that, for a time, pins wings on mortals. As Plato has Socrates tell it in the *Phaedrus* (244A): "Now, if it were a simple fact that madness [*mania*] is evil, the story would be fine. But the fact is, the greatest of good things come to us through madness when it is conferred as a gift of the gods" (trans. Carson). The desire to renew life may be a universal response to the fear of death, but eros is not necessarily concerned with reproduction. Sex and laughter seem to be the natural antidotes to tears and a means of controlling the excesses of mourning. The mourners left the funeral games, as playgoers left the theater, reminded that they still belonged to the community of the living.

The Control of Grief

Control of the expressions of grief represents power. In the small rural communities of pre-industrial Europe, where women laid out the corpse for burial and sang their laments for the dead on behalf of the community, their role in the rituals of mourning went unchallenged. But as communities grew larger, as standing armies were recruited and civic institutions developed, the state and the Christian church began to take control of mourning rituals, monopolizing and frequently politicizing the way grief was expressed. From sixth-century B.C.E. Greece to nineteenth-century Ireland we find evidence of conflict between the private and traditional expressions of grief and the attempts by various authorities to gain control over or manipulate grief. In addition to military, civic, and religious authorities, the modern funeral industry, the media, and the pharmaceutical companies have combined to manipulate grief in new and subtle ways. But however much it is controlled, there is always an element of the unexpected about grief. Its emotional potential is inexhaustible. For the angry, the ambitious, the deranged, the persecuted, and the marginalized, the energy of extreme grief may offer a unique opportunity for social mobilization and political action.

The Social Context of Death

The mechanisms for performing and structuring grief in our own age have been widely discussed in connection with the "Death Awareness Movement," which began in the 1960s.[5] The anthropology of death and grieving is a burgeoning field, but one that still leaves many questions unanswered. Many researchers continue to turn to Arnold Van Gennep's concept of death rituals as rites of passage (1960). Looking at death rituals from many different parts of the world, Van Gennep concluded that the dominant theme of funeral rites was transition rather than separation. Initially, both the dead person and the bereaved are separated from the world of the living, but during the transitional phase, the bereaved gradually move back toward the world of the living while the dead move away from the living toward the world of the dead. In the final phase, the dead are incorporated into the world of the dead and the bereaved into the world of the living.

Victor Turner (1969) carried Van Gennep's work a stage further and argued that the transitional period might be of positive value to the bereaved. In this phase normal social divisions and differences in status do not apply in many societies, and mourners in this intermediate phase may find mutual support and relief from their usual social pressures. Miller's research on the Aberfan disaster (1974) suggests that social barriers were broken down and the community was better able to deal with grief by meeting as equals to express their grief.[6] It is frequently argued that our modern world has lost touch with the rituals of mourning, and that we somehow need to get back to more satisfactory ways of grieving.[7] On the other hand, the second half of the twentieth century has been marked by an enormous intellectual and clinical interest in questions of bereavement, as well as the effects of the disasters of the century on survivors. There is a presumption, in much of the theorizing, that we understand grief as we do psychological or physical disorder, that we can help others "work it through" and eventually recover from it. In a recent lecture the director of Griefwork, a bereavement counseling service in Johnson City, New York, talked convincingly about the "five stages of grief": initial shock, a "roller-coaster ride" of emotions, "rock bottom," recovery, and relapse.[8] The phase model suggests that grief is a temporary affliction and that health consists in putting it behind us.

In the absence of a tight-knit community where the rituals of death and grieving are traditional and unchallenged, modern society has had to reassess and reinvent its attitudes to death and grief. The constant revision of knowledge, of motives for action, of response may in some ways be liberating for individuals, but when the modern, increasingly private person is faced with the death of someone close, she has more to cope with than her own grief; she must invent ways to respond to it. We find ourselves at funerals or memorial services unsure of how to act or what to say. The cultural diversity of modern society and the variety of possible approaches to mourning compound our anxiety. We pass along the aisles of available responses searching for one that fits our conception of what is appropriate.

With no community to dramatize our grief, to translate and perform it, we are increasingly forced to do it for ourselves or to turn to strangers for advice. In the isolation of our grief, we are susceptible to new kinds of manipulation. The formalized rituals of death and mourning provided a public, unquestioned ordering of grief that could, at times, be used to serve special interests, but the absence of such ordering leaves us in the hands of a new breed of "experts." Spiritual leaders and professional therapists are themselves torn between a modern notion of letting emotion hang out, and an older tradition of control that they learned from their parents and grandparents. The problem is that there are no mandatory social customs they can turn to. As traditional religious practice and belief decline, as psychologists and therapists teach people how to grieve, and physicians help people to avoid the pain of grief by prescribing pills, the bereaved suffer a double burden of grief and confusion. To cry or not to cry? To be in control and thought of as heartless, or to embarrass others by a display of emotion? To resume normal social activities and wear the same clothes, or to mark, by dress and behavior, a period of difference? In the end we usually behave in a way that is culturally acceptable. Tempting as it may seem to wail and tear out our hair when we are in the deepest grief, if we were brought up by parents tied to British culture we are unlikely to do so. The idea of encouraging people who are in distress to display it in a way they have never done may even be harmful.

In our grief over the death of those we love, we are at our most culture-bound. I was brought up in Australia, in a culture that prides itself on emotional toughness. When faced with the first real tragedy of my life, I found myself repeating the lessons of my childhood, struggling not to cry in public, repeating a talisman my mother had taught me against pain: "Be a little gypsy." But culture-bound as I was, I wanted to know how other people had lived through profound losses and emerged sound-minded, before the days of tranquillizers and counselors. I began looking at traditional laments for the dead, sung by women in rural Greece. What I found was a world of curious and forgotten expertise, one that stretched from Russia to Africa, from New Guinea to Saudi Arabia. It was an expertise that offered no comfort, a knowledge as bleak as tragedy. There was no sweetness in the art of lament, despite its poetic language and metaphors; instead there was a controlled passion that could flare into anger, dissolve into despair, become outrageously bawdy, flout all the norms of womanly expression, lead an army into battle, or avenge a murder.

The Rage of the Anthropologist

Even in the anguish of grief, we can learn much from the ways in which other societies have traditionally expressed, managed, survived, and exploited grief. Indeed, it is anthropologists, studying societies far removed from our own who have provided some of the most valuable insights into the diversity and similarities of human responses to grief.

Renato Rosaldo describes how the accidental death of his wife helped him to understand the explanation the headhunters of Luzon gave for their behavior: "If you ask an older Ilongot man of northern Luzon, Philippines, why he cuts off human heads, his answer is a one-liner on which no anthropologist can really elaborate: he says that rage, born of grief, impels him to kill his fellow human beings. The act of severing and tossing away the victim's head enables him, he says, to vent and hopefully throw away the anger of his bereavement" (1983: 178). Only after his wife's death did Rosaldo understand "the overwhelming force of rage possible in such grief" (183).

From his own experience of raging grief at his wife's death, Rosaldo was prompted to reassess not only his view of the headhunters he had been studying for fourteen years, but also Western attitudes to grief. He notes: "Although grief therapists routinely encourage awareness of the anger in bereavement, American culture in general ignores the rage that devastating losses can bring. Paradoxically, cultural wisdom denies the anger in grief even though members of the invisible community of the bereaved can be encouraged to talk obsessively about their anger" (1983: 184).

His own painful revelation led Rosaldo to question much of the anthropological and sociological literature on death, ritual, and bereavement, which tended to dismiss the place of emotions in death rituals. He notes that although the intense emotions of grief may not explain such rituals, neither do ritual acts explain the intense emotions of bereavement (1983: 187). The idea that rituals themselves express "collective wisdom" leads, in Rosaldo's view, to a conflation of ritual with the emotions of the bereaved. Rosaldo would have anthropologists consider formal ritual as only one of several ways to study what he terms the "cultural force of rage." Rosaldo's writing demonstrates that the rituals of mourning operate differently according to where the subject is emotionally positioned.

Other anthropologists have produced some remarkable studies of anger and grief without the motive of a personal tragedy.[9] In her study of Esperanza, a Mexican woman generally believed to be a witch (1993), Ruth Behar lets Esperanza tell the story of her life, a chronicle of abuse and poverty almost too terrible to believe. As the narrative unfolds in hours of taped interviews, grief and anger become so interwoven that we can understand why Esperanza and the women of her village believe that their *coraje* (rage) can be transmitted through breast milk and kill their children. The loss of one child after another is only a small part of Esperanza's suffering; like Shakespeare's Margaret or Euripides' Medea, this Mexican woman has mingled grief and rage so that it is no longer clear where one emotion ends and the other begins.

Emotional Categories and Culture

Such studies raise the question of how we categorize emotions. Emotions are difficult things to talk about. Anthropologists, philosophers, psychologists, and sociologists debating the nature of emotions have tended, as Leavitt has observed (1996: 514–515), to place them on one side or the other of the nature/nurture divide. That is, they have been regarded as either biological universals or cultural constructs specific to a particular environment. Despite the flood of recent literature on the subject,[10] faced with the difficulties of trying to conceptualize what we tend to think of as involving both our minds and bodies, most theorists opt for one side at the expense of the other.

Claude Lévi-Strauss (1987) and Clifford Geertz (1980) are probably the best-known advocates of the position that emotion is culturally specific and cognitive, although, as Leavitt concedes, Lévi-Strauss's extreme position is defined in opposition to what he sees as affective universalists (Leavitt, 1996: 519). Edmund Leach (1981) and Victor Turner (1967) account for the fact that feelings appear to be accessible across cultures by attributing them to a common biological heritage. The empathic approach raises problems that we have already seen demonstrated in Rosaldo's work on the rage of the headhunters. When a would-be empathic ethnographer is given an explanation of feelings that don't fit his or her own experience of emotion, he may become incredulous and search for alternative explanations to fit his preconceptions. On the other hand, a personal experience may help the anthropologist to penetrate what had previously seemed an opaque explanation for local behavior.

Cultural approaches to emotion have the advantage of keeping the local distinct, of dealing with the terms each culture uses to define emotion. Still, we are left with culturally specific concepts of emotion, expressed in a particular way. And if our approach is based on the "language" of emotion, how do we account for the bodily sensations that accompany our feelings? Are the tears of the grief-stricken cultural products? Is crying a social activity? The extreme position is to say yes. Abu-Lughod and Lutz (1990: 1–2), for example, tell us that emotion is "about social life rather than internal states," and that "rather than seeing them as expressive vehicles, we must understand emotional discourses as pragmatic acts and cognitive performances" (11). As if aware of the inadequacy of their own definitions, the authors concede that the emotions may be "framed in most contexts as experiences that involve the whole person, including the body" (12).

How can we get beyond what seems to be irreconcilable to the study of emotion? Among other suggestions for resolving the dichotomy, Leavitt recommends a move from empathy to sympathy. Implicit in empathy is the notion that we can feel what others feel. Instead, the anthropologist might do better by attempting to feel with and for them (sympatheia). The result would be "a re-alignment of one's own affects to construct a model of what others feel" (1996: 530). Leavitt notes, almost in passing, that this "reworking and translation of affect is what literature does" (531).

Whether or not we allow that grief is a universal emotion, it is always being consciously reworked and translated by others within our own culture, let alone by foreign anthropologists. The study of any emotion in the absence of its cultural expressions ignores the fact that emotional states are dynamic, complex, and subject to violent shifts. Literature, music, cinema, and other expressions of a culture can offer us as much insight into the emotions of a society as can anthropology. The outward show-and-tell of grief is a response to something felt. Somewhere, in the process of translation, it is conveyed, like the essence of a poem, from one language to another.

Missing Bodies

Human remains, in particular bones, appear to be universally important to the grieving process. The recovery and proper burial of the remains of soldiers killed on the battlefield, of relatives who have died far
from home, is regarded as essential if grief is to be completed. Western
literature from Homer to Rupert Brooke attests to the strength of our
desire to hold on to and control the material remains of our dead. The
absence of remains, especially when death is uncertain, exacerbates and
prolongs grief. The recovery of what are now minute fragments of soldiers who went missing in action in the Vietnam War is still a major political issue in the United States, illustrating the potency of the desire
for what is generally referred to as "closure." It is this potency that
makes the desire to put an end to grief susceptible to political manipulation. In the case of Vietnam, the national trauma of losing a war to a
smaller, less well-equipped army, the anger of veterans who were not
accorded a hero's welcome and the determination of successive administrations to exact revenge for an ignominious defeat combined to
make the bones of the dead in Indochina a commodity of greater value
than the remains of the U.S. dead in any other war. Relatives of the
dead and missing in Vietnam were a resource to be exploited in the desire for retribution. Their desire to believe their relatives were still
alive and, when they had lost hope, to recover the bodies of their dead
made them pawns in a campaign of public disinformation that continues to this day. The grief of the Vietnamese and the question of their
own missing dead were subjects deliberately downplayed or ignored
until recently. As the war itself is reassessed and animosity fades, Americans and Vietnamese are beginning to cooperate in efforts to recover
missing remains.

Another case of the political use of delayed grief and missing remains
is the phenomenon so widespread in Latin America that we all recognize the Spanish name for its victims: *los desaparecidos*. We have been
made familiar with images of the exhumation of remains from the mass
graves of Guatemala and Argentina, of the mothers of the Plaza de
Mayo holding pictures of their children above their heads. We know
that many of the victims suffered unimaginable torture for a period before they died, but the agonizing grief of the relatives is what we focus
on. The pictures of the disappeared are posed, expressionless images,

taken from student identity cards, passports, studio portraits, police mug shots. It is the women beneath them, in their white headscarves, holding the pictures of their children, who become the unwitting focus of the camera's and our attention. It requires little effort to imagine the pain of the mothers. They display it for us graphically, in a way the average mother can understand without being forced to comprehend the danger of the display, let alone the violence and bestiality perpetrated inside the Argentine prisons.

"Disappearance" is perhaps the most effective weapon in the hands of any regime, and it has been consistently and effectively exploited by many unscrupulous regimes. But even more surprising than the use of disappearance as a weapon of terror is how the relatives of the disappeared and dead in countries like Argentina and Guatemala have turned their grief into a weapon of their own, forming politically effective grassroots organizations. The mothers of the disappeared were a marginal group, united by the weakness rather than the strength of their social standing. In their unity of shared rage, they have realized their own effectiveness as witnesses, the unassailability of their silent testimony. It doesn't matter to them if the abyss of their grief is truly understood. Its display provokes a sympathetic response, and that gives them a forum to demand a public accounting.

AIDS and the Gay Community

Like the mothers of the disappeared in Latin America, the gay community of the United States was both marginal and intensely motivated by the grief and rage of a deadly epidemic. And like the mothers, gay men have mobilized their grief in surprisingly effective ways. The analogy of a plague inflicted by God on an offending population was one that occurred immediately both to the community itself and to the society observing it. The fact that AIDS initially affected the male homosexual population in disproportionate numbers confirmed the prejudices of a society that regarded anything other than heterosexual marriage as an aberration. Smug and fearful, American society drew its puritan skirts tighter around it while many homosexuals, sensitive to the dominant rhetoric, took their disease to be the wages of their own sin.[11] But as the numbers of the dead grew and the gay population began to organize, lobbying for medical research, for prevention of the spread of AIDS, for public awareness of the terrible suffering of the dying, they succeeded in transforming their own and the public's image of the disease. Their grief was channeled not only into direct political activism, but into an art of witness that has had a profound influence on the way we view death and grief.

Among the artistic responses to AIDS, the elegy is perhaps the most poignant and common. In the gay communities most affected by the epidemic, the anger and grief of those who have lost lovers and friends to AIDS has transformed the conventional elegy into a gesture of protest closer in spirit to the traditional lament than to the model familiar in Greek or English literature. As the century ends and this contemporary plague becomes no longer an automatic death sentence, the gay community can legitimately claim to have played a dominant role in achieving some progress toward a cure. Already organized as a community in revolt and able to exploit their grief as a form of political activism, gay American and European men developed a communal response to grief that was both extraordinarily original and surprisingly traditional.

Memorializing the Dead

The relationship of grief to memory is intimate and complex, juxtaposing the need to remember with the tendency to forget, and manipulating remembrance by memorials, monuments, and memoirs. In an age when there seems to be a glut of memorials, with Nazi concentration camps serving as museums and whole villages as memorials, we have to consider what function these state-sanctioned expressions of grief fulfill.

There is a necessary and unreconcilable tension between the desire to remember and the desire to forget. Memorials are a way of concretizing grief and representing memory, but the means and intent of the representation are enormously varied. The display of skulls that commemorates the victims of the Khmer Rouge in the "killing fields" of Cambodia is a jolt to memory as powerful as the heaps of shoes and spectacles at Auschwitz. On the other hand the Egyptian-inspired shrines and sculptural representations of the "unknown soldier" that graced public buildings in many parts of Europe after the First World War seemed designed, by their massive abstraction, to negate the personal pain of grief and to memorialize only the heroic aspects of war. At the end of the twentieth century we seem to be preoccupied with creating appropriate monuments to its catastrophes. From the Vietnam wall, with its list of names on a finite, solid slab, to the AIDS quilt's open-ended, communal act of remembering, to the Holocaust museums, with their multimedia displays that teach memory to a new generation, to the competitions and controversies over suitable designs for monuments, the business of memorials is thriving. Why now? Why so many? What is all this public display of grief and mourning about? Is there a fear that the dead will hover, restless and demanding, unless they are publicly acknowledged at the millennium's end?

Managing Grief's Excess

The strong emotions and social disruption engendered by death have always given grief a potential for politicization, whether it finds its voice in the laments of village women, the gay poet's elegy, or the war memorial. Human societies have understood the potential for grief to become violent and disruptive. Just as the rituals of death have evolved partly as a response to the fear of death, so the rituals of mourning have evolved as a response to the fear of the bereaved. Driven by the passion of their grief, the bereaved pose a potential threat to society. Mourning rituals and memorials are an attempt to bring order to the emotional chaos of grief. If they are ignored, disrupted, or perverted, grief may spill over from the immediate relatives of the deceased to the society at large. The danger of such extended grieving is universally recognized. Even the grief-stricken who prolong their grief deliberately to achieve revenge or to draw attention to a cause must eventually turn grief into action if they are not to be psychologically damaged.

It is a fine line between channeling grief for the benefit of the oppressed and unleashing the violent anger of suffering. Most societies have kept a lid on grief by the use of traditional or newly invented rituals and periodically allowed it to boil over if it suited their purposes. During the first months of the Bosnian war, Serbian television was flooded by images of women lamenting the Serbian dead, but the government arrested members of the organization calling themselves the "Women in Black" who put on the clothing of mourning and took to the streets of Belgrade to protest the war.

If our grief is to be managed, we should at least be aware of what is happening to us. Grief is something our society generally relegates to an insignificant position, unless there is something dramatic or glamorous about the sufferer. In the relative comfort of our society we often treat grief as a temporary affliction that can be alleviated by therapy or drugs. We have been told that the process of grieving follows a predictable pattern, and we wait for the stages of denial, anger, acceptance, and so on to pass so that we can get on with our lives. Most of us do not seek to prolong grief; it unhinges us, makes us behave in abnormal ways, divides us from the rest of society. We have not been taught to value that unhinging. Grief makes us vulnerable, but it may also empower. It tears us apart, but it may reassemble us in ways that astonish. This book offers no theory of grief; to formulate one would be as absurd as to formulate a theory of love. Instead it explores some old and well-tried ways in which pre-industrial societies have dealt with grief. Then it examines how the passion of grief has been manipulated and used for political effect in our own times, both by the state and by the grievers themselves.

~ 1

Tears

Lady Anne. Be it lawful that I invoke thy ghost
To hear the lamentations of poor Anne,
Wife to thy Edward, to thy slaught'red son,
Stabb'd by the selfsame hand that made these wounds!
Lo, in these windows that let forth thy life,
I pour the helpless balm of my poor eyes.
O, cursed be the hand that made these holes!
Cursed the heart that had the heart to do it!
Cursed the blood that let this blood from hence!
More direful hap betide that hated wretch
That makes us wretched by the death of thee,
Than I can wish to wolves, to spiders, toads,
Or any creeping venom'd thing that lives!
                    Richard III, I.ii.8–20

Queen Elizabeth. Ah, who shall hinder me to wail and weep,
To chide my fortune, and torment myself?
I'll join with black despair against my soul,
And to myself become an enemy.
Duchess of York. What means this scene of rude impatience?
Queen Elizabeth. To make an act of tragic violence.
. . .
. . . I am your sorrow's nurse,
And I will pamper it with lamentation.
                    Richard III, II.ii.34–39, 87–88

*A*N "ACT OF TRAGIC VIOLENCE," a "nurse" that "pampers" sorrow, a "helpless balm"—here we have a Dionysian juxtaposition of functions: healing and manic violence, mayhem and medicine, the twin aspects of tragedy's patron god. How do they meet in the female art of lamentation? How can they heal and nurse grief? In what sense is this act in a drama also an act of violent mourning?

Anne's grief, like Elizabeth's, is publicly displayed, intended for an audience. She has seen her husband murdered, and now her father-in-law's body lies in front of her, slain by the same hand that killed her husband. The scene is set in a London street, where the corpse is being carried from St. Paul's Church to its final resting place in Surrey. We must presume that Anne speaks not only for the ears of the pallbearers and the passersby, but to the murderer himself, who enters as she heaps her venom on him.

Anne's claim that the "balm" of her tears is helpless is disingenuous.[1] These tears are meant not to heal but to harm. The concept of tears and laments as medicinal, as nourishment for the dead and cure for the griever, is an old one. In the opening scene of Euripides' *Medea*, the nurse confides to the audience that she has gained relief from her sorrows by indulging her desire for tears but that her mistress has no such outlet. As the nurse observes, poetry and song, combined in the art of lament, heal grief (191–203). But grief that is complicated by anger and hatred cannot be cured by medicinal tears and therapeutic songs. Such grief is satisfied only by "an act of tragic violence." Anne and Elizabeth have Hamlet's "cue for passion" but no physical means to achieve their desire for revenge. The means that are available—a witch's curses—they use to full effect.

Of all the characters in Shakespeare's early historical plays, the figure who is most effective in the transformation of grief to violence is Queen Margaret. Like Helen of Troy, to whom she is compared in the last lines of *Henry VI, Part I*, she is an imported beauty, potentially dangerous. In *Part II*, when she is brought the severed head of her lover, Suffolk, she talks of grief still as an amateur, unsure of her own performance (IV.iv.1–4):

> Oft have I heard that grief softens the mind
> And makes it fearful and degenerate;
> Think therefore on revenge and cease to weep.
> But who can cease to weep and look on this?

As death follows death in the bloody feuds of the Houses of Lancaster and York, Margaret becomes an expert in the performance of grief and is able to satisfy her desire for violent action as she personally su-

pervises the torture and execution of her enemy, York (*Part II*, I.iv.67–
91). By the time she reappears in *Richard III*, Margaret is an old hand at
the art of mourning, a lamenter without peer. She, Elizabeth, and the
Duchess of York, women from two warring houses, are united in their
grief for their lost children, husbands, friends. They sit together, lamenting, but the sorority of grief does nothing to soften the violence of
their desire for revenge. Margaret demands recognition of the senior-
ity of her suffering (IV.iv.35–39):

> If ancient sorrow be most reverend,
> Give mine the benefit of seniority,
> And let my griefs frown on the upper hand.
> If sorrow can admit society,
> Tell o'er your woes again by viewing mine.

Then she reminds Elizabeth that this is no aimless, self-pitying catalogue of woes, but a cue for passion, a deliberate inflammation of hatred against the women's common enemy (IV.iv.61–62, 77–78):

> Bear with me. I am hungry for revenge,
> And now I cloy me with beholding it.
> . . .
> Cancel his bond of life, dear God, I pray,
> That I may live to say, The dog is dead!

Recognizing her need for Margaret's expertise, Elizabeth asks for a lesson in the magic art of curses (116–117):

> O thou well skill'd in curses, stay awhile,
> And teach me how to curse mine enemies!

Margaret's response is a recipe for cursing, a school for actors who
must rehearse grief to produce imprecation (118–125):

> Forbear to sleep the night, and fast the day,
> Compare dead happiness with living woe;
> Think that thy babes were fairer than they were,
> And he that slew them fouler than he is.
> Bett'ring thy loss makes the bad causer worse.

> Revolving this will teach thee how to curse.
> *Q. Eliz.* My words are dull. O, quicken them with thine!
> *Q. Marg.* Thy woes will make them sharp, and pierce like
>   mine.

When she leaves, the Duchess of York asks Elizabeth, "Why should calamity be full of words?" Elizabeth admits they are inadequate, mere "windy attorneys to their client's woes," but she returns to the theme of the therapeutic value of lament (129–131):

> Poor breathing orators of miseries,
> Let them have scope! Though what they will impart
> Help nothing else, yet do they ease the heart.

Contemporary Expertise in Grief

Tears, curses, words: they are now, as they have always been, the inadequate vehicles of our grief. If they convey little to others, they satisfy a need in ourselves. Once there were experts in the art of speaking, cursing, and singing grief. Now there are professionals in the art of dulling grief. Grief is often treated, in our society, as being like a serious illness. It is something you "get over" in time, something you are encouraged to put behind you and eventually stop talking about. This is particularly true if the relative or friend you are mourning died at an advanced age or before the age of "viability." If your mother reaches the age of ninety you may weep a little at the funeral and talk to friends about the good life she had, but you are not expected to grieve as much as if she had died at fifty. The emphasis is not on the gap the death has left in your life, not even on the stages from denial to acceptance that are said to categorize grief, but on the supposed good fortune of an exceptionally long life, for your dead relative and for yourself. If you have a miscarriage five months through a pregnancy, or if you are forced by economic or other circumstances to have an abortion, you are expected to be upset, even emotionally disturbed, but to go to work a week later as if you had got out of bed after a bout of pneumonia.[2] If, on the other hand, you give birth to a child after nine months of pregnancy and it dies a year later, you are permitted and encouraged to express grief for a prolonged period.

Grieving for those who die an unusual death—premature, violent, heroic, political, beautiful—is what gets the most attention in our society. The newspapers and television reports are full of pictures of distraught wives and mothers of those who have died in wars, accidents, a casual spray of bullets. The stunned widow of a president in her blood-stained pink suit became as much an object of fascination, for a generation of Americans, as her husband's corpse. Elton John and the playboy brother of Princess Diana were the stars of a funeral spectacular watched by more people than any previous television program in that medium's brief history. In the media age, the intensity of the grief of the bereaved can be vicariously shared and imagined in a way that death cannot—everyone has known some grief in his or her life—but the identification is fleeting; the true nature of terrible and unusual grief can be understood only by those who have experienced it. The moment of immediate shock and anguish registered by a cameraman is the beginning, not the end, for the bereaved. It is followed by a complicated sequence of shifting emotions, including rage, self-pity, and despair, not necessarily in that order.

Grieving Alone

In the face of someone else's grief, the most common reaction of our times is to encourage the bereaved to find "closure," to speak of grieving as if it were a wound that could be sewn up, provided there was no infection (trauma, denial, missing body) to prevent healing. The medical and psychoanalytic models of healing and recovery that dominate current attitudes to grief either ignore or treat as unhealthy the deliberate desire to keep wounds open or to turn grief to violent action. We grieve alone, as we dance alone, gyrating in company without touching one another, dulled by the disco beat of our work. It has been left to the community of grievers themselves and to the politically astute to exploit the passion of grief. One community of grievers who have taken their therapy into their own hands is the bereaved relatives of the victims of street violence in American cities.

Lorna Hawkins' twenty-one-year-old son was murdered in a drive-by shooting in Lynwood, Los Angeles, in 1989. Her second son was murdered in an attempted robbery two years later. The mother of the two murdered sons has started a weekly television talk show called "Drive-By Agony" that has an audience of up to half a million households across the country.[3] The people on her show, most of whom have lost relatives to street violence, use the opportunity to vent their rage and frustration, to lay blame on the police, on city officials, to complain that no one seems outraged by violence. The success of the program seems to be its public nature. The passion of unappeased grief needs a forum, a stage for its tears and imprecations. Whether or not such a program effects a change in public behavior, it fills a gap left by our modern expertise in grief, and allows the bereaved, especially the mothers of murdered children, to curse, blame, and rage like the women of the Elizabethan stage, to give visible and vocal expression to their pain.

To Weep or Not to Weep

The grief-stricken who do not attract the camera's eye have become largely invisible in our times. Even the traditional black clothes that once set them apart are no longer essential markers of mourning. The bereaved walk past us unrecognized on the street. Only if we happen to know their circumstances do we treat them as different from the rest of society. Those who seek or are given help for their grief by the medical profession are regarded as having a temporary affliction and often given drugs to alleviate their symptoms. If they seek emotional support from therapists, social workers, or spiritual leaders in their community, they are liable to meet with a variety of responses, most of them based on a belief that the pain of grief can be treated or alleviated (Hockey 1993).

A recent study of how clergymen in Sheffield, England, dealt with their bereaved parishioners found that most saw their role partly as that of healers and therapists. According to the model they subscribed to, the emotions of grief were seen, like other emotions, as both natural and contained. The therapeutic "release" of emotion was thought to be desirable as a way of avoiding the dangers of "pent-up" feelings. Despite the general agreement about the nature of the emotion aroused by grief, as a sort of pressure cooker with a lid that needed to be released occasionally if the ceiling was not to be splattered, there was considerable resistance to the idea of allowing release at the funeral. While clergy would tell their parishioners "not to be ashamed about having a cry" or "to be natural," it was agreed that not being "in control" when they participated in the service could be a problem: "and so you have an upsetting thing in the service . . . you know, someone breaks down when they're trying to speak and that doesn't help the relations . . . the last thing you want in a funeral service is for a young person to get up or even a member of the family to get up and do the reading for the family and find that it's too much for them on the occasion, which could be embarrassing" (Hockey 1993: 133). The clergy generally valued control of the outward signs of grief, especially in the context of the funeral:

> There have to be limits. I mean, I will not allow people, after a certain length of time, anyway, to cling uncontrollably to the coffin as it's disappearing down the hatch. I mean that is not on . . . and where people are very overwhelmed by their grief they tend to cry quietly . . . But people are very concerned about making fools of themselves, so I wouldn't want to reduce anybody to a state that would embarrass them . . . (Ibid.: 134)

The public display of grief is particularly embarrassing to men. Women are expected, even encouraged, to weep, provided they do it in the right place. In most societies men are discouraged from shedding tears in public. Tears have traditionally been considered unmanly, even threatening to the security of the state. In the second book of Samuel, when David learns of the death of Saul, he says: "Tell it not in Gath, publish it not in the streets of Askelon, lest the daughters of the Philistines rejoice, lest the daughters of the uncircumcised triumph" (2: 20). A few lines later, though, David enjoins the *daughters* of Israel to "weep over Saul, who clothed you in scarlet" (24).

The first of David's injunctions was quoted by an aging veteran, Shlomo Baum, in an interview on Israeli radio after television programs and newspapers had shown pictures of soldiers, male and female, weeping in each other's arms at the funeral of six soldiers killed in an ambush in southern Lebanon on October 18, 1995 (Gellman 1995). Israel's two leading newspapers published close-up photographs of the grieving solders, sparking a controversy in the country not about the intensity of grief, but about its display. "It does not add to our collective honor," said Baum, "nor to that of the individual, this new norm of mooing." The coordinator of Israel's Lebanon policy, Uri Lebrani, who was also interviewed about the coverage of the funeral, said: "When they see our soldiers crying it saps our strength . . . [it] is causing jubilation both in Damascus and Tehran." Other Israelis disagreed. One young man called in to the radio program to say: "It is an expression of strength that we are willing to cry, to risk the pain, and still continue to fight for our country" (ibid.).

What was perhaps most interesting about the controversy over tears was that older Israelis, like the veteran Baum, saw the display of "mooing" as a new phenomenon. The army, aware of a change in the behavior of mourning at military funerals during the 1980s and 1990s, took it seriously enough to order its soldiers to refrain from crying at the funerals of their comrades. The fear was, like Baum's, lest "the daughters of the Philistines exult." The chief of the Israeli General Staff responsible for the order expressed his concern "that repeated televising of hordes of weeping Israeli soldiers on Israeli TV might encourage Palestinian youngsters to step up their attacks" (ibid.). The "daughters of Israel" were free to weep; perhaps the sons too, provided they did not do so in view of the enemy. What caused the change in Israeli behavior? Is it a sign of weakness or a sign of strength that soldiers weep on TV? Have young Israeli men overcome the embarrassment of Northern Europeans and North Americans at displaying their grief in public? Have they become acculturated to the Middle East and adapted their mourning, like their diet, to a local norm of "mooing"? Or are we witnessing, in the unabashed display of emotion, a reflection of the breakdown of gender differences, inhibitions, myths of heroism?

Whatever we are seeing, it is the camera's lens through which we are viewing it. The usually anonymous witness at the funeral, the scene of the massacre, the deathbed, the execution, makes grief visible to a vast audience. What were once the most private moments of our lives are now public. The funerals of the nobility, the rich and famous, have always been, like Elizabethan funerals, "heraldic." Now anyone's funeral can be turned into a public spectacle; all that is needed is a touching story or an unusual death. The public visibility of the mourner has undoubtedly transformed mourning behavior itself. Mourners, knowing they are being photographed, must play, in some sense, to the camera. Since tears are the most visible expression of grief, the actors in the photodrama of the funeral cannot afford to play their tragic scenes dry-eyed; on the other hand, if they overdo the tears, especially if they are male, they will be thought weak, unmanly, lacking in self-control.

A System of Checks and Balances

The apparent inconsistency of allowing, even encouraging emotional relief in the form of tears at one point in the funeral and restricting it at another has something in common with the system of checks and balances built into the grieving rituals of many pre-industrial societies. In rural Greece, for example, and in some adjacent Balkan cultures, the bereaved relatives are expected to display grief openly, weeping and wailing. Women may tear their hair and scratch their cheeks until the blood runs. Bereaved relatives may try to leap into the open coffin during the funeral. But the loud wailing of laments is often led by women who are not the nearest of kin to the person who died. The dirge singers are frequently semiprofessional mourners who are gifted at improvising lyrics and expressing the grief of the family and community. It is believed that the extreme grief of the bereaved interferes with their capacity to compose a fitting lament at the funeral; they may also not be skilled improvisers of laments. Close relatives of the deceased are carefully watched and often surrounded by women of the village, who restrain them from injuring themselves and try to prevent them from excessive displays of grief. If a woman wails too long or too loud, she may actually be removed from the funeral proceedings so as not to upset the orderly display of grief.[4] When the priest is performing the funeral service, women may continue to weep, but restraint is expected, and in cases when the expressions of grief and the laments of the women threaten to drown out the official liturgy, a sort of compromise will be reached so that each party has an opportunity to play a part.

The emphasis on ordering and patterning grief in traditional funerals of the Balkans and many other cultures is part and parcel of mourning's theatrical nature. Like an ancient Greek tragedy, a funeral in a modern Greek village is a choral composition. The word *choros* means dance, and tragedy was an art of movement, of song and dance. The meters of tragic verse, like the carefully choreographed movement of the chorus, represented a harmonious order in counterpoint to the violent passions of the individual actors:

The danced song comments on, but also counterpoints, the tragedy's *dis*ordered passions: mainly those of individual characters. Order versus disorder: plural versus single. Single, mad, or impassioned minds "move out" of their right place, alone and at risk, while plural concerted bodies move in bodies emblematic of right place and security. The musical structure, violent *and* orderly, expressed through the interplay of individual actor and plural chorus, is the basis of tragic tension. (Padel 1995: 133)

To say this is to recognize that tragedy itself may ultimately be based on the interplay of the funeral, the attempt to impose order on the terrifying disorder of death, to restrain the violence of grief without losing its dramatic passion. The women mourners who lament around the body are the plural chorus; the leader of lament, like her counterpart in the theater, comments in measured verse on the dead to the bereaved and the community, reducing the risk of disorder.

In some cultures there is an elaborate hierarchy of weeping at funerals, a ceremonial display of emotion that ends as abruptly as it begins. A. R. Radcliffe-Brown noted seven occasions when the Andaman Islanders regularly wept, all of them prescribed by custom (1964: 116–117). Three of these occasions were associated with death. The friends and relatives of the dead embraced the corpse and wept over it, and when the bones of the deceased were disinterred for reburial, they wept again. There was also a customary reciprocal type of weeping that marked the end of mourning. Friends of the mourning relatives wept with them in a display of mutual grief that Radcliffe-Browne suggested was a means of reuniting the bereaved with the community. The participants in the mandatory reciprocal weeping might not all "feel" the same sorrow, at least when they began weeping, but by their own admission the display of grief engendered a genuine feeling of sadness. The social benefit of the reciprocal display was both to affirm social ties and to put an end to the temporary marginal status of mourners.

Experts in Tears

There have always been "experts" who have expressed grief on behalf of the community. Mostly they were women, women skilled in the art of composing laments for the dead. For a number of reasons, the traditional art of lamenting the dead has died out in almost all of Europe. Women, who were once thought of as having a natural affinity for conducting the rituals of death and mourning, have been replaced by clergy, by funeral officials, and by professional counselors and healers who have little or no interest in the untrained artists they replaced. What the authorities failed to eradicate, industrialization and the erosion of village life obliterated. Those who wish to understand the practice of lament must now draw on the work of anthropologists and other observers to discover the origin of the practice, how the actors played their parts in the theater of mourning, and how tears and song were thought to work on behalf of the bereaved and the community.[5]

Speaking to the Dead

In the rural villages of Greece, Romania, Bulgaria, and many parts of the developing world, the scene is repeated with minor variations. A man lies dying. The female relatives gather around his bedside. When he has taken his last breath, they close his eyes and begin to wail and sob. A woman or group of older women begin to transform their weeping into a song. The song is extemporized but almost always follows a fairly strict metrical pattern and melodic pattern. The other lamenters respond to the leader, forming a chorus to her solo. Experienced in such spontaneous composition, the women are able to anticipate the leader's words and join her in a dirge that appears, to the outsider, to have been rehearsed, but is the result of having listened to such songs for a lifetime. Often the verses or sections of the song are interspersed with sobs and sighs. The women may beat their breasts and tear their hair in gestures of mourning so ancient that we can recognize them from Egyptian hieroglyphs and ancient Greek vases, but they seldom do themselves harm. In fact anyone whose gestures or weeping threatens to get out of control is forcibly restrained by the other women. This is a performance, a carefully structured ritual that may not be disturbed.

> Who lit the candle
> when the sun was up?
> Who mourned you
> when the moon rose?

Who buried you
who buried you
when those fir trees fell?
It was they who buried me.
It was they who buried me.
Who mourned you
who mourned you
when the moon rose?
It was she who mourned me
it was she who mourned me.

These are the words of a *bocet*, or Romanian lament.[6] Like many of
her counterparts elsewhere, the singer of this dirge has addressed the
dead directly. Moreover, the dead person has responded. This dialogue
with the dead is a characteristic formula of the lament. The singer creates what has been called a "bridge between worlds" (Caraveli-Chaves
1980), acting as a sort of medium between the bereaved and the dead.
Her ability to cross this bridge through song places her in a dangerous
position. In Finland, women are warned not to "forget themselves"
while lamenting, probably in recognition of dangers inherent in their
communion with Tuonela, the world of the dead. As an intermediary,
the lamenter is too close to the spirit world not to be in some way pol-
luted by it. In many cultures there is an interval between the last breath
of the deceased and his or her passage to the spirit world, during which
the deceased inhabits a gray area between this world and the next. The
wake, the funeral, and other ceremonies following a death in such cultures are as much occasions to placate the dead and ward off the possible harm they might cause the living as they are occasions to sing their
praises.

The women who still lament the dead in certain areas of Europe are
societal in-betweens and spiritual go-betweens. Frequently unmarried
or widowed, they are persons of marginal status in society. Their art of
lament gives them a power that the community, in its need to find a
bridge to the dead, respects and fears. Their prominence as chief actors
in the drama of death is of brief and specific benefit to the community,
but it is always watched with care. Theirs is an authority not discussed
or articulated. They hold it by tradition and a recognized need for the
passion of grief to be expressed by those who have a gift for it. When

the rituals of death and mourning are completed, they revert to the margins of society.

Temporary License and Deliberate Control

We are familiar with the period of license granted armies after they have captured an enemy town. From Homer to the Bible there are accounts of orgies of rape and plunder followed by the restoration of order. The frenzy of violence is not only a reward but a means of maintaining control. If the soldiers are not permitted a brief season of madness they are likely to rebel. The cunning commander knew how long to let this insanity last, and when to rein it in. Such license is granted by a weighing of risks. It is a rope played out and hauled in. So it is during commencement festivities, when university administrators tolerate heavy drinking and a certain amount of vandalism by students celebrating their rites of transition.

The village priests in rural Greece allow old women lamenters to sing verses that contravene Christian teaching. The women tell of an underworld ruled by Charos, implacable rider on a black horse. He gathers up the living and takes them to a dark kingdom where neither Christ nor the Virgin Mary has a part to play. The vision of the afterlife that Greek laments offer is as bleak as Homer's and owes nothing to the teachings of Christianity. The priests know well that the license they grant to makers of laments is limited, that the same old women will be helping to arrange the flowers in the church for the next Sunday's service. Such license is like letting a dog off a leash in the park. You know it will come back to heel because it has established a relationship of dependence on you for its needs, and so you allow it to run in a place where it can do a minimum of damage.

Temporary license is something traditionally granted to people in a state of transition, or liminality, and to the weak. As both Victor Turner (1969) and Mary Douglas (1966) noted, groups and individuals who are marginal to the society are often perceived as having mystical power or being in some way dangerous to the community. Their difference may heighten their sense of community or give them unusual freedom. The ubiquitous court jester, for example, usually a person of low status, and sometimes physically deformed, was able to criticize a head of state with impunity, acting as a sort of institutionalized mouthpiece for the underprivileged. Among the communities of the marginalized or liminal in our own society Turner cites the millenarian religious movements, the "beat" generation, and the hippies. Comparing the properties of liminality in tribal rituals among the Ndembu and other African peoples with the attributes of such movements, he finds a striking series of similarities (1969: 111–112). Homogeneity, abolition of rank, disregard for personal appearance, suspension of kinship rights and obligations, sexual continence, or community, and simplicity of speech are among the qualities common to these groups.

As societies become more complex and rituals more diffuse, it becomes more difficult for those holding positions of authority to monitor the temporary disorder of transitional groups. The state, church, and other institutions that replace the village elders or local leaders are acutely aware of the danger of inarticulate or marginal power, of its capacity to disrupt and cause chaos. They are often prepared to grant it official license at festivals, funerals, or spectacles that they can keep a watchful eye on. But removed as they are from the rituals of everyday life, they tend to establish alternative rituals that displace the traditional and communal ones, duplicating and eventually subsuming them. The figures of authority who play the leading roles in such rituals are frequently outsiders to the community and occupy a marginal position themselves, one not determined by gender or community-perceived suitability, but by institutionally determined markers of difference: the celibate priest in his black robes, the herald, the lord of the manor, the master of ceremonies, the undertaker. Such figures represent social order. In its name they control the rituals that mark the major transitions of our lives from birth through death. They are aware of the alternate sources of power that they hold in check and of the benefits of allowing them free rein as a safety valve in the orderly system. A temporary chaos consolidates their own power.

The Threat

From time to time the European church or state has felt itself challenged or threatened by alternative sources of power. The official indictment of mourning rituals provides us with some information about the nature of the threat they posed to authority. The persistence of communities in defying official attempts to suppress their mourning rituals suggests deep and widely held beliefs about the capacity of marginal groups to order the chaos of death. There are other issues involved too. When death is violent, as in times of war, political turmoil, or social upheaval, funerals may become the site not merely of an alternative authority, but of direct political confrontation. In the sixth century B.C.E., the Greek city-states introduced new laws to curtail funeral rituals. The laws were especially addressed at women lamenters. In Athens "women's noisy and unruly behavior at funerals" was linked to their behavior in certain festivals at which they were in charge of rituals. Under laws passed by Solon, lamenting the dead was limited to close family members. One of the principal reasons for Solon's legislation may have been to put an end to the blood feuds that had disrupted Athenian society, but it also seems to have been part of a general disfranchisement of women, tied, paradoxically, to the growth of democracy.[7]

From the earliest days of the Christian era until the twentieth century the church hierarchy has periodically condemned the private rituals of death and mourning practiced by communities throughout Europe. The principal targets of criticism were, as in Solon's legislation, women mourners. John Chrysostom denounced laments as "blasphemous words" (Migne in Alexiou 1974: 29). As Alexiou (28) points out, it was not just the wailing or tearing of hair that upset the church fathers, but the dirges themselves, which seemed to them to be both self-indulgent and pagan. Chrysostom also objected to the use of hired mourners, whom he described as this "disease of females" (Migne in ibid.: 29).

During the Byzantine period, the church fathers tried to bring women's laments and public displays of grief under their control; they did not try to dispense with them, but rather to remove their pagan associations and adapt them to their own purpose. Like the British clergy of modern Sheffield, the early church authorities recognized the importance of releasing emotion, of the "pleasure of tears" (a concept familiar to them not only from ancient Greek authors but from the scriptures). They also recognized the danger of leaving this potentially dangerous resource in the control of women, women whose ritual behavior clearly had its roots in pagan custom: "And would you tear your hair, rend your garments and wail loudly, dancing and preserving the image of Bacchic women, without regard for your offense to God?" said Chrysostom (Migne in Alexiou 1974: 29). Hired mourners were not a target per se; on the contrary, the church saw well the value of the public display of grief, but it was determined to do its own hiring, order its own laments.

Philosophy versus Passion

Singing nuns provided a partial solution to the problem. Gregory of Nazianzen gives an account of the funeral of Basil of Caesarea, who died in 379. Nuns sang psalms as the body was laid out; women mourners were separated from the men and placed next to the holy sisters, who provided a safeguard against any impropriety. During the elaborate funeral procession, official pomp and splendor and spontaneous expressions of public grief alternated. The most interesting passage in the description of the funeral is Gregory's clear articulation of the church's attitude to lament. Describing the huge crowds who followed the funeral, he says: "Thousands of people of every race and age, not known before, psalms giving way to lamentations, and philosophy overcome by passion. It was a struggle between our followers and the outsiders—Greeks, Jews, and immigrants . . . and the body itself only just escaped their clutches" (Migne in Alexiou 1974: 30). Christians are pitted against Greeks and Jews, psalms against laments, philosophy against passion. Even the holy sisters themselves were not immune to the "passion" of lament. At the funeral of Makrina, sister of Basil of Caesarea, when the earth was shoveled into the grave and the final prayer of greeting was proclaimed,

> That prayer caused the people to break out into fresh lamentation. The chants had died down . . . then one of the holy sisters cried out in a disorderly fashion that never again from that hour should we set eyes on that divine face, whereupon the other sisters cried out likewise, and disorder and confusion spoiled that orderly and sacred chanting, with everyone breaking down at the lament of the holy sisters. (Alexiou 1974: 31)

Forgetting herself, the nun reverted to passionate lament. The result was a temporary confusion that threatened the authority of the church. Like his twentieth-century equivalent in Sheffield, the fourth-century representative of Christ's authority on earth was unable to deal with the "breaking down" of his congregation. Order and the sacred were synonymous to the church fathers. Tears undermined the careful control of mourning that the church had established as an alternative to traditional laments.

Ireland

In Christian Europe, from the medieval period to the beginnings of the twentieth century, the church sustained its attacks on the excesses of lament. It was more successful at controlling and eventually eliminating the practice in urban areas than in rural villages, where women lamenters continued to play a leading part in funerals. In the British Isles, "keening" survived longest in Ireland, where it was the subject of countless attacks, both by the church and by English commentators. Writing in 1588, Richard Stanihurst described the conflict between church ceremony and lament in the Ireland of his day:

> As soon as a leading member of their community expires, many women may be seen running hither and thither through field and village with wolfish and shrieking cries. I cannot easily describe the great wail with which they fill the church where the funeral rites take place. They shout dolefully through swollen cheeks, they cast off their necklaces, they bare their heads, they beat their brows, they excite emotion on all sides, they spread their palms, they raise their hands to the heavens, they shake the coffin, tear open the shroud, embrace and kiss the corpse and scarcely allow the burial to take place. (1979: 156)

Like the early church fathers, the later religious authorities saw the Irish practice of lament, especially the existence of professional lamenters, as a pagan custom that vied with their own professional control of death. Laments and the wake games that followed them were repeatedly banned, and those who practiced them were threatened with excommunication. English commentators from the sixteenth through the nineteenth centuries compared Irish lamenters to heathens. Edmund Spenser, drawing on a tradition that identified the Celts with the Scythians, noted that their lamentations at their burials with despairful outcries and ymoderate wailing . . . savor greatly of the Scythian barbarism. [Some] think this custom to come from the Spaniards for that they do so immeasurably likewise bewail their dea[d]. But the same is not proper Spanish but altogether heathenish, brought in first thither either by the Scythians or by the Moors which were African but long possessed that country, for it is the manner of all pagans and infidels to be intemperate in the wailings of the dead. (1934: 105)

The Ireland of Shakespeare, of Spenser, of Elizabeth's Irish wars, was a place of violent rebellion and terrible repression. Despite an abundance of fertile land, its population was reduced to starvation. It was calculated that 30,000 men, women, and children had died of hunger in six months of the year 1582. The "intemperate" wailing and "exciting of emotion" might be looked down on as a primitive custom; it was recognized as a political tinderbox. The crazed mother of a "traitor," drinking blood from his severed head and smearing it on her clothes, was making "an act of tragic violence" in the same way as Margaret as she comes onstage holding the head of Suffolk. She was not simply "acting out the disorder brought about by death." When the bereaved queen gets her chance to avenge her dead, her desire is to make her enemy as crazed with grief as she has become herself. Showing York a napkin stained with his son's blood, she says to him:

> Why art thou patient, man? Thou shouldst be mad;
> And I, to make thee mad, do mock thee thus.
> Stamp, rave, and fret, that I may sing and dance.
> (*Henry VI, Part III*, I.iv.87–90)

The English who ruled Ireland with a reign of terror knew they could expect no less in return. The maddened victim has no mercy. If they were to quell the potential for violent revenge, the authorities knew they must keep the women quiet, especially at funerals. In their efforts to stamp out wakes, they were aided by the established church, whose hierarchy already regarded the behavior of its rural parishioners as heathenish. Pronouncements against women keeners are found in the annals of the Church of Ireland from the seventeenth through the nineteenth centuries. The priests were enjoined to put a stop to the "heathenish customs of loud cries and howlings at wakes" unless they wished to be removed from their parishes (O'Súilleabháin 1967: 138–139). In the synod of Dublin in 1670, each priest was ordered "to make every effort in his power to bring to an end the wailings and screams of female keeners who accompany the dead to the graveyard" (ibid.: 138).

It was not only in Ireland that laments came under the scrutiny and control of the church. In Hungary during the Middle Ages, lamentation had been common practice even among the aristocracy. At his burial in 1342, the widow of King Károly Robert reportedly wailed and moaned loudly during the ceremony (Kiss and Rajeczky 1966: 79). A century later, the widow of King Matyas was shown to her bedchamber with "her hair unbraided and her face scratched" (ibid.). As late as the eighteenth century Hungarian church officials supported the practice of lamentation, but by the nineteenth century laments were generally condemned by the aristocracy and middle classes. A commentator on peasant customs, viewing them from the lofty heights of the Age of Reason, foresaw the disappearance of laments in a scathing passage: "all unseemly blubbering and bewailing, mournful songs, and other shoddy traditions of heathendom, will pass into oblivion" (Bourke 1993: 162).

Despite the injunctions against women keeners, especially those who were hired and paid, either in food and liquor or in money, the practice continued in Ireland until the late nineteenth century and in some remote rural areas into the early years of the twentieth (Bourke 1993: 167). There were sharp exchanges between the lament singers and the clergy. An Irish woman told to stop lamenting at her son's funeral told the priest to "shut up and stand up straight!" (ibid.). In southern Kerry, the practice of employing keeners was reportedly ended at the turn of the century by a parish priest who took a whip to three keeners as they sat on a coffin lamenting (ibid.: 143).

Grief as Transition: The Mad Lamenter

Grief belongs to a transitional, or what anthropologists call a "liminal," phase that follows death. Such states are often considered dangerous because they are undefined. People who are in a marginal state—young boys being initiated into manhood in many tribal societies, for example—are often temporarily segregated from the rest of their society. The rituals that keep the initiates apart also give them special license as outcasts to behave in ways that would normally be punished by the tribe. The temporary license granted to the person on the margin acknowledges the potential dangers of the state of being betwixt and between, as well as its power.

The rituals of grieving are a social means of controlling disorder, but the behavior of the bereaved may tap sources of power that are considered valuable to the community. In societies where ritual grieving is engaged in by the society as a whole and thought to be a necessary process, the temporary derangement of the bereaved is not only tolerated but expected and followed by his or her reintegration into the community.

Descriptions of lament singers from Ireland suggest that they deliberately used to "act out the disorder brought about by death" (Bourke 1993: 166). On hearing of the death of a husband or son, a lamenter would immediately set out on foot for the scene of death, avoiding the main roads and going across country. With hair uncombed, clothes loosened, and often with breasts bared, she would begin her wild lament as soon as she arrived. If the body was bleeding, a lamenter would even kneel and drink the blood of the deceased. Spenser saw a woman behave in such a way at an execution in Limerick: "At the execution of a notable traitor at Limerick called Murrough O'Brien I saw an old woman which was his foster mother take up his head whilst he was quartered and sucked up all the blood running thereout saying that the earth was not worthy to drink it and therewith also [steeped] her face, and breast and torn [hair] crying and shrieking out most terrible" (1934: 112).

The practice of drinking the blood of the dead is attested in accounts as late as the nineteenth century and appears to be a very old tradition (see Partridge 1979: 31–32 and Bourke 1993: 166). It is even attributed to the Virgin Mary, who is portrayed as a typical lamenting woman in songs about the Passion of Christ. Like her disheveled hair and exposed breasts, the lament singer's drinking of the dead person's blood was regarded as a sign of madness (Partridge 1979). The bereaved woman of the Irish tradition, including the mother of Christ, is thought to be in a temporary state in which her behavior is a mirror image of what is expected of her in everyday life. To judge from their behavior, the bereaved *were* in some sense "insane" with grief, but in nineteenth-century Ireland, as in some rural Greek villages today, the women who lamented were frequently not the next of kin, but rather professional or semiprofessional performers. Is it safe to assume, then, that their "madness" was feigned?

Angela Bourke argues that the "madness" of the lamenters in rural Ireland was a cloak to disguise subversion (1993: 166–167). The assumption of madness allowed the traditionally reticent Irishwomen to loosen their hair, bare their breasts, talk frankly about taboo subjects like their sexual relations with their husbands, about pregnancy and childbirth. The tremendous hullabaloo that accompanied the lament—clapping, the beating of fists on the wood of the coffin, and the wailing itself—may have kept the defiant words inaudible except to those of the inner circle of women listening intently to their message: "Mourners who listened carefully would hear in the words of the keener not only praise and grief but also clear statements of identity and protest and a catalogue of women's wrongs. Others listening less carefully or less sympathetically—or the uninitiated, unnerved by the experience— would hear mostly noise or would miss the small verbal clues that gave point to the familiar formulas" (167).

Whether conscious or unconscious, the putting on of madness lies close to madness. The ghost of his murdered father causes Hamlet to "put an antic disposition on" (I.v.172). As he blasts Ophelia to madness with the violence of his rhetoric, we see his cloak of madness mold to fit him: "it hath made me mad," he rants (III.ii.154), in a fury directed at his mother, not at the innocent girl before him. We wonder what is feigned and what is now a part of Hamlet's own disordered disposition. Later, when he tells the queen "That I essentially am not in madness, / But mad in craft" (III.i.187), we waver again as Hamlet seems to slip back into sanity. Madness, for the Irish lament singer as for Hamlet, is a temporary refuge, protection against the violent onslaught of grief and a means to manipulate unspeakable anger.

A Crust of Madness

In his memoir of the years he spent in Mauthausen concentration camp, the Greek playwright Iakovos Kambanellis recounts the advice he was given by a Spanish prisoner soon after he arrived. "In here, if you want to survive, you have to have a crust of madness around your brain." "What do you mean?" asks the new arrival. "It's difficult to explain . . . To put it in a few words, you must take care to go a little crazy" (1981: 86; my translation). The prisoner goes on to explain that when they first arrived in the camp, the Spanish prisoners were always asking themselves why: "Why should I work like this? Why do they beat me like this? Why do they feed me like this?" Those who continued to ask why died because of their desire to understand. The experienced prisoner gives the newcomer some advice (88):

> everything that happens in a concentration camp is unnatural, insane, unbelievable, shocking . . . If suddenly a hand were to pluck me out of here and leave me in a street in Barcelona, New York, or Stockholm and I started to talk about Mauthausen, do you know what would happen? They'd take me for a madman, they'd lock me up! You've come to another world . . . Understand that! So, begin to put a crust around your brain . . . You must go a little crazy!

The crust of madness is first "put around the brain," but the experienced inmate insists that to survive, one must "*go* a little crazy." What the dispassionate observer sees as the assumed madness of lamenters, a subversive rhetorical cloak, is close to the insanity of a "successful" prisoner of the SS. The Irishwoman who drinks the blood of her slain husband or son is committing an act so monstrous to "normal" imagination that she is thought of as insane, but to see the body of someone you love, especially if that person has died a violent death at the hands of an enemy, and to remain sane is perhaps another kind of insanity. Pascal said, "Men are so necessarily mad that not to be mad would amount to another form of madness" (1954: 184).

The lamenter, whether she assumes insanity on her own behalf or for another, performs madness until she becomes temporarily mad. She looks mortality in the eye, and for the time she engages in her dialogue with death, she undoes the complicated web of denial that holds the symbolic self together and keeps society in order. Whether she is a relative, a friend, or even a hired mourner, the singer of laments draws on her own experience of loss like an actor, translating her private pain into the larger context of the community. The songs she composes are not always intended to be understood by all members of the community. In the Finnish-speaking areas of the former Soviet Union, Karelian women performed their laments in a secret language known only to lamenters (Tolbert 1990b). Using words and grammatical forms not found in the Karelian language and disguising meaning still further by the use of metaphorical names for the deceased and musical accents contrary to normal speech, the Karelian lament singers appear to be invoking some sort of taboo on clarity. To those who understand them, however, the songs are poignant and personal as we can see in this lament of a woman for her mother:

> Listen, my dear flower sunshine,
> my mother, my dear bearer
> I wonder how you were able to endure
> all the bad days.
> The times had all kinds of sadness
> and crying.
> Oh, my dear bearer
> It was such unhappiness
> because we couldn't enjoy
> the windowsill that father made.
> And we couldn't play in the waters
> off our own Karelian shores . . .[8]

Terrible Words

If their involvement with death rituals, particularly with the singing of laments, offers women unusual liberty to express what they normally keep hidden, then what is the purpose of disguising their protest? The simple answer might be fear of retribution—the protest becoming something like the token exercise of freedom offered by double-speak and "signifyin'" among black Americans. The use of secret or special language by Finnish-speaking lament singers, though, suggests we are dealing with something more than self-protection. The art of lament has long since died out in Finland, but a few old women from eastern Finland and from the Karelia region of the former Soviet Union still remember some of the extensive repertoire of laments that once accompanied every stage of a funeral or a wedding. They sing in a language that has "terrible words . . . that one cannot understand after only one or two hearings. And if one asks what this or that means, then the lamenter as well as the transcriber is likely to forget the half of it, and it will never become clear" (Haavio 1934: 5; quoted in Tolbert 1990b: 82). What can these "terrible words" be? And why does a demand for clarification cause the collapse of the lament?

The answer may not be consistent from one culture to another, but it is clear that songs of death and grieving are generally thought to be a form of magical discourse. Among the Warao people of Venezuela, where no one is believed to die a natural death, women's wailing for the dead is an important means of finding out the "truth" behind each death (Briggs 1992: 341). The highest compliment paid to an individual woman's singing of a section of the lament is that she has created "strong words." As Charles Briggs remarks, "the 'truth' revealed by 'strong words' is not literal" (ibid.). These words are often ironic, their "truth" contradicting any literal reading of the circumstances of death. Unlike the Warao male shamans, who use a secret language in their ceremonies, Warao women do not use a special language for their laments, but their solo improvised texts are so thickly packed, their syntax so complex, that the listeners have to strain to catch their meaning. More surprising is that the laments are often full of obscenities and metaphorical descriptions of sex. Here is a section of the lament Josephina Fernandez sang for her stepson (ibid.: 342):

> My son, "because you are such a sex fiend, after you [are
>   gone] the vaginas will not be finished off."
> I, your aunt, will keep on hearing this, my son.
>   My son, oh pitiful you, my son,
> "This nephew of ours does not respect [the wives of others];
>   'when will you tire of always lying with your wife there?
>   soon your semen will be finished!'"
> this is how the shamans gossiped when they assembled, my
>   son, that's what I kept hearing about you, my son.
>   . . .
> Since I, your aunt, am ill-willed, I won't die, I will live to be
>   an old woman, my son.

> although I, your aunt, am a person who criticizes her people, now I
> will live my life praising the shamans
> Your sister died because I was always chastising the shamans, that's just what I did.

The "strong words" of Fernandez' lament clearly transgress all the taboos of normal Warao speech, especially for women, but men listen to them, singing silently along with the principal performer (Briggs 1990b: 30). They describe their experience as "crying in our hearts." All the women Briggs talked to about their laments said that their minds went blank when they sang. Unlike "dreaming," which the Warao believe helps people to alter reality according to their desires, and is related to shamanistic practices, the suspension of consciousness in laments "displaces any sense of personal investment in the discourse, thus releasing the singer from concerns with face . . . and eliminating elements of strategy and manipulation" (31). Because the Warao women do not see themselves as being in control of their wailing, they are able to overcome *tomana* (shame). They are free to express the anger and sadness engendered by death, using "bad speech" that would otherwise threaten the order of society.

Greek women from the southern prong of the Peloponnese called the Mani also occasionally use obscene language in laments. In a region where blood feuding was common, at least until the Second World War, the use of "strong words" in laments was not merely sexually transgressive. It was said that "in the laments they could kill a person with language" (Seremetakis 1991: 118). Nadia Seremetakis has argued that women, in contrast to men, manage their violence through language and sound: "For women, language and sound intensify and deintensify the presence of defilement in any social situation" (ibid.). She goes on to argue that during the ritual wailing for the dead the violence and pain expressed in language, sound, and gesture

> constructs the space of death and the separation from the everyday social order . . . The acoustic pain of singing is self-inflicted corporeal violence, like scratching the face and pulling out hair. When the violence of the singing becomes too dangerous for the singer, when the self is seen to have passed over into the autonomy of

"screaming," when screaming permeates and infiltrates every word and gesture, members of the chorus will attempt to retrieve the singer from abjection through another *moiroloi* (lament).[9]

The careful self-monitoring of violence by the lamenting "chorus" and its dissipation through a process of sharing and passing the lament from one singer to another are not inevitable (Holst-Warhaft 1992; Herzfeld 1993). Women lamenters are conscious of the power of laments to exacerbate violence, and when there is cause, they will use these powers to provoke their menfolk to violent action, even murder. When there was no man available or willing to avenge a death, women from the Mani area of Greece would occasionally carry out the murder themselves. Moreover, they commemorated their violence in long laments that may still be sung at a funeral. One such lament is recounted by a widow who waited eighteen years after her husband was murdered until her sons were old enough to avenge him, then told them to take their rifles and hunt down the killers. "If you do otherwise / may you have no joy," she told her sons, "and may my black curse follow you everywhere!" (Kassis 1979: 267–270). The reversal of the usual roles of men and women is not only tolerated but celebrated in the revenge laments of Mani. In a vendetta society where honor and violence are intertwined, a sister who kills to avenge a brother's death becomes a heroine: "Now, black Vyeniki, / woman, become a man. / Buckle up and arm yourself," says her mother, in a lament composed for her dead son and for the daughter who died avenging him. The memorizing and repetition of revenge laments that are fifty or a hundred years old and their representation in the context of another funeral suggest a social admiration among the Maniots for the violence women provoke through their pain.

Berating the Dead

It is frequently believed that the dead have voluntarily left this world, and they are upbraided for leaving a widow unprovided for, a mother bereft. Their silence is interpreted as deliberate cruelty:

> Oh N., we've been sitting here since this morning
> and you haven't spoken a word.

Why are you angry with us?
We've said nothing that might offend you.
                              (Khouri 1993: 84)

Thus sang the sister of a young Lebanese man at his funeral.

Often the anger is projected onto the dead themselves. At the same Lebanese funeral, the mother of the young man asked:

Why are you angry? Why are you angry?
What have I done, my son?
Oh my darling, my son!
Oh my darling, Mother's darling!
Oh my son! Oh my son!
What have I done?
. . .
Didn't you know, my son, that you were going to die?
Does one come to the village of Abdilly to die?
You've taken nothing with you, oh my son!
Oh my son, what is this blow you've dealt us?
Oh my little one, you haven't taken your share
of the inheritance. Neither house, nor land,
You've taken nothing!
                              (My translation)

In a similar vein, the Irish widow of a plowman sang a lament for her dead husband, calling on him to rise and start plowing again:

Look at me, my treasure,
With nobody to help me
When I go reaping or cutting!
Who will do my business at the market?
Who will go to the Hill of the Mass,
As you lie stretched from now on? Och, ochon!
                              (O'Súilleabháin 1967: 132)

Reproaching the dead seems to give some relief to the bereaved. The direct form of address confirms the continuing presence of the dead person in the thoughts of the bereaved. But the lament may also become a voice for long-suppressed resentment against the dead and the living. In Ireland and the Balkans, laments seem to have been used for centuries as an opportunity to complain about family problems, about stingy, brutal, or sexually unsatisfying husbands and cruel mothers-in-law. The mother of Dermot McCarthy used the occasion of her son's death to attack her son-in-law's brutal treatment of his wife. Beginning with a traditional praise formula, she quickly transformed it into a curse:

> My curse on you instead
> Not on livestock or harvest,
> On hearth or on home,
> But in your heart and veins
> To leave you maimed,
> You sour-tempered lout.
> (Bourke 1993: 170–171)

A Hungarian widow lamented her husband with the words: "My burning fire, my flaming fire, now you are fallen asleep, now your hands and feet are withered so that you may not beat me any more" (Kiss and Rajeczky 1966: 94). In a similar vein, a widow from Mani used a lament she composed for one of her male relatives to give voice to a lifetime of abuse from her in-laws, calling her mother-in-law "an old bitch" who "used me up" and complaining that her brother-in-law left her to "eat dry weeds / and drink brackish water" (Kassis 1981: 33). In a Warao lament, one mourner said: "Since I, your sister, have a vile tongue, I will chastise my relatives, since I am a woman, I will chastise my relatives" (Briggs 1992: 347). Such open defiance of custom in cultures in which women are expected to be reticent in public and show respect for their husbands and in-laws is part of the brief license of the funeral. Its recurrence across many cultures in the context of women's laments for the dead suggests not that women necessarily expect the social criticism they voice to provoke change, but rather that for the duration of the rituals of death they are accorded an unusual status. The dialogue they control is something they, not men, are suited for, and they use this license to turn private pain and anger into public language. The strong emotions aroused in the bereaved are felt suitable to the chaos and pain of death and are tolerated, encouraged, and finally contained as the laments subside and the next stage of the ritual begins.

The language of laments is a singular one. Its words may be subversive, secret, strong, violent. Words are only a part of the language of lament. They are generally uttered by women who punctuate each phrase or verse with sobs and cries, tearing their hair or scratching their cheeks. Tears and gestures are as much a part of this language as words. The community may regard the women who perform laments as persons of low status, but in the context of the funeral, when they become the leaders of a weeping chorus, their songs are heard with respect. Why does the language of lament demand such respect? The answer has to do with truth.

Pain and Truth

In her exploration of the relationship between torture and truth in ancient Athenian society, Page DuBois noted that the evidence of tortured slaves was thought to be reliable.[10] How could someone being tortured on the rack or the wheel tell a lie? The Athenian law courts frequently ordered the torture of a slave, holding that extreme pain would produce the truth. DuBois was not the first to note the relationship between pain and truth. Foucault (1980), Scarry (1985), and others have observed how states and other institutions have systematically used pain and confession to construct their own claims to truth. In the case of women lamenters, as Seremetakis (1991: 4–5) has rightly remarked, the sufferer can use the truth that is claimed through the emotional force of grief to challenge or manipulate social institutions. The Warao say of women lamenters: "they only cry the truth; they couldn't cry lies" (Briggs 1992: 341). For the people of Mani, the "discoursed pain and discourse in pain [in laments] constitutes truth" (ibid.: 120).

The pain of death, like the body's pain, calls up a cry that demands respect; women "sing," as the tortured informant "sings" in American gangster literature, and the song is "true" because the audience recognizes the pain behind it. In the case of the Warao women's laments, the words the women sing often do not literally correspond to reality. Their minds emptied of conscious thought, the women draw on a reservoir of images and "strong words" that produces a truth that men and women perceive as communal. Women in Greece often claim not to be able to sing without the help of other women. Frequently the structure of the laments is antiphonal, led by a soloist who improvises verses about the dead and is supported by a chorus of other women who punctuate and confirm the narrative of the leader. The truth of the narrative is thus witnessed and recorded in the course of the performance itself. It is a truth that, because of its association with the world of the dead and the pollution of the corpse, is fraught with danger. The role of spiritual intermediary, like the polyphonic character of the lament, affords both license and protection to the individual (Kim 1989; Briggs 1992; Seremetakis 1991). The dead may themselves lament through their intermediaries.

On the South Korean island of Cheju, Seong Nae Kim has shown how memories of the terrible atrocities of the 1948 April 3 uprising are expressed in the form of dreams and laments for the dead performed by female shamans. The official state "truth" about the events, in which one-third of the population of the island was massacred, is subverted by the popular narratives of the laments. "In Cheju folk religion, the dead demand that the living remember their lives and deaths—even to the extent that the well-being of the living be nearly destroyed" (1989: 257). Those who have died unnatural deaths are regarded as ambiguous and malevolent. Shamanistic rites are intended to guard the living from the spiteful dead. Through the shaman the dead lament their own deaths, and the relatives are forced to relive the painful events they have "forgotten." Kim notes that the popular memory expressed in these stories of the dead "never directly makes a truth-claim loaded with an oppositional ideological apparatus. The spirits of the dead simply lament their unfulfilled wishes and abnormal states of death and express their longing for a restful after-life" (256). Still, she contends, the retrieval of memory is a form of subversion, a telling of history that runs counter to the official version. The shamanistic laments revive the truth of the past in order to heal the living who have repressed the memory of terror.

The truth of lament is an emotional one. "Truths" can be told in laments that must be suppressed the day after the funeral. But laments are not forgotten any more than the performance of a tragedy is forgotten. Lament is both a theatrical performance of pain and the creation of a communal, as distinct from official, truth. The creation of the community's own version of the truth is generally held to be therapeutic.

Lament as Therapy

The Toraja people of the highlands of South Sulawesi, Indonesia, who usually avoid expressing intense emotions, wail and cry openly at funerals because they believe it is helpful to the survivors (Wellenkamp 1988: 492). The Toraja say the crying brings them relief by allowing them to release "hot" feelings. The open expression of feelings at Toraja funerals is not only a relief for present pain; it is believed that crying, in connection with a death, will prevent illness. Like many other societies, including our own, the Toraja could be said to have a cathartic theory of emotion.

What exactly do we mean by catharsis? The original sense of the word, in ancient Greek, was a cleansing from guilt or defilement, a purification. Rituals of purification such as sacrifice or fire could effect a cure for defilement. Aristotle extended the notion of catharsis to the emotions. The vicarious experience of pity and fear at the tragic theater, he believed, achieved a catharsis of the emotions. There is a significant shift in meaning between the literal notion of catharsis and Aristotle's metaphorical one. Aristotle is speaking not of ritual but of theater. Some would argue that the links between ritual and theater in classical Greece were close enough to be blurred, but Aristotle himself made it clear that for him, the action of a tragedy was an artistic creation quite distinct from reality. The theater was a place where death and the emotions surrounding it were presented to the public in a confined space and in a constrained artistic form. The recreation of life's most highly charged moments before an audience of Athenian citizens produced a communal response that Aristotle considered beneficial. The responses of an audience at a tragedy and of a bereaved community at a funeral were linked by the common desire for purification, cleansing, emotional relief.

Laments are not only widely felt to be salutary for the bereaved; they are even pleasurable for the performer. "I would rather lament than eat or drink," asserts a well-known Greek lament (Alexiou 1974: 125), and a Hungarian lamenter is quoted as saying, "I look forward to lamenting as one would to a shower of rain" (Kiss and Rajeczky 1966: 105). In his account of a funeral that took place on the Aran Islands, off the coast of Galway, in 1911, J. M. Synge described women keeners possessed by their art: "Each old woman, as she took her turn in the leading recitative, seemed possessed, for a moment, with a profound ecstasy of grief, swaying to and fro, and bending her forehead to the stone before her, while she called out to the dead with a perpetually recurring chant of sobs" (39). The pleasure of singing laments may derive partly from the ecstatic, trancelike state reached by the performer, a state achieved by methods that are often similar in places widely dispersed. Rocking her body, holding a cloth or handkerchief over her face, the lamenter induces a mood that may be occasioned by personal loss but that can also be reproduced more or less at will. "The essence of lament," say Bulgarian observers, "is such that once it has begun, it proceeds in the same way. Regardless of whether it is reproduced or performed at death, the lamenter falls into the same emotional state—she weeps and gives herself up entirely to her grief" (Kaufman and Kaufman 1988: 386).

The catharsis of emotion combined with varying degrees of self-induced trance gives the singer and her audience a sense that she has moved into a realm outside the everyday. The shadowy region between the living and the dead is broached by the lament singer as it is, in many cultures, by the shaman. In some cases the two are distinct, in others the line between them is blurred. The female shamans of Cheju Island in Korea perform ceremonies of magical healing in which they sing laments, assuming the voices of the souls of dead ancestors. Laments are almost always a theatrical representation of the past, but in the case of a culture with a traumatic past, too dangerous to resurrect in any literal form, the laments of the shamans dramatize the deaths of the victims of violent repression and by allowing the spirits of the dead to speak through them, "heal" their relatives. In the case of the Korean shaman's performance, tearful laments are interspersed with comic clowning. A carefully contrived exchange of tears and laughter may be a way of breaking or lightening the tragic narrative's mood and effecting a "cure" by a surreal confusion of the worlds of the living and the dead.

The Warao people say that "only with the aid of *sana* [laments] can the community overcome the acute anger . . . and sadness . . . occa-

sioned by a death. If women did not wail, the close relatives of the deceased would be unable to reincorporate themselves into the daily life
of the community" (Briggs 1992: 341). Like many other people who
sing laments, the Warao believe these songs of grief help overcome the
conflicts that either lead to a death or are produced by it. The articulation of "strong" or bitter words, including obscenities that cannot usually be uttered in public and criticism of men in positions of power, is
addressed not only to the dead person or to the object of the lamenter's
anger, but to the community. Warao women acknowledge anger as a
benefit to the expression of grief. However personal a lament may be, it
is sung in company; other women pick up phrases from the first lamenter and incorporate them into their own song. The whole group of
lamenters may join in the refrain or simply weep and sigh.

Polyphony and counterpoint are the hallmark of lament in most traditional societies. Individual interpretation is followed by incorporation; one woman's expression of grief is listened to by the community
of singers and integrated into a larger composition that comes to represent the grief of all. It is the ability of the lamenting group of women to
transform private emotion into collective pain and anger that is recognized as beneficial. In many ways this communal transformation is
what the support groups of our times are struggling to achieve. The
need to share violent emotions on a TV program with other mothers
whose children have been shot in the streets of Los Angeles, to meet
the relatives of the family members lost when a plane crashes, to talk to
people who share a common loss and to talk about it together, is acknowledged. What is lacking, in these contemporary efforts to form a
communitas of grief, is a traditional form. Laments are not simply an expression of emotion; they are poetic and musical forms that structure
powerful feelings of grief into a performance.

The transformation of rage and suffering into a performance that
seems to help the community deal with those emotions may be impossible in the absence of a small and tight-knit group. It may even be impossible without music. Among the Warao, the women who sing laments are able to cry with words and music, but men cry "in words
alone" (Briggs 1992: 340). Music is what makes the mind "go blank,"
and gives women access to the process of transforming their personal
sorrow into a collective expression. In a culture where the relationship
of poetry to music has largely disappeared, the importance of the musi-

cal element of laments may seem strange. To the ancient Greeks, it would have been perfectly understandable.

Plato believed that music imitated moral character. *Harmonia* ordered the voice as rhythm ordered the body. The sense of order that the elements of music imposed on the body and voice was what distinguished humans from other animals. To be human was to perceive beauty in the movement of the body and voice. Plato attributed the political tumult of the Athens of his day to the "mixture" of musical modes that made it disorderly (*Laws* 664b–671a; *Republic* 387–401b, 401d–402a). Music, at its best, was believed by the Greeks to order the chaos of the soul. We, who listen to music a great deal, are aware of some of its powers, but we no longer participate in it as a whole community. There is no citizen chorus, as there was in the Athens of Plato's day. There is no group of women ready to compose our laments. The musical resources for "ordering" grief are lost to us.

~ 2

Laughter

Tim Finnegan lived in Walkin' Street
A gentle Irishman mighty odd,
He'd a beautiful brogue both rich and sweet
And to rise in the world he carried a hod.
You see he'd a sort of a tipplin' way
With a love for the liquor poor Tim was born;
To help him on with his work each day
He'd a drop o' the craythur' every morn.
Wack fol' the darn o, dance to your partner
Whirl the floor, your trotters shake.
Wasn't it the truth I told you?
Lots of fun at Finnegan's wake.
One mornin' Tim was rather full;
His head felt heavy which made him shake.
He fell from his ladder and he broke his skull
And they carried him home his corpse to wake.
They rolled him up in a nice clean sheet
And laid him out upon the bed,
A gallon of whisky at his feet
And a barrel of porter at his head.
His friends assembled at the wake
And Mrs Finnegan called for lunch.
First they brought in tay and cake
Then pipes, tobacco and whisky punch,
Biddy O'Brien began to cry:
"Such a nice clean corpse did you ever see?
Tim Mavoorneen, why did you die?"
"Arrah hold your gob," said Paddy McGhee.
Then Maggie O'Connor took up the job.

"Oh Biddy," says she, "you're wrong I'm sure."
Biddy gave her a belt in the gob
And left her sprawling on the floor.
Then the war did soon engage—
Twas woman to woman and man to man.
Shelailaigh law was all the rage
And a row and a ruction soon began.
Then Mickey Maloney raised his head
When a noggin' of whisky flew at him.
It missed and falling on the bed
The liquor scattered over Tim.
Tim revives, see how he rises!
Timothy rising from the bed
Said: "Whirl your whisky round like blazes
Thanum and dial, do you think I'm dead?"

                    Traditional(?) Irish song

*T*EARS AND LAMENTS ARE, as we have seen, an almost universal response to death and grief.[1] Laughter is a less common response, one that seems inappropriate in most parts of the modern world. Jokes may be told at memorial services, but the idea of engaging in bawdy games, singing sexually suggestive songs, or courting a future husband at a funeral is offensive. We generally think of funerals as solemn events, although our view is by no means universal and appears to be a relatively modern phenomenon even in Europe. Until at least the seventeenth century and in the more remote parts of Europe, especially Ireland and the Balkans, bawdy funeral games were as common as the laments that preceded them. The Christian church, to judge by its directives against the practice, found the wake games even more offensive than laments for the dead. Except in those areas over which it had little authority, the church seems to have succeeded in putting a stop to them. Rural Ireland was one area where wake games continued to form an integral part of funeral rites well into the nineteenth century. Accounts of these games suggest that women played an unusual and prominent part, as they did in the singing of laments, with a degree of freedom that was a complete reversal of their usual subordinate role.

The games took place in the presence of the corpse and involved horse-play, drunkenness, nudity, and what appeared to observers to be blas-phemous parodies of Christian ritual.

Strange behavior this seems to us now, behavior that transgresses all the rules of mourning as we understand it. Tears and laments are al-most universal responses to death. They are, to our eyes, appropriate to the sadness and solemnity of a funeral. Most of us would be shocked to attend a funeral where tears were abruptly halted and replaced by laughter, games, and sexual play.

In an article in the *New York Times* (November 6, 1996) describing sexual pickups at funerals in Abidjan, in Africa's Ivory Coast, Howard W. French ascribes the "game of seduction that is supposedly dedicated to the dead" to a "decay in African moral values." A private funeral home in downtown Abidjan has, it seems, become the hottest place in town to pick up a sexual partner and it is common to hear "bursts of laughter more often than sobbing." The reporter contrasts the frivo-lous scene in the city funeral with the behavior of people in other west African societies, where, he says, "death is still treated with the utmost seriousness." But is laughter at a funeral an indication of lack of seri-ousness? In his study of laughter at marriage rituals among the Iteso of Kenya, Ivan Karp notes that whereas we in the West would expect so-lemnity to mark such an event, it is common, if not for the bride, at least for the other women participants in the ceremony, to treat mar-riages as an occasion of laughter and ribaldry (1987: 137). Karp argues that anthropologists have tended to ignore laughter and irony in other-wise serious events, because they tend to attribute more consistency to other cultures than they expect in their own. Clarity and order are eas-ier to deal with than subversion and disorder (138).

The reporter's view of what is appropriate behavior at a funeral echoes the rhetoric frequently directed by English observers at nine-teenth-century Irish wakes. The objections to the games played at wakes centered on their overt sexual character and the lack of proper solemnity in the face of death, especially considering that the corpse was usually lying on a table in the center of the room where they were performed. Exposed as never in life, the dead body laid out on a bier or in his coffin was the focus both of attention and of disregard, both pres-ent and not present. The rules of normal life were relaxed or inverted. Grief having been expressed in tears and laments led by the women, the mood suddenly changed. In the place of solemnity came games, jokes, laughter, sex. What part did laughter and sexual games once play in funerals? Is sexual intercourse a common, life-affirming response to death, as Bloch and Parry (1982) suggest? Or are laughter and play indulged in as a means of putting an end to grief that might otherwise pose a threat to the well-being of the community? Have we repressed and lost an aspect of mourning behavior that was possibly helpful to the mourner and to the community confronting death?

To understand what part parodic, blasphemous, and even obscene humor played in the rituals of death and the work of mourning and to arrive at an alternative understanding of the relationship between sexual jesting, the fear of death, and the work of mourning, we must travel widely in time and space.

Greece: Baubo's Strange Gesture

In ancient Greece, women's noisy behavior at festivals *and* funerals was attacked in the same breath.[2] Among the festivals in which women played a prominent part were those associated with Dionysus, particularly the Eleusinian mysteries and the Anthesteria, as well as the Adonia, where women wailed over the dead Adonis, laughed, and made ribald jokes on the rooftops of Athens. The ancient sources that link festivals and funerals and complain of noisy and unseemly behavior at both have caused modern scholars some consternation.[3] But what seems puzzling to a culture that individualizes mourning and has few social mechanisms for collectively expressing the fear, absurdity, and tragedy of death becomes lucid in cultures where the funeral and the festival are two of the central sites of a communal response to the deepest of human anxieties. At both these sites, in classical Greece, the role of women was a reversal of their quotidian reticence. This reversal was marked, in the case of the funeral, by noisy wailing, disheveled appearance, and the angry rhetoric of laments that could be used to fuel revenge (Holst-Warhaft 1992: 88–126; Alexiou 1974: 14–23). The limited evidence we have for women's involvement in the elaborate play of the festivals suggests that they had a brief license to express themselves in public and to engage in what would otherwise be unseemly behavior (Winkler 1990: 200–202).

A mythical story associated with the Eleusinian mysteries offers our first clue to the link between mourning and ribald laughter in antiquity. A curious little fragment from the so-called Orphic version of the *Hymn to Demeter* (fragment 49) tells the following story. Demeter's daughter, Persephone, was picking flowers in a meadow together with the Oceanids. When she bent to pick a narcissus, Hades appeared and carried Persephone off to the underworld. Demeter heard her daughter's cry for help and roamed the earth searching for the girl. While the goddess was lamenting by a spring, the daughters of the king of Eleusis, who had come to fetch water, discovered her. Demeter was disguised as a woman, so they failed to recognize her, but they invited her to visit their home, where she was given a child named Demophon to nurse. She took a liking to the child and tried to make him immortal by anointing him with ambrosia and placing him in a fire. The child's mother, Baubo, caught the goddess but did not succeed in saving her child.

In the Orphic fragment 50, ascribed to Clement of Alexandria, Baubo is mentioned again. This time she receives Demeter at Eleusis and offers her the *kukeon*, the traditional drink of the initiates at the mysteries. When Demeter refuses to drink it because of her sorrow, Baubo raises her skirt, exposing her genitals and causing the goddess to laugh. Demeter then agrees to break her fast (N. J. Richardson 1974: 213, 810). Another interesting version of the story is given by Arnobius.[4] Here Baubo first depilates her pubic area, making it "as neat and smooth as a little boy whose skin is not yet tough and hairy. She comes back to the grieving goddess. Then, in the midst of the other things that are customarily done to assuage grief and bring it to an end, she exposes herself, and showing her organs lays bare all the parts veiled by shame. The goddess' gaze falls on the pubis and feasts on the sight of this extraordinary sort of consolation." In the "Homeric" version of the *Hymn*, the figure of Iambe replaces Baubo, and the episode of exposure is absent, but Iambe's name is still associated with the humorous language of insults.[5] There is evidence from a number of sources to suggest that *aischrologia* (the trading of insults accompanied by obscene gestures) was common at the festivals of Demeter as well as at the Dionysian festivals.

There has been much discussion of the relation of Baubo/Iambe to the mysteries at Eleusis and to a group of terracotta statuettes found at Priene in 1898 by German archaeologists in the ruins of a temple of

Demeter and dubbed "Baubo" by the classical scholar Hermann Diels (Olender 1985: 3–55). The figures' large heads, hair drawn up on top, rest directly on the legs so that the face is where the belly should be, and the genitals are reproduced on the chin. The "Baubo" statuettes are serene, plump, faintly smiling. If they echo Baubo's gesture, it is to reveal her belly as symbol of fertility and perhaps to assure ease in childbirth. Diels's dubbing of the figurines was based on his work on Empedocles, who defined Baubo not only as the name of a nurse of Demeter but as a synonym for *koilia* (cavity or belly). He also noted a recent discovery of the use of the word *baubon* in a masculine form to mean a leather phallus or dildo (Olender 1985: 39).

The associations of Baubo's name are varied. She may be nurse, demon, and maenad, but she is always linked with Demeter's mourning. As Maurice Olender's summation of the evidence suggests (1985), the means used to end the goddess' mourning in the various accounts are all connected with sexuality. Whereas Iambe chatters and uses obscene language, Baubo's gesture appears to be a last-ditch attempt to persuade the goddess to break her fast and end her mourning. The wordless gesture replaces serious behavior with a comic revelation of what should remain hidden, as the versions of the tale by Clement and Eusebius stress. Baubo raises her skirts and displays her genitals. For its comic effect, the gesture depends on the gaze of the observer, in this case the goddess. Demeter must be sufficiently impressed by the absurdity or comic indecency of the gesture to break into laughter and out of mourning. The goddess does not merely smile; she bursts out laughing. The gesture achieves what words failed to obtain, a respite from grief for Demeter and a consequent relief for the earth: a reprieve that cheats death of its power.

The controversy over the origins of Baubo are as heated as those over its meaning. Olender dismisses attempts to reduce the Baubo/Demeter story to a fertility-oriented theory that combines etiological and apotropaic arguments, but he ends his own discussion with an interpretation of Baubo based more on the statuettes at Priene than on the literary accounts; his Baubo becomes "the locus of a glance fascinated by the chaotic topography of an outrageous sexuality" (1990: 105), one whose effect is viewed in relation to other Greek figures, specifically Hermaphroditus and Priapus. This approach seems as reductive, in its way, as those Olender dismisses. What is interesting about Baubo's gesture is precisely that it conforms to a type, one that is proven effective in interrupting cases of intense and potentially destructive mourning.[6] If the statuettes, emphasizing a single feature of the anatomy, usually but not always the sexual organs, are commonly found in connection with rites of initiation, as Victor Turner (1967) and others have observed, the "Baubo" figurines may be viewed not merely as the plastic depictions of a frozen gesture, but as predictable cult objects in such a context.[7]

An Egyptian Tale

The resort of exposing the genitals to break a mood of mourning or depression is one found in a number of mythical stories. Clement of Alexandria, the principal source for the Orphic version of the Demeter myth, may well have been familiar with the Egyptian myth of the goddess Hathor, who made her father laugh and go back to work by exposing herself.[8] The god Ra-Harakhti, master of the universe, had been insulted during a heated meeting of the gods. He retired to his pavilion for a whole day and lay down in a huff. Nothing would persuade him to emerge until his daughter, Hathor, arrived and exposed her genitals to him, causing the god to burst out laughing. Immediately he became reconciled to the other gods and returned to his duties (I. Levy 1936).[9]

N. J. Richardson (1974: 217) cites tales similar to the Baubo story, including ones from Sardinia and Romania about the Virgin Mary being made to laugh, while mourning her son's death, by a joking frog or toad. At first sight these tales may seem far removed from the figure of Baubo. However, Baubo's association with demons and dark powers, especially Hecate, includes an identification with toads. Indeed the female toad becomes a metaphor for Baubo in Old Comedy. The ugliness of Baubo in her aspect of old woman and the vulgarity of her gesture may be what links her to toads; the toad that breaks the Virgin's mourning still carries a trace of Baubo's role as coarse jester.[10]

Japan: The Shaman's Exposure

Far removed from the Mediterranean, a Japanese Shinto myth also suggests that exposure of the genitals is the ultimate comic gesture, one that may successfully put an end to intense mourning. The story, which predates the version found in the eighth-century *Kojiki* but is told there in convenient form, relates the cosmogonic myth of Izanagi and Izanami (Philippi 1969: 48–86). The two creators of the world, Izanagi and Izanami, are sent by the heavenly *kami*, or spirits, to solidify and complete the earth. Izanami, the female creatrix, gives birth to the islands and various *kami*, including the fire *kami*, who burns her genitals, causing her to "die." Her spouse crawls around her feet weeping. From his tears is born a deity whose name suggests women's laments.[11] Izanagi kills the child, buries Izanami, and sets out for Yōmï, the land of the dead, to seek his beloved. He finds her, but she tells him that, having eaten from the hearth of Yōmï, she cannot return without seeking the permission of the *kami* of the realm of the dead. She asks her spouse to wait outside, but he is too impatient. He enters the Hall of the Dead and sees her rotting corpse, covered with maggots. Disgusted, he flees and is pursued by the ugly women of Yōmï and by his spouse, but he manages to pull a stone across the door, thus sealing off the world of the dead from the world of the living.

To purify himself from the pollution of death, Izanagi performs elaborate ceremonies that result in the birth of more *kami*, daughters and sons. A power struggle develops between Izagami's sun-goddess daughter, Ama-terasu, and her brother, Susa-No-Wo, who weeps uncontrollably, mourning his father's death. The behavior of the brother includes a series of acts that threaten the prosperity and fertility of the agricultural cycle and frighten his sister so much that she opens the heavenly rock cave and shuts herself inside, causing universal darkness. The many *kami* devise a plan to lure Ama-terasu from the cave and restore light. Elaborate rituals involving sacred objects are performed, and a female *kami* regarded as paradigmatic of the female shaman dances on top of an upturned barrel, becomes possessed, and exposes her breasts and genitals, causing all the *kami* to laugh. Ama-terasu is curious. She opens the door a crack to see what is going on, and the *kami* tell her that the singing, dancing, and laughing she hears mean there is a deity superior to her. Ama-terasu steps out of the cave, a hidden deity takes her by the hand, and a rope is pulled behind her. She is told, "You may go no further than this" (Philippi 1967: 85). With her emergence, light returns to the world; the usurping brother is subsequently punished, and order is restored.[12]

In the Japanese myth, laughter caused by a female shaman's exposing her genitalia is instrumental in restoring light and fertility to earth in the form of Ama-terasu and ending the chaos caused by the excessively mourning Susa-No-Wo. The goddess' voluntary interment in the cave is a form of death, one that the *kami* overcome by trickery. In the Orphic myth of Demeter, light and fertility are restored by an agreement with the ruler of the underworld soon after the mourning mother is diverted from her excessive mourning by a mysterious female figure exposing her genitalia and causing the goddess to laugh. The Egyptian myth of Hathor differs slightly in that the figure to be distracted is the father of the goddess, but the effect is the same: life and light are restored to a world by the catalyst of laughter occasioned by indecent exposure.

The stories are far apart in time and space, but in all cases there seems to be an association of female genitalia and sexual humor with the capacity of laughter to interrupt potentially dangerous or excessive mourning and to restore fertility, light, and life. The three tales taken together raise some intriguing questions. What is so hilarious about female genitalia? And what is the nature of the laughter? Why does it bring relief? Is the exposure of what mankind, unlike all other animals, keeps concealed the original joke? Is it the breaking of a taboo that shocks and attracts? Does the reversal of codes of behavior, especially of female behavior, cause laughter? We will return to these questions after surveying other contexts in which laughter, sexuality, and the grotesque are linked to death and mourning.

The Medieval Carnival

The classic investigation of role reversal, parody, and "grotesque" behavior in the context of folk festivals and carnivals is undoubtedly Bakhtin's. In his studies of Rabelais (1984a) and Dostoevsky (1984b) and in *The Dialogic Imagination* (1981), Bakhtin elaborates a theory of the "carnivalesque" or "popular grotesque" as a salutary expression of ordinary people's opposition to authority. According to Bakhtin, the manifestations of this folk culture of the European Middle Ages can be divided into three forms: (1) ritual spectacles, such as carnivals, the Feast of Fools, the "Paschal Laughter," and harvest festivals; (2) comic verbal compositions such as parodies; and (3) popular slang, oaths, and curses. Characterizing all these forms are laughter, ambiguity, uncrowning, or the debunking of authority.

For Bakhtin, the carnival world of mocking laughter existed as a parallel but self-sufficient realm, creating a double aspect of life that was once accepted as part of official cultic behavior:

> But at the early stages of pre-class and pre-political social order it seems that the serious and the comic aspects of the world and of the deity were equally sacred, equally "official." This similarity was preserved in rituals of a later period of history. For instance in the early period of the Roman state the ceremonial of the triumphal procession included on almost equal terms the glorifying and the deriding of the victor. The funeral ritual was also composed of lamenting (glorifying) and deriding the deceased. But in the definitely consolidated state and class structure such an equality of the two aspects became impossible. All the comic forms were transferred, some earlier and others later, to a non-official level. There they acquired a new meaning, were deepened and rendered more complex, until they became the expression of folk consciousness, of folk culture. Such were the carnival festivities of the ancient world. (1984a: 6)

In the Middle Ages, Bakhtin continues, the comic rituals were not religious, nor did they have any aspect of prayer or ritual about them. Rather, these carnival spectacles and humor belonged somewhere on the borders of art and life.

Bakhtin includes a vast variety of behavior and manifestations in his theory of the carnivalesque, and his purpose in investigating the genre is primarily to illuminate what he sees as the progressive, rejuvenating influence of the popular forms of the marketplace on Rabelais's work.[13] But for all the breadth and insight of his investigation of ancient and medieval sources, he pays surprisingly little attention to what I take to be the deeper psychological motivations of much of this humor. Nor does he sufficiently consider its other primary site: the wake.

While Bakhtin paints a picture of the carnival as a licensed forum for mockery and "uncrowning," the sports of the funeral, like the laments of women mourners, far from being licensed, seem to have been a continuous locus of contention with the authorities.[14] The prominent part played by women in the rituals for the dead was undoubtedly one reason for the controversy that surrounded them. The medieval marketplace, like the medieval church and state, was dominated by men. Sexual license and role reversal, often made explicit by the exchange of costumes, were common features of the carnival and could be tolerated as part of the temporary topsy-turvyness it engendered; but the funeral was a site where women exercised a traditional and unusual authority. As handlers of the corpse and chief mourners they were already key players in the rituals that surrounded death, and their participation in "obscene" wake games was a natural extension of this prominence. Another reason for the antipathy of church and state authorities to the "play" of the funeral was that, unlike the sanctioned festivals of the marketplace, death rituals appeared to preserve a cultic character that was not well understood and that clearly predated Christianity. Finally, in the event of untimely or violent death, the funeral became the focus for expressions of anger and outrage that sometimes led to violence. Far from being apolitical, it was frequently used as the forum for inciting private and popular opposition to authority.[15]

Bakhtin's work on the carnival is centered in medieval Europe but refers frequently to the comic literature of ancient Greece and Rome. The problem in such comparisons is the limited number of surviving Greek sources: a handful of comedies by Euripides and a single example of the satyr plays that followed a trilogy of tragedies in the Attic theater, drawing on and satirizing the material that preceded it. The sources are more numerous for Roman comedy, including information about popular carnivals, but we still know very little about the popular or cultic origins of ancient comedy. We don't even know whether comedy preceded tragedy or vice versa. It may be that they were always intertwined, that the comic and the tragic masks were, if not identical, interchangeable. By the sixth century B.C.E., it seems, they had already been separated (Carrière 1979: 26). We are left with two well-developed literary genres, one with its mouth turned down, the other with its mouth turned up.

The literary distinction between tragedy and comedy, established at the theater of Dionysus, was not inviolable. Euripides already prefigures the irony and comic relief of Renaissance drama; later prose forms would blur the distinction still further. The ambiguity that was undoubtedly linked to ritual practice may be irrecoverable in the Greek case, but accounts of the practices that surrounded funerals in certain areas of modern Europe until recently offer us more helpful insights into the deeply intertwined "tragic" and "comic" aspects of ritual play than we glean from the more public and licensed buffoonery of the carnival proper.

The Fun in the Funeral

The games that were once a common part of the wake or funeral rituals across much of Europe were enacted in the presence of the corpse, a constant reminder of the fragility of life, and of the ever-watchful dead. However hilarious and ribald the funeral became, the corpse was a terrifying observer to be reckoned with. As long as it was present, it was hard to trivialize or tame the wake. To "wake" the dead is to inhabit, for a brief period, the same space—to imagine one's own death. The primordial suspension of disbelief is not that of the spectator but of the players. For there is only one spectator of importance: the dead man or woman, laid out on a table, dressed in his or her best clothes, waiting for the show to begin. Not merely an observer, the corpse was believed to be the host of the wake.[16] The displays of grief, the games of skill or sexual conquest, the obscene gestures were all addressed to the single silent watcher, the constant reminder of the common fate of the players. Every tear was shed, every joke made in the face of death.

In rural Ireland and parts of the Balkans funeral games were once as much a part of the funeral as laments.[17] Both practices were integral to conceiving of death as a lengthy ritual process rather than as a discrete event, a view that made the dead accessible to the living, and vice versa.[18] Both were vigorously opposed by the Christian church and have virtually disappeared, but accounts of the wakes and the record of their condemnation provide at least a shadowy picture of what was once, apparently, a widespread European tradition.[19]

Finnegan's Wake

> Even the dogs in the street in West Kerry know that the "otherworld" exists, and to be in and out of it constantly is the most natural thing in the world.
>
> Nuala Ni Dhomhnaill (1995)

In rural Ireland we have accounts of funeral games dating back to the medieval period, but by the time ethnographers began to describe the

actual nature of the practices, either they were in decline or their details had been suppressed because of alleged obscenity. There is general
agreement about the consumption of large quantities of alcohol by
both sexes at the wakes, and about the smoking of tobacco. Besides this
there were games of various sorts, storytelling, singing, and dancing
(Prim 1853: 334; Morris 1938: 123; Evans 1957: 290; O'Súilleabháin
1967: 16–18). Among the best indications we have of the behavior of
those attending the wake, and of the persistence of the rural Irish in
maintaining their traditional games, are the numerous directives issued
against them by episcopal synods and individual bishops. The condemnation of the wake games occurred in a context of organized cultural
repression following a series of bloody campaigns against the Irish
during the sixteenth and seventeenth centuries. Eighty-five percent
of Irish lands were transferred to English colonists during the seventeenth century. At the same time, despite severe penal laws attacking
Catholic property, clergy, and civil rights, the Catholic church, en-
trenched in the towns and among the upper classes, was becoming increasingly anglicized (Whelan 1999: 253).

In the traditional wake, with its loud lamentation, drunkenness, and
sexually explicit games, the hierarchy of the Catholic church saw traces
of older religious practice, of a "primitive" Ireland that negated their
desire to be accepted by the English. In the archdiocese of Amagh, the
synod of bishops on three occasions (1660, 1668, and 1670) ordered
that drinking be abolished at wakes (O'Súilleabháin 1967). Similar directives were issued at Tuam, Clones, Waterford and Lismore, and Kil-
more in the same period. Drunkenness was only part of the problem
for the church. In 1614 the Synod of Amagh issued a statute declaring
that "the pious feelings of devout people were outraged by the singing
of lewd songs and the playing of obscene games by silly fellows, conduct which would not be permissible even on occasions of merrymak-
ing. This misbehaviour was carried on under cover of darkness; the
fear of Death was absent, although Death itself, as represented by the
corpse, was before the eyes of all present" (ibid.: 147). In a similar vein
the diocese of Waterford and Lismore in 1676 requested the clergy
who might be present at wakes and funerals "to ensure that Death was
uppermost in the minds of those who attended" (ibid.). In 1730 the
Dublin archdiocese ordered its clergy to "compel those who sang
smutty songs or played unchristian games on these occasions to do

public penance" (ibid.: 48). Some of the amusements were spoken of as "travesties of the sacraments" or "in mocking imitation of the sacred rites of the Church, especially the celebration of marriage" (ibid.: 150). The penalties for continued disobedience were severe, and included excommunication.

There are as many directives from the church concerning women keeners at funerals as there are about the wake games.[20] Indeed so closely are the two practices linked that the games were once termed *Cluichthe Caointe* ("Games of Lamentation").[21] The practice of hiring professional keeners at wakes was already well established by the seventeenth century, as we know from the numerous attempts to suppress them (O'Súilleabháin 1967: 138–143). In a series of pronouncements that uncannily echoes the legislation passed in the sixth century B.C.E. in Athens and the complaints of the early church fathers, the Church of Ireland condemned "exaggerated crying and keening at wakes" (1631), "the practice of employing female keeners at wakes and funerals" (1660), and "the wailings and screams of female keeners who accompanied the dead to the graveyard" (1670). A lengthy pronouncement by the diocese of Leighlin in 1748 stated that "the heathenish customs of loud cries and howlings at wakes and burials" were contrary to the teaching of St. Paul, and the diocese imposed a series of penalties for the offenders, the ultimate one for a recidivist being excommunication (ibid.: 139).

The condemnation of professional lamenters involves issues that may be somewhat different from the games themselves, but the confluence of the laments with wake games in the rhetoric of the church's denunciation suggests that there were other concerns than lewdness and debauchery. The church hierarchy, as distinct from the village priests, who apparently failed to carry out their directives, seems to have understood little of what went on at wakes. To these more distant clergy it was as if the Irish peasants had neither fear of death nor respect for the dead. The games and loud wailing were so alien to the Christian church's institutionalized solemnity of death that they believed the participants were ignoring the presence of the corpse instead of performing for it. They did, however, recognize such behavior as outside their control and perhaps stemming from a system of beliefs that conflicted with Christian doctrine.

In the nineteenth century directives were still being issued about wake behavior with suggestions for suitable alternatives to the games such as prayers for the dead, the saying of rosaries, and the reading of spiritual books. A pastoral letter issued in 1800, in the archdiocese of Cashel and Emry, urged parishioners who were present at funerals or wakes "where such odious, pernicious and detestable practices take place, to give immediate notice thereof to the Parish Priest" (O'Súilleabháin 1967: 20). Not only were the ordinances issued all over Ireland, but they were repeated time and time again in the same parishes.

The Church of Ireland was not unique in condemning wake games. Similar ordinances were issued by churches in Germany, Norway, and France (O'Súilleabháin 1967: 157–158). The Church of England took an equally strong stand against them (ibid.: 23). A canon issued in the reign of Edward III (1312–1377) aimed at "putting an end to the misbehaviour which took place when people assembled to wake the dead before burial" (ibid.: 156). The canon forbade any but the nearest relatives of the deceased to attend the wake on pain of excommunication. In rural Ireland, where priests were often in hiding because of the penal laws, the difficulty of enforcing such laws was considerable. The local clergy, too, were reluctant to enforce unpopular laws in the villages where they lived. The result was that what seems to have been a common medieval practice endured in Ireland long after it had disappeared from most of western Europe.

The Nature of the Games

Of the many games that were played at wake gatherings in Ireland, some were contests of strength and agility such as arm-wrestling, picking up horseshoes with the teeth, and other games that only the men competed in.[22] Games that involved verbal taunting and mockery frequently led to the exchange of missiles such as potatoes or clods of turf, or to blows, and the wakes were sometimes used as occasions to settle old scores (O'Súilleabháin 1967: 65–66). Other games were reenactments of procedures in the courts of law, of crafts such as shipbuilding, of weddings, or of visits to the doctor. A nineteenth-century observer described the funeral games as a complex series of presentations:

> The "game" usually first performed was termed "Bout," and was joined in by men and women, who all acted a very obscene part

which cannot be described. The next scene generally was termed "Making the Ship," with its several parts of "laying the keel," forming the "stem and stern," and erecting "the mast," the latter of which was done by a female using a gesture and expression, proving beyond doubt that it was a relic of Pagan rites. The "Bull and Cow" was another game strongly indicative of a Pagan origin, from circumstances too indelicate to be particularized. The game called "Hold the Light," in which a man is blindfolded and flogged, has been looked upon as a profane travesty of the passion of our Lord; and religion may also be considered to be brought into contempt by another of the series, in which a person caricaturing a priest, and wearing a rosary, composed of small potatoes strung together, enters into conflict with "Borekeen," and is put down and expelled from the room . . . In a game called "Drawing the Ship out of the Mud" the men engaged actually presented themselves before the rest of the assembly, females as well as males, in a state of nudity, whilst in another game female performers attired themselves in men's clothes and conducted themselves in a very strange manner. (O'Súilleabháin 1967: 291)

As tantalizing as it is informative, this account of the wake games typifies the prudery and self-censorship of most observers. Oscar Wilde's mother, writing in 1887, went so far as to call the wake games "orgies" (Mercier 1962: 50), but her account of them suggests something quite different. For example, she described a play with "a symbolic meaning" enacted just after the keeners had performed their dirge. Called "The Building of the Fort," the play was performed by masked players who fought mock battles with an enemy band until the fight was settled by a duel between the two champions. When one fell as if mortally wounded, hooded women keened over him, and pipes played martial tunes. "An herb doctor" muttered incantations as he waved a bundle of herbs above the "dead" man until he sat up and was carried off in triumph by his comrades (Morris 1938: 125). "Details can seldom be obtained," wrote Lady Wilde, "for the people are afraid of the priesthood, who have vehemently denounced [the games]. Yet the peasants cling to them with mysterious reverence and do not see the immorality of the wake practices. They accept them as mysteries, ancient usages of their forefathers to be sacredly observed, or the vengeances of the dead would fall upon them" (ibid.).

Despite her condemnation of the games, Lady Wilde seems to have understood that they were no mere frivolities. She concluded that what seemed to be sarcastic parodies of Christianity in several of the plays were actually remnants of older pagan, probably druidic rites meant to propitiate evil spirits. "It was against these two plays [that] the anathemas of the Church were chiefly directed, and they have now ceased to form any portion of the wake ceremonies of Ireland" (Morris 1938: 125).

The church, too, understood that what the games represented offered an alternative and potentially threatening ritual response to death, one that conflicted with its own teachings. Had the games been merely wanton, it is unlikely that they would have been so severely condemned from the pulpit. The problem with trying to analyze what was most offensive to the church is that the observers who wrote about the wake games belonged to a different class from those who participated in them; they also spoke a different language. There are no surviving accounts in Irish of the games, and by the time they became a topic of interest to folklorists, they had already been banned by the church and were being performed in a manner very different from what they must once have been.

Observers were apparently attracted as well as repulsed by what they regarded as the obscene aspect of the festivities. William Gregory Wood-Martin, writing at the turn of the century, quoted "a gentleman who had the opportunity of collecting accounts of many wanton orgies which disgraced wakes, particularly in the province of Munster" (quoted in Mercier 1962: 51). According to his informant, "The highly obscene manner of the dance called 'Droghedy' is very objectionable." William Carleton recalled seeing a performance of a solo dance at a wake which "could not be danced without the emblematic aids of a stick and a handkerchief. It was addressed to an individual passion, and was unquestionably one of those symbolic dances that were used at pagan rites" (quoted in Mercier 1962: 51–52). Coy though these descriptions may be, they leave little doubt that phallic dances were performed at wakes and that the association of the wake with sexuality was explicit.

Sex, Death, and Laughter

Sexual and scatological elements are as common in ritual humor as role reversal. The contrary behavior that Bakhtin sees as a feature of the medieval carnival is as essential an ingredient of the ritual humor of many non-European societies as it once was in Europe. The absence of social control during rituals may be what encourages what would, in another context, be regarded as obscenity (Apte 1985: 158). Among the Hopi, Zuni, Arapaho, and Mayo Indians, for example, ritual clowns wear huge artificial penises made of wooden sticks or knives. Obscene horseplay and humor plays an important part in the funerals of many other cultures. During the final phase of the funerals of the Tiwi tribe of Australian aborigines, for example, there is mock fighting between actual and potential spouses present at the ceremony. The funeral ends in wild laughter as the grappling couples begin to tickle one another (ibid.: 162). Among some East African tribes, certain individuals who have established a "joking relationship" with the deceased are supposed to make jokes at his funeral and ridicule him (ibid.).

Noting the links between death and uninhibited sexuality in many cultures, ethnologists and anthropologists have tended to ascribe the association to a common fertility cult.[23] Death is seen, according to this view, as part of a cyclical process that is followed by the regeneration of life. In his study of Irish humor, Vivian Mercier links the grotesque and comic elements of the wake to vestigial fertility rites perhaps exemplified by the stone carvings known as "Sheela-na-gigs" (1962: 53–54). These female figures, varying widely in date and form, are characterized by a skull-like face, skeletal ribs, and huge genitalia, often held open with both hands. Sheela-na-gig, in Mercier's view, belongs to a familiar type of figure that combines sexual potency and death. The pregnant hag is a common figure in medieval Europe, one that Bakhtin associates with the carnival. Mercier notes that "neither she nor the wake games become truly humorous—sometimes even porno-graphic—until much of their primary significance has been forgotten" (54). Mercier postulates that Sheela-na-gig may be associated with an earlier Celtic goddess of war, but concludes that whether or not this is the case, she is a powerful symbol of what "the most archaic and conservative people in Western Europe" never lost sight of: the con-nection between sex and death: "death, as we have seen in the wake games, implies sex and offers an incitement to reproduction. We can look away from the scowling face and skeletal ribs of . . . Sheela-na-gig to her distended fount of pleasure and fruitfulness—and laugh with re-lief" (56).

With Sheela-na-gig we have come full circle. The ugly figure who

exposes her genitals and appears mysteriously on the roofs or graveyards of Irish churches cannot help but remind us of Baubo. She has
none of the serenity of the Baubo figures, but her gesture of exposure
is equally outrageous, especially in its conjunction with consecrated
Christian sites. Is she, as Mercier suggests, designed to make us laugh
with relief?

A Metaphor of Exposure

Michael Herzfeld's illuminating exploration of an apparently obscene
metaphor in a Greek island song (1979) suggests some promising ways
of approaching not only the figure with her genitals exposed but also
the accounts preserved in English of Irish wakes. The metaphor, which
links the penis of a man who habitually exposed himself when drunk
with the holiest of Greek icons, the Epitafios, or Christ Entombed, is
shocking to the observer living outside the village context. Needless to
say, such songs are rarely anthologized, but Herzfeld's analysis suggests
a logical congruity between the terms of the metaphor; the icon that is
kept hidden from public, especially female eyes, for most of the year, is
taken out on Good Friday, a day when women play an unusually prominent part in church ritual. Just as they play an unusually prominent
role in secular funerals, singing laments and keeping watch over the
dead body, Greek women sing the Virgin's lament for her dead son on
Good Friday and decorate the bier carrying the Epitafios with flowers.
"Above all there is a sense of reversal," Herzfeld notes (290), one that
gives women unusual prominence and exposes what the church usually
keeps hidden in its inner sanctum. The period of forty days during
which the icon is exposed is generally regarded as a dangerous period
when evil spirits wander freely among the living. The use of the word
epitafios as a euphemism for a man's penis in the popular song expresses
not a leniency toward such exposure but its opposite. In a culture
where nudity, drunkenness, and loss of face are all frowned on, the
man's revelation of what should remain hidden is a serious breach of
community norms. The metaphor, amusing as it is, reminds the listener of the gravity of the impropriety without necessarily implying
blasphemy.[24]

The suppression of songs like the one Herzfeld describes from the
national folk song corpus is predictable. To the folklorist anxious to

present the best face of Greek culture to the outside world, the song appears both blasphemous and obscene. But to the villagers, the use of a religious icon associated with the death of Christ and the *eksotika*, or evil spirits, as a metaphor for a man's sexual organ marks the parallel "between two potentially dangerous sources of power, in which the maleficent term is restated as the beneficent" (Herzfeld 1979: 301). Here the "euphemism" of the Epitafios icon is, as Herzfeld stresses, apotropaic. It does not avoid but indirectly confronts deeply held fears.

Both the wordplay of the Greek village song and the Irish wake games, in which sexual exposure and "obscene" gestures contradict the norms of everyday behavior, may be thought of as examples of what Clifford Geertz described as "deep play" (1973). In both, fear of death and exposure of what is normally kept hidden from the public gaze are closely linked. The seriousness of the play doesn't mean that laughter and fun were absent from the wake games and the ribald songs of a Greek village. On the contrary, the humor undoubtedly gained intensity from its proximity to fear and death.

Humor, Exposure, and Death

Freud claimed that the two purposes of jokes, when they were not ends in themselves, were aggression and, in the case of the obscene joke, exposure (1960: 97). Sexual jokes, according to Freud, begin as smut intended to arouse desire in the female, but develop an aggressive dimension if the male meets with rejection. A third person, often of a lower social order, may be enlisted as an ally by the male in his effort to win the woman who is thus exposed before a witness (100). Smut becomes a joke only in more refined circles, where allusion and other techniques of joking circumvent the refined woman's intolerance of undisguised sexuality. "When we laugh at a refined obscene joke," Freud said, "we are laughing at the same thing that makes a peasant laugh at a coarse piece of smut. In both cases the pleasure springs from the same source. We, however, could never bring ourselves to laugh at the coarse smut; we should feel ashamed or it would seem to us disgusting. We can only laugh when a joke has come to our help" (101).

Freud refined and elaborated the work of H. Spencer K. Fisher and other theorists of humor and laughter in his investigation of the mechanisms and effects of jokes. Laughter and humor, according to his theory, concern the lifting of the "inhibitory cathexis." The purpose of an obscene joke is exposure:

> A chance exposure has a comic effect on us because we compare the ease with which we have enjoyed the sight with the great expenditure which would otherwise be required for reaching this end . . . Every exposure of which we are made the spectator . . . by a third person is equivalent to the third person being made comic. As opposed to this, witnessing an exposure is not a case of the comic for the witness because his own effort in doing so does away with the determining condition of comic pleasure: nothing is left but the sexual pleasure in what is seen. (1960: 222)

In a short paper written in 1916, Freud referred to Reinach's account of the Baubo legend and to the statuettes found at Priene in connection with a case of what he called a "visual obsession."[25] The patient he treated had repeated visions of his father in which the facial features were represented on the abdomen in a manner that resembled the Baubo statuettes. Freud interpreted the images, which occurred in conjunction with the repetition of the word *father-arse* (in German this can be construed as humorous wordplay on the term *Vaterarsch*, "patriarch") as being related to the patient's fear and respect for his father, whom he also regarded as a debauchee. The obsessive image of the father was, according to Freud, a replacement of the whole person by the genitals (1963: 346). Freud was not aware of the Baubo story or the Priene statuettes when he wrote about jokes. Reinach's article, which he acknowledges as his source, postdates his discussion of humor, but he must have been struck by the confirmation of his intuition about exposure and its fundamental relation to jokes.

The combination of prudery, sexism, and class consciousness that makes Freud's interpretation of humor seem dated does not diminish its remarkable insights. The Baubo and Hathor tales suggest that exposure (*contra* Freud) is intrinsically comic or at least productive of laughter, without the presence of a third person. In the Japanese tale of Amaterasu, the goddess is a sort of absent witness to the joke, but as with Finnegan at his wake, the hilarity is directed at her and causes her to emerge from her cave/death to see what the cause of such laughter could be. Freud believed that sexuality and obscenity offered "the amplest occasions for comic pleasure alongside sexual excitement; for they can show human beings in their dependence on bodily needs (degradation) or they can reveal the physical demands lying behind the claim of mental love (unmasking)" (1963: 346). Like Bakhtin's, Freud's understanding of the comic involves the breaking of taboos and the notion of unmasking/uncrowning.

As explanations of the "comic grotesque" and sexually based humor, both Bakhtin's and Freud's theories suffer from what I take to be a modern and Western absence of connection to the tragic, to death and mourning. One of the major criticisms leveled at Freud, both by such followers as Adler, Jung, and Rank and by later scholars of human behavior, notably Ernest Becker (1973: 93–105), is his failure to deal with the question of death. His late formulation of the notion of a "death instinct" allowed Freud to retain his earlier instinct theory by claiming that humans have a built-in desire to die, a theory he used to explain human aggression. As Becker remarks (88–89):

> He seems to have been unable to reach for the really direct existentialist level of explanation, to explain both man's continuity and his difference from the lower animals on the basis of his *protest* against death rather than his built-in instinctive urge toward it . . . The fiction of death as an "instinct" allowed Freud to keep the terror of death outside his formulations as a primary human problem of ego mastery. He did not have to say that death was *repressed* if the organism carried it naturally in its processes.

Otto Rank commented: "even when he [Freud] finally stumbled upon the inescapable death problem he sought to give that a new meaning also in harmony with the wish, since he spoke of death instinct instead of death fear. The fear itself he had meantime disposed of elsewhere, where it was less threatening" (1945: 116).

Freud's own displacement of primal fear from death to sexuality may be helpful in trying to understand what links the obscene gestures of the wakes, the carnival, and the mystery cults. Exposure of the genitals is both the symbolic defeat of death and the display of the forbidden. Female genitalia, being both by nature more concealed and yet revealed in alarming extension in the process of giving birth, are more likely to be invested with magical powers than male. Sheela-na-gig may be a representation of death and rebirth but her main value is probably apotropaic.[26] She belongs to a type of "shameless woman" found in Asia, Africa, and the Pacific, often placed in prominent positions on churches or other buildings or on boats. The association of the evil eye and its homeopathic double, the apotropaic eye, with genitalia is common in the Mediterranean. What is concealed is feared. What is feared can cure fear. The unexpected reduction of human to animal has shock value. It causes fear and laughter, the sort of out-of-control laughter that is both close to tears and capable of interrupting them, both tragic and comic. The beneficial effect is to halt grieving, to put an end to the excess of mourning that can harm the individual or society.

It is dangerous to try to explain anything so culturally specific and fragile as humor. To look for common elements in the humor of cultures widely separated in time and space is even riskier. We still have only a sketchy idea of the humor of the Irish wake games; it may have been not so very different from the humor at Irish weddings or other events. As Apte warns, theories of ritual humor, especially functional theories, often ignore the fact that such humor may serve several functions or may simply be an epiphenomenon, designed to entertain (1985: 175). Still, it is difficult to argue that the humor associated with the wake games and the laughter that is induced by exposure of the genitals are not different in kind from other types of humor. What makes the humor different is its apparent incongruity. The emotions aroused by death are not, I argue, culturally specific. The fear of death and the grief of bereavement, however they are displayed, are universal experiences. Tears and laments are among the most common responses to death; humor, especially sexual jesting, seems once to have been widespread. One response now seems to Western observers appropriate, the other bizarre.

Perhaps the theatrical analogy may be useful again here. Imagine sitting through the three tragedies of the *Oresteia*, and then watching a farce that turned some of the same material into an absurd and scatological comedy. Initially it might be a shock, but undoubtedly a relief too. Rather than argue what has caused the ancient Greeks, the nineteenth-century rural Irish, or the present-day inhabitants of certain parts of the world to follow tears with laughter, the deepest grief with the most irreverent humor, perhaps we should ask why we view it as shocking or inappropriate to juxtapose the two.

The answer may be that modern Western societies are increasingly removed from the calendrical and life-cycle rituals that once linked us to seasonal changes and marked the passage of individuals through life as a series of important, potentially dangerous events. The rituals that punctuated the life of the individual and the community were occasions for drama, for the performance of music and dance, for clowning. All of them were designed to appease nature and promote human well-being. The rituals of death must always have stood out as a particular sort of ritual, but as many observers have noted, weddings and funerals often have common elements, and most rituals are marked by suspension of normal social controls. A temporary instability is introduced into the community, a time of excess, license, reversal. For a time, there is no apparent care for propriety; what is normally hidden is exposed.

Perhaps Freud's idea of the importance of the spectator as an essential component of exposure can be resurrected, provided we realize that the witness to the primal joke is Death. Like the other fun and games at the funeral, the exposure of the genitals is a joke that depends, for its effect, on the figure laid out on the bed, Finnegan at his own wake. It is Death who must be appeased with games, confronted with the only weapon humans have to counter the terror of nonbeing—the continuity of life through reproduction. And there is always the hope that Death may be defeated, at least for a while. The story of Demeter and her daughter unites the themes of the appeasement and defeat of death. Baubo's gesture empowers Demeter, enabling her to exchange tears for laughter and to ensure the regular cheating of death. The interruption of intense mourning by laughter and sexual jesting seems to have been the "natural" way of managing grief. It was at the funeral, not the marketplace, where emotions were most likely to unhinge the community and tip society into chaos. What the authorities of state and church succeeded in suppressing was the self-regulation of grief. There was a time, it seems, when we understood the need to counter tears with laughter, death with sex. What followed the free-for-all at Finnegan's wake was not a riot but a return to life.

What happens now that the community has lost or abdicated its role in managing death? Is it possible for a community to take back its control of grief? If not, who will do it for us?

~ 3

Bones

At that time, saith the Lord, they shall bring out the bones of the kings of Judah, and the bones of his princes, and the bones of the priests, and the bones of the prophets, and the bones of the inhabitants of Jerusalem, out of their graves:

And they shall spread them before the sun, and the moon, and all the host of heaven, whom they have loved, and whom they have served, and after whom they have walked, and whom they have sought, and whom they have worshipped: they shall not be gathered, nor be buried; they shall be for dung upon the face of the earth.

Jeremiah 8:1–2

The hand of the Lord was upon me, and carried me out in the spirit of the Lord, and set me down in the midst of the valley which was full of bones.

And he caused me to pass by them round about: and behold there were very many in the open valley; and lo, they were very dry.

And he said unto me, Son of man, can these bones live? And I answered, O Lord God, thou knowest.

Again he said unto me, Prophesy on these bones, and say unto them, O ye dry bones, hear the word of the Lord.

Ezekiel 37:1–4

*F*IVE TIMES we hear it repeated in one biblical verse: the most terrible punishment the god of the Hebrews can inflict on a disobedient people is to dig up the bones of their ancestors and leave them for dogs to devour. Again and again the prophet Jeremiah utters the word, reminding his readers of the terrible fate that will overtake the backsliding nation of Israel. Bones are all that remain of the fragile body, the solid evidence of a past life. It is no wonder they have been disinterred and reburied, washed and carefully wrapped, arranged and worshipped by so many peoples. If they can withstand the passage of time they can buy us a little immortality. The prophecy of doom and the prophecy of redemption are closely related. The dry bones can conceivably be reassembled, clothed in flesh. Life can be breathed back into them. They are both the reminder of the absolute end of life and a promise of its renewal.

If bones and tangible remains are central to mourning, depriving families of the bones of their dead is a powerful weapon. It may be one of the most effective means of manipulating any population, but it is undoubtedly especially effective in cultures where the bones of ancestors are held to be sacred.

Burying Bones and Ashes

> The god of war keeps a shop
> where he deals out portions of glory
> for measures of blood and tears.
> The weights in his scales are corpses
> and urns of ashes, the crop
> of the battlefields of the earth.
> Aeschylus, *Agamemnon* 367–372

I would feel better with bones in my hands.
> Christopher Cuny, brother of an American
> disaster relief expert executed by Chechen
> rebels (*New York Times*, August 18, 1995)

Nineteenth-century opponents of the new practice of cremation in England saw it as inconsistent with a belief in resurrection (Eassie 1875: 53–62), although the Native Americans of the Pacific coast and other areas burned their dead to allow the soul to reach the land of the dead. The ancient Greeks began cremating their dead around 1000 B.C.E., partly to prevent enemies from molesting their dead on the battlefield, partly to liberate the souls of the deceased from their bodies. In almost all societies where cremation has been practiced, the bones and ashes are gathered for reburial. The second burial of the ashes, as Hertz has demonstrated, corresponds quite precisely to the disinterring and reburial of the bones in societies where double burial is practiced (1960: 42–45). Indeed even mummification, which appears to be the exact opposite of cremation, can be a form of desiccation caused by the air or soil. Smoking the corpse on a wicker frame or leaving it temporarily in the fork of a tree is a more primitive means of drying the body, but the result in both cases is to reduce putrefaction of the body and retain what appear to be the incorruptible remains for burial.

In the first century the Roman gladiators often fought at funerals while the body of the deceased burned on a pyre nearby. After the body had burned the mourners collected the bones and washed them in milk or wine. In the *Aeneid* Virgil describes the careful regathering of the bones of Misenus after his cremation:

> . . . Heaped offerings
> blazed up and burned—food, incense, food in bowls.
> And when the flame died and the coals fell in,
> they gave a bath of wine to the pyre's remnant,
> thirsty ash, then picking out the bones
> Corynaeus enclosed them in an urn.
> (4.315–320, trans. Fitzgerald)

Bones are about holding on to the dead and about letting them go. To deny people who bury their dead the bones of their loved ones has always been the most terrible of punishments. There is perhaps no more moving account of mourning in literature than book 24 of the *Iliad*, where the proud and aged King Priam abases himself before Achilles for the right to bury his son Hector's bones (509–514, trans. Fitzgerald):

> . . . And take
> pity on me, remember your own father.
> Think me more pitiful by far, since I
> have brought myself to do what no man else
> has done before—to lift to my lips the hand
> of one who killed my son.

And Achilles, a man not easily moved by appeals to pity, dissolves in tears, weeping with the father of the man whom he has killed and whose corpse he has deliberately defiled by dragging it behind his chariot around the funeral mound of his own friend Patroclus each morning for twelve days. When they have wept together Achilles urges Priam to eat and drink, reminding him of his own bodily needs. Then he not only accepts the ransom Priam offers for his son's body but agrees to suspend the war for eleven days so that the Trojans can carry out the prescribed rites of mourning. At the end of ten days of weeping and laments around the corpse, the body is burned, and mourners and the mourned are released from their involvement with the body. Then the war can be resumed.

During the Peloponnesian War the Athenians gathered up the bones of the soldiers who had died first on the battlefield and put them on public view in a special tent for two days so that relatives could bring offerings to them. Then the bones of members of each tribe were gathered into a single coffin, and an empty bier was decorated and carried in the procession to the cemetery. This was a symbolic coffin for the missing, whose bodies could not be recovered (Thucydides 2.34).

In cultures in which bodies are burned, something is still kept—a jar of ashes, a piece of evidence to bury one day or to scatter in an appropriate place. Among the Toda people of Indonesia, bones and ashes may be gathered up and buried in elaborate ceremonies (Van Gennep 1960: 149). Even when there are neither bones nor ashes, the desire for some tangible remains is strong. After the crash of a Boeing 737 in Pennsylvania in September 1994, the National Transportation Safety Board, against the wishes of the airline company that owned the plane, brought dozens of relatives of the crash victims to a hangar near the Pittsburgh airport to view parts of the wreckage from a special catwalk built for the purpose. The relatives had demanded to see the pieces of the plane. An airline company spokesman stated: "We don't think it helps the families to closure." But Donna Snefsky-Gingerich, the widow of one of the victims, was reported as saying: "My husband was unidentified. I had no remains. I wanted to see what would kill 132 people all at one time, to the point where they were in little body parts" (*New York Times*, January 27, 1995).

It appears that even in this society, where death is conceived of as a moment rather than a process, a discrete event marked on a screen by the cessation of bodily functions, there is a desire to see the last flicker on the graph, to hold the hands of the dead, to comprehend the most incomprehensible fact of life, its absence.

Second Burial

In many cultures the custom of disinterring the bones of the dead and reburying them in an ossuary marks the end of a long process of mourning. This process is, as Van Gennep and other anthropologists have noted, "a transitional period for the survivors, and they enter it through rites of separation and emerge from it through rites of reintegration into society (rites of the lifting of mourning). In some cases the transitional period of the living is a counterpart of the transitional period of the deceased, and the termination of the first sometimes coincides with the termination of the second—that is, with the incorporation of the deceased into the world of the dead" (1960: 147). In many cultures in which reburial of the bones is practiced it is believed that the dead arrive at a final resting place only after the flesh has decomposed and only the skeleton remains. Among the Melanesian Islanders, "it is believed that the soul remains weak for as long as putrefaction lasts . . . Death is finally consummated only when decomposition has ended; only then does the deceased cease to belong to this world so as to enter another life" (Hertz 1960: 47). There may be additional cultural reasons for temporary burial followed by reburial, such as the preparation of expensive and elaborate ceremonies, but as Hertz and others have noted, they do not fully explain the custom: "the obligation to wait until the bones are dry before proceeding with the final rites is, without any doubt, the direct cause of the period of delay and determines its length" (ibid.: 31).

The necessity for the body to decompose fully before final burial is, according to Hertz, related to the Indonesian belief that the body is inhabited, during the period of putrefaction, by evil spirits. These spirits threaten the welfare of the living. Among the Olo Ngaju, he notes, the body is kept in a sealed container, from which putrid fluids are drained or collected, preventing the escape of the evil power residing in the corpse and allowing the bones to dry. Hertz's observation about the dangers posed to the living by the decomposing corpse have been observed in many cultures. Closing the body's orifices with coins, tape, or beads are indications of similar precautions to keep evil from escaping the body and polluting the living, but they are also intended, as Hertz notes, as a means of protecting the corpse, which is thought to be in a fragile state until the final burial, subject to attack by evil spirits (1960: 33). The unburied corpse, then, is both endangered and dangerous. Its twilight status extends to the grieving relatives, who, in many societies, must conform to a rigid set of taboos. They share in the pollution of the corpse and it is their task to set a watch on the corpse, protecting it from harm. They are generally expected to remain in their houses, wear special clothes, eat special foods. Remnants of these customs that mark the bereaved as marginal to the rest of society are still seen in the black clothes worn at funerals, the torn neckties, the expectation that bereaved women, at least, will spend time at home receiving friends and relatives.

At the ceremonies of reburial the bones are usually handled by the women relatives who laid out the dead body. This second burial, with its display of clean bones or ashes, not only marks the release of the fragile corpse from pollution and evil spirits; it signals the liberation of the mourners from their initial phase of grief and isolation. The soul, which has hovered in a sort of limbo, is finally freed to eternity. For the mourners, and in particular the female relatives, who are frequently regarded as sharing the pollution of the corpse and treated as outcasts during the period before reburial, the second ceremony is a time of reintegration into the community and of relief. Whatever the metaphysical beliefs of the society, it is clear that seeing the bones also has a practical therapeutic function. It permits the living to witness death a second time in a form that may be comprehensible, to "know" what some part of the mind has refused to know, to bring one period of mourning to an end and begin another.

The ritual process of transition that begins with the funeral and continues through the memorial services and the ultimate reburial of the bones is a cultural process of ordering the disruption and chaos brought about by death. When rituals are performed in a way the community knows and respects, the pain of separation is integrated into the life of the survivors.

The American-Greek poet Olga Broumas, born on the island of Syros, describes in two poems the reburial of her father's bones (1989). The exhumation takes place four years after the first burial, allowing time for the bones to be dry and clean. She and her mother find the bones already unearthed:

> an armful of bones in a tin ossuary bathed in red wine
> is set in the sun and the long night through evening
> to another dawn under stars to dry. ("Perisprit")

In the long poem "On Earth" Broumas describes the ceremony in detail:

> We waited for the man
> whose job it was to see the bones were ready.
> Sometimes the flesh is slow.
> Sometimes a daughter buries her mother
> twice in the reddish earth as mother had.

But her father's bones are dry, as they should be:

> Good bones. Thick bones. Bones drinking deep.
> I carried them,
> with the woman whose job it is,
> further behind the chapel
> for their day in the sun and the vaulted night
> and wrote a number on the box in magic marker
> I gave back to the woman with a tip.

Good bones are dry ones, clean ones, washed in wine or milk or anything else that removes the traces of flesh or earth, the lingering reminders of decay. Old women in rural Greece carefully read the exhumed bones, especially the lines "sewn" on the skull. They will tell you from a person's bones what sort of life he lived, whether he was a good husband or harbored secret evil in his soul. Seeing the bones, handling them, and re-interring them, in cultures that practice exhumation, marks the beginning of the final stage of grief. It seems to be universally disturbing and satisfying, fulfilling a deep human need to see in order to believe.

A Vietnamese Exhumation

The Vietnamese writer Nguyen Thi Vinh describes the powerful effect of reburying bones in a story called "Exhumation" (trans. Le Van Hoan

1959: 35–38).[1] As the protagonist, Fan, stands at the cemetery waiting for the coffin to be unearthed, she remembers the day of her mother's death, how she had disobeyed custom and lifted the sheet of white paper covering her mother's face to look at her for a last time. When the coffin is opened her heart is thumping, but everyone is kept busy preparing for the ritual washing of the bones, making offerings of food and lighting joss sticks. At last the bones are handed to the next of kin to wash:

> Fan was given the skull. She solemnly held it in her hands and cleaned every inch of it with scrupulous care. When she poked her fingers into the deep hollows of the eye-sockets, she grieved so deeply for the deceased that her eyes were brimful of tears. Through the veil of her tears, she felt as though her mother gazed at her, as real and lovely as ever. All the happy days of the past whirled though her mind.

There is a brief moment of revulsion as her fingers touch something still soft in the skull:

> She shuddered, clenched her teeth, then more resolutely she poked her finger into the eye-sockets to take out all that viscous substance, trying to clean the whole thing neatly.
>
> Holding the main part of the body, the head of her mother in her hands, she tried to find some insight or thought of her dear departed . . . So the body was of little importance, she thought, for death was inevitable and inevitably flesh would suffer decay. Bones remained but they were as inanimate as earth. Only now she understood clearly the saying that it is only the soul that matters.

The process of washing complete, the bones of Fan's mother are neatly arranged in a new coffin and reburied. Then Fan sobs with her relatives beside the grave. Fan moves away with her sister and is struck by the resemblance between her sister's eyes and those of her dead mother. She is deeply moved and feels "as though the soul of her mother hovered about in the pattering of the rain and the rustling of the wind and finally lived again in herself and her brothers and sisters."

What strikes the Western reader about Nguyen Thi Vinh's description is the combination of familiar emotional reaction with what appears to be gruesome detail. It is not that Fan feels less affection for her mother than we would expect, but that she is able to overcome her initial revulsion to handle and prepare the skull for reburial with the same care as she would the whole body. She has comprehended and accepted death in a way that is quite different from our own. We immediately identify with Hamlet's combination of disgust and fear at the sight of Yorick's skull, a revulsion that causes him to fling the skull away, despite the tender relationship he once had with the court jester. The notion of "caring" for bones was already foreign, it seems, to an Elizabethan audience. The custom of washing and dressing the corpse of one's relatives for burial lasted longer, but in most of the developed world even this is now done by professionals. But however far removed we are from the physical care of the dead, we still expect bodies to be buried or burned in a ceremony that we witness. We still visit the graves of the dead and make offerings above the bones—flowers, flags, statues, photographs, trees. It may be that Fan's handling of her mother's bones led her more quickly to acceptance of death, but we are all eventually forced to imagine what we cannot comprehend, the transformation of the living into inanimate objects. We need a site of mourning removed from our daily lives where we can focus grief and leave the dead behind. The cemetery, the ossuary, the crematorium mark off a space that has always been a source of fear as well as sorrow. The marking-off of that space for the dead is as much a protection of the living as an honoring of the dead. It is not only the fear that the dead will come back to haunt us that keeps them confined. We have a need to confine grief to a place where it can be "visited" and left behind. In societies where there are double burials or where there are a number of memorial services after the funeral, prayers and laments for the dead cause the bereaved relatives to weep as they did at the funeral. But when the ceremony ends, they go home, leaving at least some part of their grief behind them.

The Vietnam War Dead and the MIAs

To say, "I'm okay, you're okay, but him, he's dead!" is, for the living, a kind of comfort. It is why we drag rivers and comb plane wrecks. It is why MIA is more painful than DOA. It is why we

have open caskets and classified obits. Knowing is better than not
knowing, and knowing it is you is terrifically better than knowing
it is me.

Thomas Lynch, "The Undertaking"

There are facts,
and there are facts:
when the first missing man
walks alive out of that green tangle
of rumors and lies.
I shall lie
down silent as a jungle shadow,
and dream the sound of insects
gnawing bones.

W. D. Ehrhart, "POW/MIA"

The issue of the return of remains of American servicemen classified
as missing in Vietnam, Laos, and Cambodia is still one of the most
inflammatory political issues in the United States. The only flag that
has ever flown over the White House besides the Stars and Stripes
is the black-and-white POW/MIA flag depicting a shackled prisoner
with bowed head. It is now flown on Memorial Day at post offices, police stations, and other public buildings across the country. A postage
stamp honoring prisoners of war and those missing in action was released on Memorial Day 1995. In his address to mark the occasion,
President Clinton said that although "we can only imagine the pain"
experienced by families of the missing, "We know very well our obligation to them and their families to leave no stone unturned as we try to
account for their fate and if possible to bring them home" (*New York
Times*, May 30, 1995).

What or who could they bring home? Were there still POWs in
Southeast Asia? Could any be alive still? If not, why did the president
feel compelled to speak as if there were live prisoners, as if unaccounted-for dead in the Vietnam War were still numerous, and the
recovery of both a stumbling block to the normalization of relations
with Hanoi? Why were the families of servicemen classified as MIAs
plagued with the additional grief of uncertainty? And why, as the cen-

tury ends, are units like the Army Central Identification Laboratory in Hawaii expanding their activities, spending millions of dollars identifying each set of remains? Why is there such a focus on the recovery of remains from Vietnam when approximately 78,000 U.S. military are still officially listed as MIAs from World War II and about 8,000 from Korea?

The Remains

Their B-26's flight was last seen on its way back to Da Nang. Two years ago the Vietnamese government turned over to the U.S. what was left: a few bones, some teeth, a pair of socks, boots, a first-aid manual, a .45 pistol and a Sears credit card . . . Employing anthropologists, odontologists and the latest DNA genetic testing, U.S. army forensic experts took two years to make what they consider a positive identification of the fragmentary remains. If a Pentagon review board agrees, the 2,233 Americans still listed as missing in action from the war, including 1,642 in Vietnam, will be reduced by three.

Chicago Tribune, May 29, 1994

The remains of Air Force Sgt. Frederick T. Garside, who was shot down over Laos in 1961 and became one of the first US servicemen to be missing in action in the Vietnam War, returned home yesterday.

In morning drizzle, under the watchful, weeping eyes of two of his sisters, Garside's casket was lowered from a jet at Logan Airport and taken by hearse to Plymouth, where he will be buried with full military honors tomorrow.

Boston Globe, December 15, 1991

There is no mention, in the second report, of bones. Unlike Fan in the Vietnamese story, the sisters of Frederick Garside did not handle their brother's bones or even look at them. Nevertheless an honor guard carried the box of bones as if it contained a body; there were a hearse and a motorcade, just as at a regular funeral. All that the relatives had to prove the identity of the bones in the box were the reports of forensic experts, anthropologists, dentists. At best there might be a metal tag, a plastic card. Even if they had cared to open the casket and look at the remains they would probably have found only a handful of fragments, none larger than a wristwatch. In the tropical climate of northern Laos, where many of the MIA remains have been recovered, bones and teeth disintegrate quickly, and planes were immediately stripped of anything the local farmers could steal or use. But even though such boxes contain only a few scraps of solid material that might once have been a brother or a son, for most families they bring a measure of relief.

The acceptance of the scant remains as a positive step in the grieving process is common but not universal. It is not as satisfactory as a body or a full set of bones. Air Force Captain Mark Danielson's remains were brought home to his family in 1993, twenty-two years after his gunship went down over South Vietnam's A Sau valley. His widow, now remarried, was relieved by the discovery of the remains and by the funeral at Arlington National Cemetery: "For me, putting those remains in the ground at Arlington means completion and a certain kind of peace," she said. But for the mother and sisters of the dead man the remains were insufficient to assuage their grief. As his sister said: "Two teeth isn't his body—big difference . . . When you hear 'remains,' you're thinking a skull and arms and legs. You're not picturing two teeth in a box" (*People*, November 28, 1994). The mother of the dead airman had never been able to accept the reports of the survivors of the crash that there was almost no possibility of his survival and the three women had been active members of the POW/MIA movement. For them, even the most tenuous hope was preferable to the acceptance of Danielson's death.

In some cases the remains returned to the families have been not only scant but dubious. Anne Hart, widow of an airman whose plane was shot down in southern Laos, disputed the identification of her husband's remains by the Hawaii laboratory. The bones were fire damaged and difficult to identify, but they and other fragments of bones were found in the position one would have expected them to be in the wreckage. Hart's litigation lasted for years, until the Eleventh Circuit Court of Appeals ruled that the government had the right to "use its discretion" in such cases. The result of the protests against the finding was to force the laboratory to adopt even more rigorous standards for identification, and thus possibly to deprive other families of missing men of information.

The most extreme case of such persistence in denying the evidence of a death in Vietnam, both by the relatives of the missing man and by the military authorities, may be that of Air Force Colonel Charles E. Shelton, whose widow opposed an Air Force attempt to declare her husband "presumed dead" in 1980. Despite their conviction that he had died in captivity in Laos soon after his plane went down in 1965, the Air Force continued to pay his active-duty salary until 1994 and retained his POW status "as a symbol of U.S. commitment to obtaining the fullest possible accounting of the still missing and unaccounted-for Americans in Southeast Asia" (*San Diego Union Tribune*, October 5, 1994). In 1990 Shelton's widow took her own life. Four years later a memorial service with full military honors was held for Shelton although no remains had been found. The suicide of Shelton's widow lends support to the widely held belief that the prolongation of doubt and unreasonable hope causes more pain than the acceptance of death. It also suggests how powerful a political lobby the relatives of the missing had become.

Clifford Kirk, spokesman for the forensic laboratory at Hickam Air Force Base in Hawaii, said in an interview with the *Chicago Tribune:* "If it weren't for the families, we wouldn't be here . . . We are trying to provide closure and some answers for people" (May 29, 1994). The administration itself was aware, it seems, that the certainty of death is better than the vague hope held out for twenty-five years by the designation "MIA." But is the U.S. government spending approximately $100 million a year on some sort of grief therapy for the families of the Vietnam War veterans? And if not, why the enormous investment in recovery of remains in this war compared to others? And why does the president continue to speak as if there were still prisoners of war, when no one who has investigated the issue believes this to be true?

The answer is connected to the deep trauma that lingers in this country over the defeat in Vietnam, both the humiliating military defeat abroad and the socially divisive defeat at home. Far from satisfying the grief of relatives, the government, especially the military leaders but also civilian politicians, deliberately inflamed and extended the suffering of many families, flying them on military planes to Washington and parading them as exhibits in a campaign of self-justification, designating thousands of what they knew to be dead soldiers as MIAs, and fostering a myth that there were still prisoners in the Indochina peninsula long after they knew there were none.

The desire to punish the Lilliputian enemy and salvage some self-re-spect is perfectly expressed in the series of movies that began with *Rambo*. It can be recognized in postwar rhetoric urging the government to "make Vietnam bleed" and "squeeze Vietnam." It is only now, when trade relations have been normalized with Vietnam, and the Stars and Stripes hangs on a flagpole in Hanoi, that the myth of the missing may slowly and consciously be reburied at an official level in America, but it is not a myth that will lie easy in its grave: it has become a national religion.

The Making of the Myth

The most convincing exposure of the Vietnam POW/MIA myth has come from H. Bruce Franklin, a professor at Rutgers University who formerly served as a navigator and intelligence officer in the Strategic Air Command. First in a long article in the *Atlantic Monthly* and later in his book *M.I.A., or Mythmaking in America* (1993), Franklin meticu-lously examined the evidence for MIAs and live POWs and found little more than a dogged persistence in keeping the myth alive. As Franklin points out, there is nothing unusual about combatants' dying in wars without being identified. In fact even the official total of 2,273 "unac-counted for" in the Indochina war is a far smaller number than that for any other war in the nation's history. Moreover, 1,101 of these were never considered either missing in action or prisoners but were "known at the time of their loss to have been killed in action; they are listed as 'unaccounted for' only because their *bodies* have not been accounted for" (1993: 11). At the time Franklin published his article, only one man was still even officially listed as either missing in action or a pris-oner of war, "and he is known to have died more than a quarter of a century ago" (ibid.).

From the end of the Vietnam War the POW/MIA figures were sys-tematically inflated. The 1,101 who were known to have been killed died in circumstances that prevented recovery of their bodies. The of-ficial designation for such cases is KIA/BNR (killed in action/body not recovered). Franklin discovered that it was only after the Paris Peace Agreement was signed in 1973 that this category was conflated with the POW/MIAs. But the designation POW/MIA was itself "an unprece-dented invention, purposely designed to suggest that each and every missing person might be a prisoner, even though most were lost in circumstances that made capture impossible" (1993: 13). The distinction between the two was maintained internally by the Department of Defense, which continued to apply "POW" only to those known or believed to be prisoners while lumping the two categories together in its public announcements. The Pentagon listed as a POW anyone reported as a possible prisoner in Indochina between 1963 and 1973, whether or not there was any evidence of capture or of subsequent death. "After the Paris Peace Agreement, all but fifty-three men on this internal list were either released or reported to have died in captivity. In the next three years, intensive analysis of these remaining cases resolved all but a handful" (ibid.: 14).

Administration officials themselves referred to the continued listing as "a symbolic gesture of the Administration's commitment to this issue" (Franklin 1993: 15). It has been a remarkably effective gesture. While *The Economist* could report in 1994 that "although some eccentrics persist in spreading rumors of pilots festering in an Indochinese gulag, sensible people do not believe that Americans remain alive as prisoners of war," a 1991 *Wall Street Journal*/NBC poll indicated that 69 percent of Americans believed that U.S. prisoners of war were still being held in Southeast Asia (Franklin 1991: 45). The spreading of the rumors has been the work of determined men, aware that they could exploit the grief of the relatives, the widespread desire for revenge against the Vietnamese, and the dissatisfaction of the veterans to gain popularity. The Nixon and Reagan administrations were particularly active in fostering the myth, but no administration has failed to respond to the pressure of the Pentagon and other interested parties, including the motion picture industry, to keep the MIA question alive. In the political game of saving face that followed a catastrophic blunder in foreign policy, the POW/MIAs were a trump card, a bid to win a trick in a game that was being lost at home and abroad.

In 1968 presidential candidate Richard Nixon had pledged "to bring an honorable end to the war in Vietnam." Amid public disgust and controversy over the treatment of North Vietnamese prisoners, tortured and executed both by U.S. troops and by the South Vietnamese government, Nixon was able to drum up support for his campaign by cleverly shifting the focus of attention to the missing and imprisoned Americans. It may have been the single issue that allowed the administration to extend the war for another four years. Franklin notes that during these years, more than 50 million POW/MIA bumper stickers were sold, a measure of the success of the Nixon administration's relentless exploitation of the issue (1993: 49).

The families of the MIAs were the pawns in the campaign. Wives were flown to the Paris peace negotiations; children were photographed praying "Bring our Daddy home safe, sound and soon," in advertisements paid for by Ross Perot, who also flew 152 wives and children to Paris, and had his own private jet flown to Laos loaded with Christmas presents for the "POWs." State Department officials toured the country meeting with families of MIAs; rallies of the families were officially encouraged and supported. Displays featuring models of prison cells infested by cockroaches and rats, and inhabited by simulated shackled prisoners, were set up in state capitals across the country. Veterans' Day was even officially renamed "Prisoner of War Day." The Victory in Vietnam Association (later renamed the Voices in Vital America Association), formed to counteract the antiwar movement, was given official status as a charitable institution and began manufacturing bracelets engraved with the names of POWs and MIAs. Launched in 1970, the idea was an extraordinary success. Movie stars and national leaders, Billy Graham and General Westmoreland wore them. By the time of the Paris Peace Agreement more than 4 million bracelets were being worn. One of the conditions of wearing the bracelets was that the wearer swear not to remove it until his or her POW/MIA was either returned home or declared dead. The name on the bracelet created a relationship, however tenuous, between the wearer and the missing serviceman, extending the pool of people who could be relied on to continue to foment the issue of the MIAs. In addition to the emotional manipulation of the relatives, large numbers of people with no personal connection to the missing men were being drawn into a political game that would prove even more effective than the administration hoped.

The 1973 peace agreement called for the return of all living prisoners of war and for lists of those who had died in captivity. The North Vietnamese apparently complied with the terms of the accord. President Nixon made enormous political capital out of "Operation Homecoming," stating that he had achieved his goal of "the return of *all* of our prisoners of war." The issue of the POWs seemed about to be put to rest, but it was not allowed to die. The successful revival and perpetuation of the myth began almost immediately after Nixon's moment of triumph and is still implicit in the flags' being flown in almost every town in the United States.

The first official step in the long-drawn-out process of investigating reports of prisoners and remains after the war was the creation of the Select Committee on Missing Persons in Southeast Asia. The initiative for the Select Committee came from a conservative representative from Mississippi, Gillespie "Sonny" Montgomery. In 1976, after fifteen months of investigation, including a trip to Southeast Asia, the committee issued its report, concluding that "no Americans are still being held alive as prisoners in Indochina, or elsewhere, as a result of the war in Indochina" (Franklin 1991: 52). They added that "because of the nature of the circumstances in which many Americans were lost in combat in Indochina, a total accounting by the Indochinese Governments is not possible and should not be expected" (Franklin 1993: 15). Montgomery's admission of disillusionment at the end of the investigation is particularly interesting. His belief in the existence of live prisoners was, he said, "based more on hope than fact and more on rumors than hard evidence . . . like so many others I wanted to believe they were alive, so I did" (ibid.: 15).

The desire to find that there were prisoners alive in Indochina persisted long after the evidence convinced even an enthusiast like Montgomery to abandon his dreams. For the families of the men listed as "missing," the deliberate manipulation of the myth added an intolerable burden to their grief. A study published in 1979 by Navy Captain Douglas L. Clarke, of the National War College, who had flown on 300 missions in Indochina and had many friends listed as MIAs, concluded that not only were the findings of the Select Committee correct, but the "matter of the missing men has worked against the best interests of the United States." Noting that there was no more likelihood of accounting for all the men missing in the Indochina war than in any other, Clarke concluded: "The government did the families—and therefore the lost men—a tragic disservice by encouraging the belief that there would be such an accounting" (Franklin 1993: 15).

Despite this report and others that followed, the Reagan and Bush administrations continued to exploit the issue of the POW/MIAs, insisting that the Vietnamese government was withholding information. While successive administrations and the Department of Defense encouraged the POW/MIA myth, Hollywood did an even more effective job of manipulation that sometimes overlapped the official one and at other times conflicted with it. Movies like *The Deer Hunter, Rambo: First Blood Part II, Uncommon Valor,* and *Missing in Action* created the myth of a war in which American servicemen, secretly kept in inhuman conditions in the jungles, could be rescued only by the heroism of individuals acting independently of their government or in loose cooperation with it. In the new epics of heroic exploits in the jungle, the recovery of bones and the needs of the grieving relatives were a secondary concern. Revenge and individual daring were the themes; the recovery was one of lost American self-esteem.

The Reagan administration and Hollywood had cooperated to create a new script of the Vietnam War, with the families of the MIAs as a sort of *tableau vivant* in the foreground. Now the fantasy took a surprising turn. The real villains of this mythical reshaping of the MIA issue were less the Vietnamese than the Washington bureaucracy that had covered up its knowledge of prisoners still held in Indochina. The release of *First Blood Part II* soon created a "Rambo faction" of POW/MIA activists who believed there had been a government conspiracy to conceal the truth about prisoners still alive in Indochina. So effective was their lobby that the government could not afford to ignore it. In 1985, National Security Advisor Robert McFarlane commented at an official function that "there have to be live Americans there" (Franklin 1991: 80). Following the conspiracy allegations came a stream of reports of sightings of prisoners.[2]

The Bones on the Other Side

One of the most memorable images of Peter Davis' documentary film about the Vietnam War, *Hearts and Minds* (1974), is of a Vietnamese funeral for a young man killed in the conflict. The women relatives are wailing and sobbing. A woman kisses the boy's photograph. The weeping mother has to be restrained from leaping into her son's grave. There is a cut to an interview with General Westmoreland: "The Oriental," he is saying, "doesn't put the same high value on life . . . Life is plentiful, life is cheap. As the philosophy of the Orient puts it: life is not important."

The idea that the Vietnamese experienced grief in the same way as

Americans, that they were as much in need of recovering the remains of their dead as the relatives of the MIAs, did not occur to the makers of the POW/MIA myth, or if it did it was deliberately suppressed. The myth rested on the assumption of the inequality of the opponents, on a notion that one Caucasian life was worth countless Asian lives, that the Vietnamese relatives felt less grief than the American. The documentary film *Lament of a Warrior's Wife* (1991), directed by American filmmaker Bob Kane, effectively dispels the myth. Kane, who did not serve in the war although he volunteered and later backed out of a marine platoon-leaders' program, was provoked by the strength of the POW/MIA movement in his own country to investigate what the Vietnamese felt about the issue of unequal grieving. How many MIAs did they have? Did they feel, as many people suggested to him before he set out for Vietnam, less grief? Were they a heartless people?

The film begins with a woman's voice saying:

> We didn't have much time together, because all his life he was only with me for one month total, but the thing I remember most was that every night my husband would go into the jungle to bring me sugar cane to give it to me in preparation for my giving birth to my first child . . . His friends' remains were collected later, but they never found those of my husband. So each time I visit the cemetery I take some soil and bring it home to the altar to pray for him . . . I thought I was prepared to receive any sacrifice, but the grief is that my daughter never saw her father. I only kept the wildflower. I still have it in my armoire, my flower—yellow. In the South almost every family during the Tet holiday has that kind of flower. It is the flower of memories, the flower of lament.

She is the first of the women to speak, but there are others, all of them still overwhelmed by grief. Like the Americans, the Vietnamese counted as "missing in action" those soldiers whose remains were not discovered. At the end of the war, the Americans declared 58,000 dead, 2,302 MIAs. The Vietnamese count their MIAs at somewhere above 300,000, their dead at 1 million. In addition there are 1 million permanently disabled, 1.5 million civilians severely wounded, and 2 million affected by dioxan. Another million civilians are calculated to be suffering severe mental disorder as a result of the war, and by 1991, when

Kane made his film, there were more than 700,000 orphans. As Kane remarks, how can we demand anything of the Vietnamese when it would take a wall five and a half times the size of the Vietnam War Memorial to contain their names?

Like the Americans, the Vietnamese have been searching for the remains of their dead since the war ended. The villagers are generally cooperative, according to Ho Xuan Dich, of the North American division of the Vietnamese Organization for the Seeking of Missing Persons. They ask no reward for handing over the remains of soldiers who died in or near their houses, but the offers of rewards by some U.S. groups has led to a black market in bones. One family, he tells the director, had stockpiled 456 remains over a period of four years. Most of the "recovered" remains offered for sale by boat people and villagers anxious to make money were stolen from Vietnamese cemeteries. Now the government is faced with demands from Vietnamese people for the return of their own relatives' remains.

What surprised Kane most was the lack of bitterness and anger among the people he interviewed. Bui Thi Lien described how she was told her husband had been killed. In 1968 he had returned briefly on leave for the birth of their second child. She never believed her husband was dead, and she did not remarry. Then, in 1985, she set out with fifteen other women to visit the cemetery where she was told her husband was buried. All of the women wandered in the cemetery searching for their husbands' graves. Lien found her husband's grave but some could not find the graves they were looking for and burst into tears. "That's why I feel such deep sympathy for the American wives," says Bui Thi Lien:

They suffer the same as our people, maybe more than me because even though I had to suffer such loss, I was lucky because at least I had the remains of my husband. I *am* luckier, because I could see my husband's grave and be with him if only for that moment. I feel quite happy now, but since my husband was killed I carry constant grief. In my dream I always wish that my husband is still alive and for a moment I think it is true and I cry out.

The grief that Bui Thi Lien carries with her seems to have left her capable of functioning normally. There are many other women in Vietnam who suffered severe mental disturbance because, as Vietnam's director of mental health says in an interview, "Those who could not find remains have nowhere to go to pray for their loved one." For the Vietnamese, a sense of the place of death is almost as crucial, it seems, as the bones themselves. Nguyen, whose son was declared MIA in Quang Tri province, traveled to the area where her son was last seen: "I stood at the crossroads and prayed because I thought his remains might be somewhere around there. I put a cloth on the crossroads and I prayed for the soul of my son and of all the soldiers killed there."

Kane wonders if he is encountering such extraordinary politeness and lack of anger because he is interviewing people in Hanoi. He decides to travel to the countryside, to areas where the enemy was not a faceless load of bombs dropped from the sky. At Dam Ho village he talks to Mr. Sam, whose son was killed in the fighting, and notices, the day after his first interview, that Mr. Sam has removed the photograph of his son from the room and seems reluctant to talk openly. Kane wonders if Mr. Sam feels that his son would not approve of his showing hospitality to an American. But in the same village, a woman named Pham Kim Hy comes to visit him, carrying a copy of a lullaby she used to sing to her missing son. She has kept all his belongings, his baby clothes, even a diaper. "On Chung Sun Mountain you sleep soundly. / Sleep, my son, my beloved child," she recites.

> My spirit reaches out to you.
> Your pure soul rests in the mountains.
> Jungle birds sing my lullaby to you.
> Sleep, my son, my beloved child.
> I send love echoed by my country's love.

"For fifteen years I have been searching for the remains of my son. The suffering and loss I have will never stop," she continues, and then, addressing her absent son again: "It seems your voice is mixed with the wind. / You drift in and out of sight as you drifted in and out of my life." Mrs. Hy ends her lullaby and continues:

> I have suffered a great loss but little in comparison to others. The American mothers suffer more than we do because their government sent their sons to die in a lonely, faraway country, not in their

homeland. Now they demand the return of all American remains when there are a great many Vietnamese wives who, up to now, have not found the remains of their relatives . . . It is ridiculous that the United States government does nothing about Vietnam, the direct victim of the war.

Mrs. Hy's anger about the discrepancy between U.S. insistence on the recovery and return of their MIA remains and their lack of concern about the Vietnamese remains is common. Mr. Dich, of the Vietnamese Organization for the Seeking of Missing Persons, lost his own brother who accompanied a U.S. search team looking for remains in the jungle. His brother contracted malaria and died, according to Mr. Dich, without the benefit of drugs or hospital treatment, although the U.S. team carried medical supplies with them.

The last section of Kane's film is shot in the town of Cu Chi, thirty-five kilometers northwest of Saigon. Known simply as "The Battlefield," the Cu Chi area was designated a freefire area; it was customary for bombers to dump any leftover munitions there after a raid. Life above ground became impossible, so the inhabitants dug 250 kilometers of tunnels and lived underground. In the tunnels were schools, markets, hospitals, even concert halls. Twenty thousand of Cu Chi's residents were killed, 5,000 were disabled, 2,000 were designated MIAs. In 1968 the area was flattened by American bulldozers, and the bodies of all the dead lying on the ground were pushed into the bomb craters and covered without any markers. Many of the survivors of Cu Chi still suffer from severe emotional problems. As the district chief says: "The mothers of Cu Chi locked up their hearts; they suppressed their sorrows, stopped their tears. The reason was that if they cried and celebrated their sons' or husbands' funerals, the U.S. or South Vietnamese troops would arrest them. So they tried to keep their feelings hidden."

Bob Kane asks Mai Thi Buoi what she thought of the mothers and sisters of men lost in Vietnam. "They [the men] abandoned wives and sons to come here . . . What am I to do? I had four sons and now I have nothing," she answers. Another woman he talks to about the continued anger against Vietnamese in America is surprised. "Why hate us?" she replies. "I lost my husband, and I have no remains of my father, no possession or grave of my husband. Of course I hated the Americans at the time . . . not now . . . Why hate us? Our graves are not in your country."

Vietnam's director of mental health says that all MIAs are now considered dead in Vietnam. The relatives feel that they have fulfilled their duty to their missing after they have made an effort to find the remains. Some travel thousands of kilometers in their search, and if they are unsuccessful, they worship and pray for their relatives, or buy a dish at the market and invite the MIA to have a meal with them. Mr. Dich suggests that Vietnamese society helped the bereaved women to deal with their grief better than American society. He has heard that American women felt lonely and were not helped by their neighbors. In Vietnam, neighbors would come on the anniversary of the death and pray with the women who had lost sons and husbands.

Kane's film ends with an interview with a woman who seems to fit the picture he was given before he left the United States of the tough, heartless Vietnamese woman. All five of Doan Thi Sang's sons were killed, one fighting against the French, the other four against the American and South Vietnamese armies. Her husband, who lost both eyes in the war against the French, died in 1983. Her face, as she smokes a cigarette, is difficult to read. She shows Kane her anger and resentment, telling him that her grief is greater than the American mothers': "My sons fought for liberty, but you didn't stop your sons, so I found much more grief," she says. While the U.S. army took care of its soldiers, who lived comfortably in the cities, her sons got no payment for their services; they were "not for hire."

In the last shot of the film, Kane accompanies Doan Thi Sang to the monument for the dead and missing of Cu Chi and is astonished by the transformation in her behavior. She lights incense and begins to pray. "I don't know if you are here. I feel terribly wounded," she says, brushing the tears from her eyes, "because I don't know where you are. I came to see you, to light some incense for your sacred soul to witness my soul . . . I feel a mother's failure because you, my sons, died nameless, without a grave." She turns her back on the camera to wipe her eyes again, and we hear a woman's voice, the daughter of one of the Vietnamese MIAs, saying she would like to come to America to see the Vietnam War Memorial with all its names. "In some way I identify myself with all these mothers and wives," she says. In Vietnam, "We cannot do it, even if we had the money—we don't have the names."

Mutual Recognition

Since 1991, when Kane's film was made, some veterans' groups have realized that shared grief and a common need to recover and bury the dead may provide more answers than commando-style raids into the jungles of Laos. In Hanoi in May 1994, James Brazee, national president of the Vietnamese Veterans of America, handed a briefcase to Major General Le Cu, representative of the Vietnamese Veterans Association. In it were photos, identification cards, letters, and other items taken from dead Vietnamese soldiers as souvenirs during the war. As he handed over the briefcase he said, "Our Native Americans have a saying that things taken in anger and pain must be returned in order to free one of that pain . . . In that spirit, we return these items to you" (*Cleveland Plain Dealer*, October 10, 1994). Together with the objects returned were detailed maps provided by another American veteran, Jim Kapucinski, showing where the Vietnamese could find a mass grave. Kapucinski had helped to bury 216 North Vietnamese soldiers, many of them teenagers, in April 1969. Using the map Kapucinski provided, Vietnamese officials excavated the battle site and recovered the remains of ninety-five soldiers. The remains were then reburied, and a videotape of the ceremony was made. What is most interesting about the veterans' initiative is that it was accompanied by an entirely new rhetoric about the Vietnamese, and a recognition that they were experiencing grief in a similar way. "To the Vietnamese people, location of the remains of relatives is a very important issue, part of traditions that date back thousands of years," said Jack Clark, vice-president of the Vietnam Veterans of America (ibid.).

There is nothing new about realizing the horror of the war or the suffering it caused in Indochina, but the idea of sharing a common grief and participating in a common search for remains with no other motive than a need to help put an end to mourning was surprising to many Americans. Veterans who learned about the initiative or watched a report about it on *Sixty Minutes* were impressed by the possibilities of such a private, nongovernmental initiative: "For over twenty years, we have not felt we've gotten a satisfactory response from our government or their government," said one veteran. "Now you have two veterans [groups] sitting down and saying, 'Hey, I'll tell you what happened to your people and you tell me what might have happened to my people.'

That's exactly what's going on" (*Cleveland Plain Dealer*, October 10, 1994).

The unofficial efforts of veterans continue alongside the extraordinarily expensive official operation of searching for, recovering, and identifying remains. Press reports carefully note that the Vietnamese have, as an inducement, the promise of most-favored-nation trading status. But it is not reported that the United States has as much to gain by remaining on good terms with a country whose economy is expanding as rapidly as Vietnam's.

As he proclaimed the extension of full diplomatic recognition to Vietnam in 1995, President Clinton used metaphors of wounding and healing. Echoing the words of Lincoln at the end of the Civil War, he stated: "This moment offers us the opportunity to bind up our own wounds. They have resisted time for too long. We can now move onto common ground . . . Let this moment, in the words of the Scripture, be a time to heal and a time to build" (*New York Times*, July 12, 1995). At the same time, Clinton insisted that the government would press Vietnam for a full accounting of the missing. Noting that the Vietnamese had handed over hundreds of pages of documents and the remains of twenty-nine missing Americans since the trade embargo had been lifted in February, the president claimed that "our strategy is working," suggesting that normalizing relations between the two countries would aid rather than hinder the recovery of remains and of information about the missing.

The Care of the Bones

Whether bones are burned or buried, exhumed and reburied, or hidden in boxes never to be seen, almost all people feel the need to know where they lie. Grief is prolonged and unassuageable when there is doubt about a death, but also when there is nothing tangible to grieve over. In Greece, Vietnam, China, and many other cultures where the bones are examined and cleaned after exhumation, it is important that they should be clean and white. One of the aims of relatives who tend the graves of the dead in rural Greece is to ensure that the flesh falls away from the body like wax from the funeral candle. The soul is then thought to be free from sin.

Caring for the bones of the dead is, and has been since antiquity, the responsibility of the entire community. When a village was forced to move, as in the case of the village of Parga, which was ceded to the Turks in 1819, its inhabitants burned the bones of their ancestors before they left to prevent them from being desecrated by the enemy.[3] The ancient Athenians, as Thucydides tells us, were similarly concerned that the bones of their dead be recovered for burial (4.97–99). The bodies of those who died in war were transported back to Athens and buried with unusual ceremony in the most beautiful part of the city (2.34.6). Even when the Athenian empire expanded and men died in battles far from the city, their bodies were burned individually and the ashes brought back in urns to their families (Garland 1985: 92).

The bones and ashes of the dead belong to the living, who have always, in their grief, demanded to dispose of them according to some tradition. The need to see, even in one's imagination, what lies in a box or urn may be a means, for some, of distancing themselves from the dead just as flesh has been separated from bone. For others, like the Greek village women who cradle the skulls of their dead, or like the Vietnamese daughter Fan, who overcame her revulsion and cleaned her mother's skull, it may be a way of drawing closer. In either case, there is a finality in viewing or handling the dry remains which seems to satisfy a need. The withholding or hiding of bones is an effective means of manipulating the bereaved because it denies this finality. In the second half of the twentieth century we have seen that the desire to recover the bones of the dead is as powerful as ever, but there has been an important change. The bones of one person can no longer be substituted for any other. The identification of remains has become an exact science that has enabled people from Guatemala to Kosovo to claim their dead, even to determine how they died. There are no more anonymous bones. The political effectiveness of the Tomb of the Unknown Soldier as a substitute for the missing war dead is finished.

~ 4

Disappearance

Only those who have died are ours, only what we have lost is ours.

Jorge Luis Borges, "Possession of Yesterday"

They took my daughter away when she was with her children. I ask my grandchildren, "Did you see them take your mother away?" "Yes," they answer. I tell them, "If you saw that she was alive, I am asking for her alive, because if she isn't, I want to know who killed her and I want that assassin to be put in jail. If I ask for her as a corpse, then I am killing her, not the one who assassinated her." If my grandchildren can understand that, an adult can.

Mercedes Mereno, member of the Mothers of the Plaza de Mayo (Bouvard 1994: 138–139)

$\mathcal{T}$HE VERB "to disappear" is intransitive in English: "to cease to be visible, die away from sight or existence, be lost" (*Oxford English Dictionary*). To disappear is another way to die. As W. H. Auden put it in his elegy on W. B. Yeats, "He disappeared in the dead of winter."[1] It is as if the two terms of the metaphor have been mysteriously exchanged. The landscape, though "dead," will reappear as before. The poet, having "disappeared," has suffered an irreversible change, unless he can be said to survive in verse. That is, of course, what elegies are usually about. The younger writer of the elegy has the power to revive his mentor and at the same time assert his right of succession by the brilliance of his verse. Disappearance, here, becomes a particularly appropriate metaphor for the dead poet, something of whom reappears in the verses of the younger poet.

If "to disappear" is synonymous with "to die," what happens when disappearance becomes a transitive verb? To "disappear" someone must also mean to kill him. To make someone invisible to his family or friends is already to cause his social death. If, after torturing him to extract information, you then kill him, you merely extend his disappearance—infinitely. The "disappearing" of political opponents is not a Latin American invention. Herodotus and Xenophon use the transitive verb *aphanizein* (to remove from sight, make away with) in reference to state criminals. The practice of removing enemies from sight is at least as old as politics itself and has always been an effective means of dealing with opposition. In the pages that follow I am concerned with the effects of this removal from sight not on the person who is "disappeared" but on his or her relatives. If, as we have established, certainty and physical remains are essential to mourning, what is the effect of the purposeful uncertainty of disappearance? How can grief be put to rest or mobilized in the labyrinthine vagaries of a state apparatus designed to keep it on hold?

In the 1970s it was the military dictatorships in Chile and Argentina that made the transitive use of the verb "to disappear" common currency, first in Spanish and then in English. In Argentina, under the junta, the "disappearing" of suspected dissidents was used as a means of terrorizing the population. For the most part it appears to have been successful. Those Argentines opposed to the regime who weren't murdered or imprisoned during the seven years of the dictatorship were cowed into submission by the fear of losing someone close to them. There was no mass rebellion or political revolt. There was, however, a curious form of organized opposition to the regime. The mothers of the *desaparecidos*, or "disappeared," none of whom had been involved in any political activity before, formed themselves into a grassroots organization to discover the fate of their children. As their numbers swelled and they began to march regularly in the central square of Buenos Aires, they became known as the Mothers of the Plaza de Mayo. Their story is one that shocks and inspires. It is a story of women transformed by the intensity of their grief not into reckless individual heroines, but into a community of determined political activists.

The Mothers

From 1976 until 1983, during seven years of military dictatorship in Argentina, thousands of people were taken from their homes or picked up on the streets. Human-rights organizations estimate that there were at least 30,000 of them.[2] Most were tortured and killed; hundreds, perhaps thousands, were drugged and thrown into the sea from helicopters.

Many of the "disappeared" in Argentina were intellectuals, and a disproportionate number were Jews.[3] There were also a large number of pregnant women who were kept alive until their babies were born and then killed. The babies were given to childless military families. After the restoration of democracy in Argentina, a series of presidential decrees prevented any full-scale investigation of the atrocities of the dictatorship. The "full stop" law held that no more claims of human-rights violations against members of the junta would be heard by the courts after February 1987. Then came the "law of due obedience," which absolved all members of the military beneath the rank of colonel for actions they had committed during the period. In 1988, after a series of attempted coups, President Raúl Alfonsín issued a general amnesty that extended to the officers responsible for ordering the executions and torture of thousands of men, women, and children. His successor, Carlos Saúl Menem, came to office promising to reverse the amnesty, but as soon as he was elected in 1989, he pardoned the remaining 210 officers convicted in trials held during the 1980s.

During the dictatorship and the years that followed, the Mothers of the Plaza de Mayo maintained a constant pressure on the military leaders and the civilian governments that succeeded them. With no access to the institutions of power, no political experience, and no financial support, a group of mothers and housewives turned themselves into a political force so effective that they drew worldwide attention to their campaign to learn the truth about the disappeared. What turned these women from housewives into activists? And how did they pursue their campaign in the face of opponents who never hesitated to intimidate and eliminate opposition? The organization of the "Mothers" is an object lesson in the politicization of grief.

The stories the women told about their disappeared children were similar. Without warning, usually late at night, a large group of armed men from the security forces dressed in plain clothes would ring the doorbell of an apartment in Buenos Aires or some provincial town. Sometimes they would give an excuse—they were searching for a thief, they wanted a son for questioning. They began beating the people they were arresting in front of their parents or children and dragged them off to an unmarked Ford Falcon parked in the street outside. Most of the people they took away were never seen again. Two young physicists, a son and daughter-in-law of Noemie de Álvarez Rojas, were among those who were taken away. In the early hours of the morning a group of armed men broke into their apartment and assaulted them in front of their three children, aged twelve, nine, and two. The men stole some valuables and the family car, then took the parents away, leaving the children in the apartment with the maid. Noemie de Álvarez Rojas lived in Mendoza, 1,000 kilometers from Buenos Aires. As soon as she heard of the abduction she came to the capital to look after the children and began searching for her son and his wife. Despite hundreds of letters of inquiry from the son's scientific colleagues all over the world, and despite the family's continued requests for information, there was never any response.[4] Álvarez Rojas had no preparation for becoming an activist. Like most of the women who became members of the Mothers, her initial reaction was a feeling of complete helplessness. Some women whose children were disappeared lay on their beds for days unable to move. Most felt they were going mad. Because few of the women were employed outside the home, it was they who were free to spend their days searching for their lost children. Other family members often discouraged them, but the mothers were driven by their frenzied grief to continue their search. As they waited in line at police headquarters, ministries, or prisons for hours, only to be turned away at the end of the day with no information, each woman thought at first that she was the unique victim of a grotesque mistake. Slowly mothers began to recognize the faces of other anxious and grief-stricken women, to exchange information, and eventually to combine resources.

The Ministry of the Interior, in its attempt to gain more information, ironically helped to unite the women. The office that ostensibly helped the distraught mothers find information about their children was actually a means of gaining more information about the children's friends and associates. Beatriz de Rubenstein described how the office operated:

They played with us. It was a form of psychological torture. Sometimes they would tell us not to continue because it would endanger our other children. They tried to paralyze us in this way. There I met mothers from all over Argentina, women of all ages and backgrounds. Someone would come in every now and then to tell us not to speak to each other so we all sat there in silence holding the number that gave us an appointment with some official. That piece of paper was the only thing we had which gave us some hope that we would find our children. (Fisher 1989: 27)

By comparing their stories, the women began to realize the danger of giving more information to the police and the army. Soon they started meeting in one another's houses. After a year of meetings and group representations to various offices, one of the women, Azucena de Villaflor de De Vincente, had the idea of holding a meeting in the Plaza de Mayo, outside the government offices, where they could present a petition demanding information. Many of the women were afraid at first, and only fourteen attended the first meeting, but gradually the meetings became regular weekly events. It took two months before the president eventually received them. By that time their numbers had swelled to sixty. When they were ordered to disperse, they continued to walk in a circle around the pyramid in the center of the square (Bouvard 1994: 70–80; Fisher 1989: 28–31). They were threatened with guns and dogs and sprayed with teargas. When the square was barricaded against them, they tried meeting in the cathedral. They were denied access to the cathedral by the cardinal, so they tried other churches, most of which shut their doors. In the end they returned to the square.

Meanwhile the Mothers were transforming themselves into an increasingly efficient political organization. They began collecting testimonies from prisoners who had been released, finding out the names of torturers and the most common methods of torture. To discourage them, the security police sent them pictures of their tortured children, but still they met. To distinguish themselves, they began wearing white shawls on their heads. At first they used babies' diapers, later baby shawls to symbolize their ties to the disappeared. Although they never stated it, the choice of white rather than black was symbolic of the Mothers' determination not to give up hope of finding their children alive. In October 1977, when the number of women circling the Plaza each week had grown to hundreds, the Mothers placed a paid advertisement in the daily newspapers listing the names of the disappeared, each name accompanied by a photograph. They signed the advertisement and attached their addresses.

Not realizing they had already been infiltrated, the women collected money for a second advertisement. In December, as they prepared to place the advertisement, two of the Mothers and a French nun helping them were arrested and taken away. On the day the advertisement appeared, Azucena de De Vincente was arrested with a second French nun. They were not seen again, and there were reports that they had been badly tortured.

The disappearance of three of the Mothers and their helpers was the first of many attempts to intimidate them, including the disappearance of more of their children. Often the women faced opposition from their husbands and other family members. Others felt guilty for abandoning their household duties as their political activities took up more and more of their time. Some families broke apart under the strain; others were strengthened. The financial burden on most of the women was crippling, but they worked at whatever they could, often sewing or knitting at home to earn money for their struggle. In the words of Aida de Surez: "All the Mothers felt the same. If we had a ring, we would sell it. Mothers came to Buenos Aires from all over the country because this is where the government is and this is where the Plaza de Mayo is. Whatever way you could, you came here. We knew women who walked miles from the suburbs to be at the square on Thursdays" (Fisher 1989: 55).

It was not long before the international press began to pay attention to the weekly gatherings in the Plaza de Mayo. In an attempt to discredit them, the government labeled the Mothers *Las Locas* (The Crazy Women), but by 1977, international hostility toward the junta was mounting, and Lisbeth Den Uyl, the wife of the Dutch prime minister, created the first of many international support groups for the Mothers of the Plaza de Mayo. The following year the Mothers sent a delegation to the United States and Europe. Although none of them had previously traveled abroad or could speak a foreign language, the three women delegates spoke to representatives of the press and human-rights organizations, government officials, even to the Italian president. They continued to travel and spread their message in countries as remote as Canada and Australia. Eventually they would be nominated for the Nobel Peace Prize and awarded the Norwegian Peace Prize of the People.

The Mothers were not the only group seeking information about the disappeared; there was also a group of Grandmothers of the Plaza de Mayo, whose main concern was to find grandchildren born in captivity or disappeared with their parents. The Center for Legal and Social Studies, formed in 1979 by a father whose daughter was disappeared, provided legal advice and drew up writs of habeas corpus. But it was the Mothers of the Plaza de Mayo who set in motion this protest movement that eventually became so internationally respected that it could not be squelched.

What Makes a Mother a Political Activist?

In most cases the initial motivation for political action was personal grief. The story of Hebe de Bonafini, who became president of the organization after the disappearance of Azucena de De Vincente, is an almost unbelievable account of grief transformed into political activism. Two of Hebe's sons were disappeared, tortured, and eventually murdered. She had no education beyond primary school, no experience in any sort of social or political organization outside the home. Hebe's reaction to the disappearance of her first son was one of despair and disbelief. She began, as any mother would, to search frantically, going from one police station to another, only to be told there was no information. Relatives were afraid to help her. She contacted friends and friends of friends, who also refused to help her. About two months after her son's disappearance, Hebe began to change her behavior. After a day's fruitless search for information in the waiting room of the army barracks in Palermo, she started shouting at the officers and was hustled out of the barracks. She wrote a letter to President Videla asking for information. Four months after her son's disappearance, a fellow detainee contacted her and told Hebe and her husband about the terrible torture their son had suffered. Hebe strode into the police headquarters where she knew he was being held and screamed at the police, calling them assassins until she was thrown out on the street.

In December 1977, Hebe's younger son, Raúl, was disappeared. She admitted that her grief temporarily robbed her of all her energy.

Shortly after this second terrible blow Hebe's pregnant daughter-in-law, the wife of her first son, was disappeared from a café where she was sitting with a group of her friends. Like her sons, the daughter-in-law has never been seen again, and Hebe has never been able to learn whether a child was born to her in detention. An anonymous letter, written by a young man who was released from the prison where Hebe's second son was held, described the strength and humanity Raúl had displayed under the brutalizing conditions of torture, filth, and humiliation in which the prisoners were held. Hebe claimed that her sons' strength and courage helped her to resume her work not only on their behalf but on behalf of all the disappeared. Initially Hebe was supported by her husband, but his death from cancer in 1982 left her with no family assistance. Despite her grief, Hebe de Bonafini continued her dangerous and energetic work as leader of one of the most unusual political organizations in the world.

Far from destroying her, Hebe de Bonafini's grief transformed her into an international activist, a witty speaker, a compassionate advocate for the rights of others. Clearly, the junta's methods were calculated to have exactly the opposite effect. In a country where the family is still a traditional and inviolate structure, where home and children are expected to be the center of women's lives and few women work outside their own homes, the practice of disappearing young people, many of them girls who were raped and otherwise sexually abused before they were killed, was intended to instill terror and absolute obedience.

As the voluminous *Nunca Más: Report of the Argentine Committee on the Disappeared* documents, violence against women, many of them pregnant, and against children, who were often forcibly separated from their parents, was a particular specialty of the authorities. From the accounts of the few women who survived their torture and captivity, it is clear that the torturers lost interest in finding information, even in the identities of the victims (*Nunca Más* 1986: 286–340). So intent were they on terrorizing the population that almost any victims would do, and the most vulnerable and formerly sacred unit of the population—the family—was their prime target. For the most part, the junta's methods were successful. The state propaganda convinced many Argentines that the authorities were targeting only extremists and terrorists. What seems to have transformed women like Hebe into activists was a combination of grief and rage against the murderers of their children.

Like the other Mothers, Hebe began organizing when she believed she could still find her sons alive, and thought her activities could help to gain their release. But she and the other Mothers continued their activities after they knew their children to be almost certainly dead. What kept these women motivated, even after they knew their efforts to find their children alive were doomed to failure? As the women themselves acknowledge, the organization they created gave them a new social unit to belong to that was entirely different from a traditional family and yet in some ways a substitute for one. Observers have stressed the humor, solidarity, and good spirits of the women (Bouvard 1994; Fischer 1989). It may be a rare exception to the destruction of the social fabric of Argentina during the period, but the Mothers of the Plaza de Mayo was a remarkably successful social organization. From the chaos of despair, the women who joined it moved toward individual and then collective action, structuring their lives and their emotions in ways they could not have envisioned before their loss. Their white head shawls, emblematic of their gender and status as representatives of family values, angered some feminists, but the women never aspired to change their social role. Their effectiveness was precisely their refusal to abandon their role as mothers and wives, even when their children were gone and still later, when the junta had fallen.

From Protest to Justice

Despite the success of the Mothers and other grassroots organizations in drawing attention to the plight of the disappeared, it was probably a combination of economic failure and the debacle of the Falklands War that brought down the junta.[6] The fall of the junta was, however, by no means the end of the Mothers as an organization. The Mothers were both politically experienced and well informed about the activities of the military and the police during the junta years when President Alfonsín came to office. They were in possession of a unique archive. Some of them felt that they must work with the new and fragile democracy to achieve their original goals of finding any of the disappeared who might still be alive. They were also determined to see that those responsible for the atrocities committed during the seven years were punished. Others were distrustful of the new government's resolve to punish those responsible for the torture and murder of their children.

In their search for information they had become aware of the extent of the military's power in their country, and they intended to put constant pressure on the government to bring the leaders of the junta as well as the lower-ranking members of the military and security police to justice. On their leaflets and banners they wrote "Jail for Those Who Committed Genocide," a slogan that reminded the population of the Nazi sympathies and antisemitism of many of the torturers. Their uncompromising stance made the Mothers unpopular not only with the new government but with many in the general population.

The Mothers' distrust of the new government was well founded and based on a political sophistication they had acquired through years of desperate struggle. Despite what many regarded as a courageous decision by President Alfonsín to bring members of the junta to trial and the prosecution of the nine junta members for crimes committed during their seven-year rule, the simultaneous arrest of a number of leaders of left-wing organizations suggested a parity of responsibility for the terror. At the same time, the fact that military courts were made responsible for judging most of the cases of abuses of human rights made nonsense of the government's claims about a fair investigation of the armed forces. The Mothers continued to challenge the government, calling for a parliamentary commission to investigate the disappearances. Eventually the president compromised again and appointed an advisory panel of ten prominent citizens, leaving the parliament to appoint six others. The commission was to review the testimonies of witnesses and send criminal cases to the courts. The commission had no power to subpoena or to compel testimony. Not surprisingly, there was no testimony from the torturers, but despite its limitations, the massive report of the commission, published in book form under the title *Nunca Más* (Never Again), combined with the discovery of mass graves and spontaneous testimony from witnesses grown bold in the new climate of revelation, had a profound effect on the population at large.

The Refusal of the Bones

The bones don't interest us. What are we going to do with the bones?

Beatriz de Rubenstein, member of the Mothers
(Bouvard 1994: 136)

As we have seen, there seems to be an almost universal desire to view, to possess, to re-inter, at least to know the whereabouts of the bones of one's dead. In general, this applied to the Argentine people who had lost their relatives during the seven-year reign of terror. Soon after the return to civilian government, the courts began ordering the exhumation of hundreds of corpses from unmarked graves all over the country in an attempt to identify what were presumed to be the remains of the disappeared. Photographs of the bodies were published daily in the newspapers until most people were surfeited with horror. They wanted to bury their dead and close an ugly chapter of their country's history. The Mothers felt differently.

The Mothers were accustomed to being pressured to accept the deaths of their children. During the junta years, in response to constant requests for information from the families of the disappeared, two laws had been passed. The first, passed in August 1979, allowed for the "presumption of death because of disappearance." The second law granted economic reparation to families of the deceased, allowing them to claim pensions after the first six months of absence (Bouvard 1994: 139). In order to continue collecting the pension, the family had to make a legal declaration of death after three years of a person's disappearance. The state could declare dead anyone missing between November 1974 and September 1979.

The purpose of the legislation, as the Mothers immediately recognized, was to prevent them from making further inquiries about their missing children. It was also a form of incrimination, since in passing the legislation, the minister of the interior had stated that apart from those who might be in hiding or who had left the country secretly, "there exist reasonable possibilities that others have died as a result of their own terrorist activities."[7] President Alfonsín replaced the laws passed by the junta with similar laws. Some mothers were sent telegrams inviting them to collect their children's remains together with an indemnity payment. Others received a box of remains in the mail.

In November 1984 Beatriz de Rubenstein, president of the La Plata branch of the Mothers' organization, received a package of bones identified as those of her daughter, Patricia, who was "disappeared" in 1977. With the package came a letter from a military commander. The letter began:

Dear Madam

In response to your incessant search for your daughter Patricia, we have decided to send you part of her remains which should satisfy your anxiety to be reunited with your dear daughter . . .

The letter stated that Patricia had been condemned to death for crimes she had committed with her husband. They were "Betrayal of her country, concealing the activities of the enemy and collaborating actively with the Montonero assassins." The last sentence of the letter read: "For these reasons she was condemned to death. May God have mercy on her soul" (Bouvard 1994: 140).

The bones were subjected to a forensic analysis and found to be those of a man between twenty and forty years old. Beatriz de Rubenstein's response was to refuse the bones, insisting on her daughter's innocence. She reminded the authorities that her daughter had been taken away alive and was still missing.

In the months that followed, the Mothers carried banners proclaiming "no" to the exhumations, "no" to posthumous homage, "no" to economic reparations. They condemned the practice of exhuming hundreds of bodies as a gesture meant to paralyze the public. They were not against exhumation per se, but most of them recognized the deliberate manipulation of public sentiment involved in the wholesale, unsupervised exhumations. This was a time of painful controversy among the Mothers. Some were ready to accept the bones they were sent so as to be able to have a burial and say the mass for the dead. These were the Mothers who were ready to close a chapter of their grieving. The more radical Mothers were not ready. As Graciela de Jeger explained:

Alfonsín took power on 10 December. On the 11th the spades were ready to exhume bodies in cemeteries all over the country. They brought a very important forensic specialist from the United States who worked with a very special method, like an archeological dig, moving the earth carefully, with little spoons. Argentine students of medicine were working with him and it was terrible, paralyzing. Moreover, when Alfonsín took power the sensationalist press began the "show." People were saturated with horror and they didn't want to know any more about it, because horror has its limits. That was their intention . . . With the exhumations they want to eradicate the problem of the disappearances, because there are no more *desaparecidos*, only dead people . . . they have re-turned people who disappeared from the street, or from their houses, saying they died in *"enfrentaientos"* [confrontations]. If you accept this in your desperation to have the remains of your loved one, you lose all your rights.   (Fisher 1989: 128–129)

Graciela de Jeger, like other Mothers, did not deny the need to bury the bones of the dead. The refusal of bones was, like the refusal of repa-rations, a refusal to mourn and a determination to bring the guilty to justice. In 1984 the Mothers adopted a new slogan: *Aparición con Vida*, or "Bring Them Back Alive." They were criticized by many people for what seemed like an obstinate and unrealistic stance, but as one Mother expressed it: "Why should we accept cadavers, so the murderer can go unpunished? For my son to be dead, his murderer has to go to jail. Peo-ple think you have to have a tomb to go and cry in front of. I don't want to go and cry at a tomb because if I do, I am going to allow thousands of other youngsters to die" (Fisher 1989: 128–129). Naming the dead, for the Mothers, was always linked to naming the one responsible for the death, and they succeeded in forcing an end to exhumations under-taken without the consent of the families.

Keeping the Wounds Open

Keeping the issue of responsibility alive meant keeping pain alive, and that is an extraordinary choice, but it is one we have seen women make in other societies. The Mothers deliberately asked questions about the tortures endured by those who had been released from the jails and camps. They read reports and heard testimonies that forced them to endure vicariously the appalling suffering of their children. Why did they do it? Hebe de Bonafini claimed that the knowledge of atrocities gave them strength: "The ferocity of the enemy gives us the strength to face him. I mean, how are you going to allow him to go on? The other very important step is to go on fighting even though we may not find our children, so that it will not happen to someone else and another child will not have to suffer" (Bouvard 1994: 147).

Not all mothers were strong enough to make such a choice. It is one that refuses the comfort of traditional mourning. As Bouvard wisely says: "Contrary to the normal process of grieving, during which the agony of loss moves away from the centre of one's concerns, the Mothers have made a deliberate decision to keep the wounds open, in order to maintain their purpose and momentum" (1994: 151).

The decision the more radical Mothers made did not mean that they didn't wish to heal themselves. Their ability to function efficiently as an organization is ample evidence of the fact that these women have effectively healed themselves. They claim that their healing is a result of their combined sense of purpose. Although they will take no part in memorial services, their organization is arguably a living memorial to their sons and daughters. In their monthly newspaper, *Madres*, in October 1985, they stated: "Let there be no healing of wounds. Let them remain open. Because if the wounds still bleed, there will be no forgetting and our strength will continue to grow" (Bouvard 1994: 151). We must conclude, I think, that it is possible to let one's wounds bleed and yet be psychologically sound. To refuse artificial "healing" is to be "healed" and to "bleed" simultaneously.

The organization of Mothers of the Plaza de Mayo has fragmented, and many have accepted the necessity for compromise. The Mothers who refuse to compromise may be regarded by many as unrealistic, but they are still politically active. Given their relentless struggle, it was surprising to read, in an op-ed article in the *New York Times* of December 12, 1994, the question: "Why is there no rage in Argentina?"[8] The article concerned the November 1994 trial in which the Buenos Aires district court awarded $3 million, $1 million from the state and $1 million each from two former military chiefs, to the son of Hugo and Blanca Tarnopolsky, who were "disappeared" together with their daughter and another son and his wife in 1976. The unprecedented decision was immediately appealed by the government. The author of the article lamented the failure of successive Argentine administrations to investigate the circumstances of the disappeared: "Today the only memorial to the thousands of *desaparecidos* is a small forest in Israel, planted a few years ago by a private organization." But the author's surprise is answered by the obduracy of the Mothers and by his own cousin Daniel, who has the last word. As the lone survivor of a disappeared family, Daniel realized his family's murderers would soon be released and decided to file a civil suit for damages against them. In an article he wrote in a Buenos Aires newspaper the day after the decision, one passage could have been written by one of the Mothers: "Why this lawsuit? The law of due obedience and later, the amnesty sought to throw a blanket of oblivion over the acts that took place under the junta. They strove to silence everything, to cover, to erase, to deny. This is why. Argentines, do not forget. Memory is the only barrier against the recurrence of barbarism" (quoted in ibid.).

The Argentines have periodically been forced to remember the disappearances whether they liked it or not. In March 1995 a retired naval officer, Adolfo Scillingo, admitted to taking part in what most of the relatives of the disappeared already knew about: a particular form of disappearance known as the "death flights." In an apparent attempt to clear his conscience, Captain Scillingo said he had participated in flights over the Atlantic in which up to 2,000 people had been drugged and pushed into the sea. He noted that military priests had sanctioned the flights, claiming it was "a Christian way to die" (*New York Times*, April 5, 1995). The disclosures of Captain Scillingo set off new debates about the disappearances and the government's offers of compensation. Protesting the revelations, representatives of the Mothers threw flowers into the River Plate, which empties into the Atlantic.

The Case of the Disappearing Corpse

That the exhumation of corpses became a regular subject on prime-time television in Argentina seems to bear out the contention of novelist Tomás Eloy Martínez that his fellow countrymen have "a tendency toward necrophilia" (*New York Times*, July 30, 1995). The figure of Eva Perón has captivated Argentina for more than forty years. Her life was the subject of the successful musical *Evita*, but it is her dead body that haunts Luisa Valenzuela's *The Lizard's Tail* and is the subject of Martínez' novel *Santa Evita*. When she died of cancer in 1952, Eva Perón's body was embalmed with meticulous care. Her embalmer made wax and vinyl replicas that were used by the military to deceive her followers. The embalmed corpse was put on display at the headquarters of the General Confederation of Labor. That was the beginning of the cult of Evita-as-Saint, a saint worshipped by thousands of Peronists in candlelit masses. In an attempt to quell the tide of Peronist support, the military removed the body, hiding it in an attic until they transported it to Italy, where it was buried under a false name. In 1971, when one military ruler displaced another, the body was exhumed from a cemetery near Rome and transported to Juan Perón's villa in Madrid. There Perón and his third wife, Isabel, kept the body in an open casket on the dining-room table before building a shrine for it in the attic. In November 1974, after the return to power and subsequent death of Juan Perón, Eva's corpse was brought back to Argentina by Isabel, who succeeded her husband as president. It lay in state in the presidential palace until Isabel was overthrown by the junta. The military rulers were so afraid of the aura surrounding Evita's corpse that they had it buried under three plates of steel in the Ricoleta Cemetery in Buenos Aires.

Martínez believes that the fascination of Argentines with the body of Eva Perón was symbolic of a more widespread preoccupation with corpses. In 1987 Juan Perón's tomb was broken into and the corpse's hands sawn off. And in 1989, President Carlos Saul Menem brought back from England the remains of Juan Manuel de Rosas, a nineteenth-century Argentine warlord, as a symbol of the futility of nurturing old hatreds. His purpose was to justify his pardoning of military officers responsible for crimes committed during the dictatorship. The refusal of the Mothers to join in the mass hysteria and turn the corpses of their tortured and murdered children into objects of veneration is all the more remarkable in a culture where the remains of the dead appear to have an exaggerated symbolic value.

Eva Perón's disappearing corpse, with its plastic substitutes, makes a perfect metaphor for the atmosphere of mystery and sinister intrigue created by the dictatorship. Like Borges' mazes and forking paths, the methods of the dictators created a deliberate, nightmarish confusion. There was no real escape because the society had become a surreal landscape of secrets and terror, but the fearlessness of those who had no more to lose was a constant reminder of another reality outside the labyrinth. Even now, the Mothers continue to remind Argentines that the nightmare they have awakened from was created by men, men who have not been held accountable for their crimes. As Hebe de Bonafini said in a 1995 interview: "Pardon is divine for those who still believe in God, but we don't pardon" (*New York Times*, March 25).

Bones of a Dead Hero and the Disappeared

In a continent where the exhumation of the bodies of the disappeared has become a common occurrence a bizarre episode took place on October 20, 1995. It was a story that linked the disappeared of Argentina to the disappeared of Guatemala and the strange story of Eva Perón's corpse to another famous corpse. More than forty years after he was ousted as president of Guatemala in a coup engineered by the U.S. Central Intelligence Agency, and nearly twenty-five years after his death in exile, Jacobo Arbenz Guzmán returned to Guatemala. The bones of the man who had tried to redistribute some of the land owned by Guatemala's tiny group of wealthy landowners and to institute modest democratic reforms were exhumed from a cemetery in El Salvador and flown to Guatemala City, where thousands of people crowded to catch a glimpse of the coffin.

What lay behind the extraordinary decision to bring back the bones of Arbenz Guzmán? And why has he been reburied in the National Cemetery beside the mausoleum of Colonel Carlos Castillo Armas, the man who overthrew him and began a violent war of repression? A possible answer might be suggested by the fact that although the majority of pilgrims to Guzmán's tomb are from the left of the political spectrum in Guatemala, the military have also laid claim to his bones. The defense minister himself went to the airport to receive them and to restore the dead president's military rank and honors. The image of the Guatemalan army abroad has been damaged by the revelations of the American lawyer Jennifer Harbury, by the Nobel Peace Prize recipient Rigoberta Menchu, and by many others. The bones of a dead hero who was also a military man might come in handy.

Like the body of Eva Perón, the remains of Arbenz Guzmán are pawns in a complicated policy of controlling grief by the public spectacle of reburial. And like the other bones that have been disappeared, the whereabouts of these remains have always been known to the authorities. The decision to stage a new funeral is a conscious attempt to divert private grief into displays of communal, state-sanctioned grief. Just as the tragic theater performed its function of catharsis, allowing the population of ancient Athens to experience violent emotion in a controlled space, the reburial of a dead hero's bones or the exhumation of the bodies of the disappeared is unlikely to inflame the audience to actions that threaten the status quo. Instead, by allowing the population to grieve in public, it briefly opens a pressure valve, giving an illusion of remorse that has much to do with theater and little with reality. It is to the credit of the Mothers and their counterparts in Guatemala that they understood that their grief was being manipulated by the authorities and resisted the impulse to join in the publicly sanctioned catharsis.

Doubt and the Impossibility of Mourning

The mothers and wives of the disappeared were deliberately subjected to a form of torture as agonizing as their children and husbands suffered. When disappearance, torture, and murder become commonplace, secrecy is difficult to maintain. In the end most Mothers discovered the fate of their children from fellow prisoners or informers, but there was always an element of doubt, even when the bodies were exhumed.

That element of doubt made traditional mourning impossible. Mourning rituals are social. They may be imposed by religious organizations or developed by a community, but by consensus, they order and contain grief. They cannot take place when there is any ambiguity about death, or when the individual no longer has faith in the institutions that control public mourning. As the Argentine poet Etelvina Astrada writes:

> In my country
> nothing is permitted
> not even being a corpse,
> laid out beautifully,
> immensely poetic and immortal,
> or thinking death to be personal,
> as property, our very own and private.
> . . .
> there are no gravediggers,
> elegies go unsaid,
> no one buys a little snippet of eternal peace.
> The dead are not laid to rest.
> In my country

you can't hear the tolls of bells for the dead,
personal demise as a custom
is a thing of the past.[9]

The absence of the corpse made the passion of the Mothers' grief a
continuous but not a steady state. Like a slow-burning flame, it flared,
then settled, never losing its heat. As the Mothers described it, there
was an initial period of numbing despair, followed by a frantic, frus-
trated search for information, the coming together of helpless individuals into a group and eventually an organized movement. There has
been much postmodernist feminist rhetoric about bodies, lived bodies,
and written bodies.[10] In their weekly gathering in the Plaza de Mayo,
the mothers of the disappeared of Argentina deliberately emphasized
the bodily link between themselves and the absent bodies of their children. The diaper-as-headscarf (later replaced by the baby shawl) was a
reminder that the mothers had a physical right to know the whereabouts of their children, a right they claimed by their bodily presence
in the square. Their insistence on representing themselves by the most
basic of corporeal symbols was also a reminder that the junta, for all
its rhetoric of Christian values, had violently severed the most sacred
of Christian bonds. As they said themselves: "We made maternity solidarity."

Eloquent Bodies

Argentine poets and writers may have used texts as substitutions for the
bodies; the Mothers of the Plaza de Mayo used the eloquence of their
own bodies together with the representations of their children's absent
bodies in the form of photographs and black silhouettes on newspaper.
Their means and gestures were instinctive and effective, particularly in
Buenos Aires, where foreign journalists soon began to attend the regular gatherings in front of the presidential palace. At first, as Elsa Santí
de Manzoti told me in an interview (March 3, 1997), "We had none of
the social sense of our children . . . we learned solidarity from them."
As the struggle of the Mothers grew and became internationally recognized, the absence of bodies became a metaphor itself. Their political
raison d'être was based not only on recovery of bodies—the hope of recovering their children alive soon faded—but on holding those responsible for their deaths to account. The offer of officially exhumed bones

was, they recognized, an inadequate gesture of compensation, a ghoulishly sentimental attempt to settle accounts. By now, however, the authorities were dealing with a hard core of professional activists proud to be carrying on the tradition of their children. Grief, for these women, had become a path to a life they never dreamed of, one with its own rewards.

The grassroots organizations of women in Argentina, Guatemala, and other Latin American countries, formed as a response to grief, are not unique. In Johannesburg in the 1950s, in Tel Aviv in the 1980s and 1990s, in Belgrade in the Bosnian war, and more recently in Chechnya and St. Petersburg, women in black have taken to the streets to protest violence. Often the women risked their lives to protest, and usually they were originally motivated by personal grief. What is unusual about these women, in Argentina and in other countries where disappearance was used as a weapon of terror, is that they refused to put on the trappings of mourning, the "outward signs of grief." By refusing to mourn they consciously avoided both self-pity and condescension. They could be called crazy but never pathetic.

These women inspired by the passion of grief to defy a regime remind us of the heroines of Greek tragedy. In the tragic theater, the grief of an Antigone or Electra begets disorder. Death follows death in a cycle that threatens to overturn the state. The grief of mothers and widows of the disappeared of Argentina is no less threatening. The immediate aim of each grief-stricken mother may have been to discover the whereabouts of her missing relative, but once she had combined her loss with the losses of others, she was transformed into a member of a citizen chorus that demanded information and passed judgment on a regime. The citizen chorus, like the lament singers at a village funeral, contained and focused individual grief. Within its ranks, individuals found not the banality of comfort, but the satisfaction of ordered defiance. Some chose to put grief away and mourn with the means they were offered—the exhumed bones, even if the wrong bones. The women who continued and still continue to demand an accounting from those responsible for the disappearances wear their grief like open wounds, proudly displayed. They divide grief from mourning, refusing one and transforming the other.

~ 5

Plague

In the city of Athens it appeared suddenly, and the first cases were among the population of Piraeus . . . Words indeed fail one when one tries to give a general picture of this disease; and as for the sufferings of individuals, they seemed almost beyond the capacity of human nature to endure.

Thucydides, *History of the Peloponnesian War* 2.48–50

We are all mourners on this mortal earth who daily choose the measure of our participation in the world's fate, which is to say its mortality, which is to say its grief. It's just that HIV—with its extended incubation period, its prolonged illnesses, its often horrifying complications, its impact on close-knit neighborhoods and communities—is forcing gay men to acknowledge what our life—and youth-obsessed society—prefers to deny.

Fenton Johnson, *New York Times*, December 24, 1994

THE ELEMENTS of the Chinese character for leprosy are "heaven" and "punishment." Periodically, it was thought, God strikes down the unclean, the sinner, perhaps the whole imperfect human race. When disease or calamity strikes an already marginalized group—the poor, prostitutes, homosexuals—there is always a tendency to identify the victim with the disease, to see the relationship as not an accidental one, to shudder with relief that the disease cannot possibly touch us. Sexually transmitted diseases like syphilis and gonorrhea seemed, to nineteenth-century observers, a particularly fitting example of God's wrath striking the wicked. When the AIDS virus was first identified among male homosexuals, it was also regarded by many as the quintessence of disease as punishment. One of the earliest jokes about AIDS suggested that the new acronym for AIDS should be WOGS—Wrath of God Syndrome.

The view of AIDS as punishment for past sins was predictably adopted by conservative religious leaders, but it also appeared in surprising places. In an editorial in the *Southern Medical Journal*, Dr. James Fletcher expressed the view forcefully:

> A logical conclusion is that AIDS is a self-inflicted disorder for the majority of those who suffer from it. For again, without placing reproach upon certain Haitians or hemophiliacs, we see homosexual men reaping not only expected consequences of sexual promiscuity, suffering even as promiscuous heterosexuals the usual venereal diseases, but other unusual consequences as well.
>
> Perhaps, then, homosexuality is not "alternative" behavior at all, but as the ancient wisdom of the Bible states, most certainly pathologic. Indeed from an empirical medical perspective alone current scientific observations seem to require the conclusion that homosexuality is a pathologic condition. (1984: 149)

Whatever statistics are published about heterosexuals with AIDS, Haitians with AIDS, Africans with AIDS, Thai prostitutes with AIDS, the epidemic remains, in the mind of most Americans, a disease of gay men. Even the most enlightened, including gay men themselves, have, if only in a soft inner whisper, told themselves that the disease was some sort of retribution for the lifestyle of the gay community during the late 1960s and 1970s. Everyone concerned with AIDS in the United States has at some stage, by choice or by force, been confronted by the fact that AIDS was first identified in the male homosexual population, that it attacked an already stigmatized group. As Sander Gilman pointed out, "the idea of the person afflicted with a sexually transmitted disease, one of the most potent in the repertory of images of the stigmatized patient, became the paradigm through which the AIDS patient was categorized and understood" (1988: 247).

The timing of the outbreak was significant. In an era when medical science seemed on the verge of eliminating epidemics, when many forms of cancer seemed to be curable, a mysterious virus appeared that was inevitably fatal. At a time when homosexuals had won unprecedented social acceptance, when most not only had come out of the closet but were reveling in an era of sexual liberation that made the bath houses and gay bars of New York and San Francisco a garden of earthly delights, a disease as grotesque in its symptoms as any the medieval artist could depict decimated the worshippers of male beauty.

The fact that the first cases of AIDS identified in this country were members of a group organized as a self-conscious minority determined to fight their cause, made the response to the epidemic swift and strong. But the strident response of the gay community to what they and the world first saw as a "gay plague" may have intensified the public's perception of the disease as punishment for abnormal sexuality.[1] As the AIDS epidemic spread and sufferers were identified outside the gay community, it was still possible for the dominant majority to perceive the disease as sexually and racially removed from themselves. The "4H's"—homosexuals, heroin addicts, Haitians, and hemophiliacs— were a caste apart, the untouchables of American society. Whatever the realities of AIDS transmission and the epidemiology of the disease in the 1990s, the 1980s construction of the typical AIDS patient as urban, gay, a drug user, and sexually promiscuous has remained the dominant public image.

Grieving for the Sick and Dying

> For when people were afraid to visit the sick, then they died with no one to look after them; indeed there were many houses where all the inhabitants perished through lack of any attention. When, on the other hand, they did visit the sick, they lost their own lives, and this was particularly true for those who made it a point of honor to act properly.
>
> Thucydides 2.51

For people dying of AIDS and their families, the expression of grief that normally accompanies illness and death in this society has been a process complicated by the social stigma of the disease, the sexual predilection or ethnic background of the sufferers, the fear of contagion even among members of the medical profession, and the rage that was an inevitable concomitant of all this. How did the sufferers express their grief? Did their grief take on a new form? Were the grief-stricken families and friends politically manipulated, or did they politicize their own grief?

Grief for the victims of AIDS was never just like other grieving. It still isn't. In the small town where I live in upstate New York, I spoke to two counselors from the local AIDSWORK office and asked them how families and relatives of people dying and dead from the disease typically expressed their grief. "They don't," said Georgette. "People are still lying about the cause of death of family members who die of AIDS, telling people they died of cancer or some more socially acceptable disease. Children in schools are not telling their teachers or friends that their father is dying of AIDS; there are families denying there has been a death at all. Teenagers who contract the disease are afraid to go to doctors, hospital workers and dentists are reluctant to treat patients."[2] This is a college town, a liberal community where there is a large gay community. There are collection boxes for AIDS victims all over town, and small red ribbons worn on hundreds of lapels. But a local dentist would treat an AIDS patient only after his usual office hours and then only when he had covered all his equipment and office furniture with dust sheets. At the local hospital, some medical staff have refused to enter the rooms of patients infected with the HIV virus, while others, according to AIDSWORK officials, have failed to take even the most elementary precautions to protect themselves from infection.

That teenagers should keep quiet about a father's disease or even their own is hardly surprising. The two counselors at AIDSWORK are so overwhelmed by the physical demands of their job, by the need to combat prejudice and ignorance, that they have almost no time to think about the grief of the families. "How can you grieve," said one worker, "when you're in total denial? The families we speak to don't want to admit they lost someone to AIDS. The ones who have it are forced to deny it to keep their jobs. The families are forced to deny it because they live in a neighborhood and they don't want to be treated like pariahs."

The Gay Artists' Response

Such people felt ashamed to think of their own safety and went into their friends' houses at times when even the members of the household were so overwhelmed by the weight of their calamities that they had actually given up the usual practice of making laments for the dead.

Thucydides 2.51

One community in the United States was determined not to deny its grief for the suffering caused by AIDS but to channel that grief into a political campaign of extraordinary force. Gay men were disproportionately represented in the arts. They had always enjoyed an exceptional freedom in the theater, in dance, as painters, photographers, poets, and playwrights. As they watched their colleagues and friends sicken and die in ever-increasing numbers during the 1980s, members of the gay artistic community of New York, San Francisco, and other large cities decided not to retreat into the familiar pattern of denial from which they had fought so hard to liberate themselves during the preceding decades. The metaphor of sexual self-revelation, the "coming out" that had galvanized them into political action, could, gay men realized, be equally well applied to the disease that was sweeping through their community, a disease so shocking in its virulence and specific in its epidemiology that it was wreathed in secrecy, misinformation, and denial.

The motivation for making AIDS a public affair was partly a hope that attention would make more funding available for medical research and that research would lead to a cure. But there was more to it than a rational campaign for a solution. The lovers and friends of the first to die of AIDS were living in a state of shock, experiencing what Aristotle had isolated as the two emotional responses evoked by tragedy: fear and pity. Grief for their loved ones complicated by the terror of infection; in mourning the other they anticipated mourning themselves. The gay community was also lamenting a brief era of sexual freedom. Avoiding one another "like the plague" meant reversing a way of life that many gay men had established in flagrant denial of the accepted norms of social behavior. It was not surprising that they responded with rage toward the disease itself and toward a society that blamed it on an aberrant lifestyle.

The Language of War

From the beginning, the language of the gay community writing about AIDS was the language of war, a rhetoric they shared with the media and with those who believed that some concerted federal government action in the form of "a war on AIDS" was the only way to approach the disease.[3] As critics have pointed out, the war metaphor had many problems. For one thing, it made it necessary to create an enemy. To some, the disease itself was the enemy; to others, the government, the medical profession, even the society at large became targets of bellicose rhetoric. Activist Larry Kramer proposed the Manhattan Project as a model for action against AIDS: science and the massive resources of government pitted against a faceless enemy. The same war rhetoric could be used against the gay community by the fundamentalist right with terrible irony: in Patrick Buchanan's words, "The poor homosexuals—they have declared war upon Nature and now Nature is exacting an awful retribution" (1989).

The use of the Nazi Holocaust as a metaphor for AIDS was less common than the allegory of war, but it was adopted by a number of the more radical members of New York's gay community. The rhetoric of Larry Kramer and his organization ACT-UP (AIDS Coalition to Unleash Power) defines the most polemic of the political responses to the horrors of AIDS. The very name ACT-UP suggests antisocial behavior, a childlike, theatrical attempt to attract attention. Many would claim that Kramer's methods achieved no more than that. Borrowing a slogan familiar in literature about the Holocaust, "Silence = Death," Kramer equated what was being done by society and the Reagan administration to the gay community with the atrocities of the Nazis. Charging gay men with complicity in their own destruction, Kramer both participated in the dominant rhetoric and turned it into a powerful force for chastising everyone who neglected the epidemic, especially the press. In Kramer's play *The Normal Heart* Ned says: "Do you know when Hitler's Final Solution to eliminate the Polish Jews was first mentioned in the *Times* it was on page twenty-eight. And on page six of the *Washington Post*. And the *Times* and the *Post* were both owned by Jews. What causes silence like that?" (1985: 50–51).

The failure of the press to deal with AIDS was one of Kramer's main complaints. Not only was the mainstream press guilty, but the gay press too: "With the exception of the *New York Native* and a few, very few, other gay publications, the gay press has been useless. If we can't get our own papers and press to tell us what's really happening to us, and this negligence is added to the negligent non-interest of the straight press . . . how are we going to get the word around that we're dying?" (1989: 44).

For some of the gay men affected by AIDS, particularly those who were Jews, but also those aware of the extermination of the homosexual population of Germany by the Nazis, the identification must have afforded a sense of status, of belonging to a larger class of now sanctified victims. Still, it did not address their astonished rage at finding themselves an endangered species in the middle of the peaceful, prosperous 1980s. Were they, in part, responsible for the catastrophe that had befallen them? Kramer's consistently belligerent stance and his inclusion of the gay community in the combined guilt of the epidemic were bound to anger many members of the gay community and to complicate the grief of others. In a "Personal Appeal" to the community, made soon after the first press reports of the outbreak of the disease, Kramer warned the gay men of New York City that "the many things we've done over the past years may be all that it takes for a cancer to grow from a tiny something-or-other that got in there who knows when from doing who knows what" (1989: 8).

Kramer's extreme position reflected a personal ambivalence toward the gay community that predated the outbreak of the epidemic. His 1978 novel *Faggots* had already portrayed the homosexuals of New York as a dissipated, drug-ridden community with few redeeming graces. If his pronouncements on AIDS came close to blaming the community for their own disease, it may simply indicate how affected even gay American men of the 1980s were by the dominant rhetoric of the day. The combination of guilt and anger that dominates Kramer's writing was an expression less of grief than of a generalized rage against society, including the gay community. At its worst, as David Bergman remarks, Kramer's voice was like that of a teenager trying to shock his respectable parents. His warning to the community to "get up off [our] fucking tushies and fight back" seemed designed as much to humiliate as to promote effective action (1992: 180).

The suggestion that AIDS was the wages of sin, together with Kramer's insistent focus on the dead rather than on the sick and dying, alienated many of those who supported his initial attempt to draw attention to the epidemic. It may even have handicapped the gay community in their attempt to come to terms with their grief. They were watching friends and lovers die. It seemed pointless to talk about blame when you were overwhelmed by fear and loss. Not only gay men but fellow artists of both sexes felt the need to turn their pain and rage into art. For some gay artists, already established as writers, painters, or photographers, the task seemed straightforward, the means traditional. They would eulogize the dead, lament their passing, and be as open about the cause of their friends' deaths as they were about any other death. Other gay artists deliberately sought new forms of artistic expression that would shock a society they saw as indifferent into a form of response—any response, so long as it brought attention to the epidemic. Funerals often became elaborate and stylish displays. Mark Doty describes such a funeral in a poem called "Tiara" (1989):

> Peter died in a paper tiara
> from a book of paper dolls;
> he loved royalty, sashes . . .

The most flagrant of such displays of grief was probably the strewing of the ashes of a number of men who had died of AIDS on the White Houses lawn in October 1994.[4]

The Language of Grief: Singing of Heroes

Like any artist working in the midst of a catastrophe, the gay writer affected directly or indirectly by AIDS felt impelled to express his horror and grief in his art. But there was something unique in the population of artists who wrote about AIDS. They were more often than not writing about the loss of homosexual lovers or the demise of a golden age of erotic adventures and the worship of male beauty. The brief duration of their liberation made it seem like some butterfly-summer. For many writers, the grief of the loss of a lover or friend was compounded not only by guilt or rage but also by a sense that an entire world had been lost.

The epigraph to Paul Monette's novel-length memoir of his lover's illness and death *Borrowed Time* ("Unsung the noblest deed will die") tells us a lot about the purpose of his book and about the particular nature of grieving for gay men. A translation of Pindar's Greek (fragment 126), it is about heroism. The affinity that gay men, especially those who have some knowledge of classical Greek art and culture, have always felt for Greece is predictable; in Monette's case a visit to Greece with his lover, Roger Horwitz, was the crowning moment of his life:

> impossible to measure the weight of the place for gay men. We grew up with glints and evasions in school about the homoerotic side, but if you're alone and think you're the only one in the world, the merest glance is enough. The ancient soil becomes

peopled with warrior brothers equal to fate, arm in arm defending
the marble-crowned hill of democracy from savage hordes. The
source of such heroics is buried very deep—for me it lies in History 1 at Andover, the stone swell of the athletes' muscles and
Marathon battle statistics, war after war till it all disappeared.
(1988: 20)

At Delphi, the atheist Monette had the nearest thing to a religious
experience he ever knew. When he ran on the grass of the ancient
arena,

> I knew I was poised at the exact center of my life. I belonged at last
> to a brotherhood where body and spirit were one. When a victor
> at the games returned in triumph to his home, the city wall was
> breached to show that a place that possessed such a hero required
> no further defense. In the pitch of the moment it seemed to me
> that Roger and I and our secret brothers were heir to all of it.
> (Ibid.: 22–23)

In Monette's passionate elegy for Horwitz, "Your Sightless Days," the
memory of those Greek days returns for an instant among the references to his lover's terrible ordeal with blindness—he remembers "how
clear Aegean blue your eyes were," and finally in outraged identification, he assumes the role of the blind Roger: "I am shut tight Oedipus-
old leave me alone" (1989: 168).

Greece and Greek literature had always offered a model to gay writers of a society in which their sexual predilection was the norm rather
than the exception, at least in their youth. The cult of youth and
beauty, of bath houses and gymnasiums, of transient passion and sen-
sual indulgence, of Fire Island and San Francisco in the late 1970s and
early 1980s must have seemed, especially to the literary-minded males
in its orbit, a Hellenic paradise, no sooner won than lost. And when disaster struck, the perfect model of mourning was appropriately Greek.

The impulse to sing of the wrath and death of heroes, of men who
have died in the full flower of their beauty, is as old as our culture and
common to most. The novelty of Monette's account of his lover's death
is that AIDS is not most people's idea of the heroic death but its opposite. AIDS is a relentless assault on the body and the spirit; it robs the

handsome of their beauty, the proud of their dignity, the private of their integrity. All deaths from serious illnesses tend to share these qualities, but those that undermine the body's immune system are especially repellent in their symptoms. How does a man who worshipped beauty, liberated sexuality, the light of Greece, face the steady decay of his lover? It is a tribute to Monette's love and humanity that he could always see the man behind the dying body of his friend, and a tribute to his lover that he could preserve his sense of humor to the end and retort to those who asked how he felt: "Read *Job!*" (1989: 168).

Monette's project of heroizing his friend's death is, surprisingly, a success. The struggle of two men, no longer in the first flush of their passion but still deeply in love, against a disease that closes in on them, decimating their circle of friends and finally themselves, is a tale of modern heroism in the setting where most of us will have to perform our heroics. In an age in which conventional battlegrounds are no longer places of heroism, where death comes from afar and a soldier rarely sees his enemy, the opportunities for conventional heroism are few. The young may run risks merely to taste the fear of death, but as adults we are likely to be voyeurs of heroism, of death as entertainment, until we are faced with the diseases and deaths of the people we love, finally with our own. Our struggle with the fear of death will be the most demanding moment of our lives, and many of us will meet it too drugged and debilitated to rise to the occasion, make a brave face or laugh it off. But for some there will be moments of lucidity, of bravery in the face of pain, the cracking of a joke to dispel the gloom of relatives and friends. The metaphor of war is not uncommon in descriptions of the struggle of the body and mind to cope with pain and death. Monette's achievement is to carry the metaphor of heroic struggle into the daily battles of his lover against a humiliating, stigmatized, and deadly disease.

Not many victims of AIDS are fortunate enough to have the support, the undivided love, the resources of Roger, whose days ended in a dream of Greece, reading and discussing the last dialogues of Plato with his lover:

Then we turned to the *Apology*, Socrates' defense, delivered in the Agora, below the Temple of Hermes. Two years before we had wandered the very spot, our guide books out like dousing rods, trying to make a city out of the fallen stones . . . There was nothing to figure out or understand at all. Just the clarity of it, unfiltered by vanity or bullshit or the need to kiss ass. And how tough Socrates is as he goads the pompous and self-deluded and dares them to put him to death. (1988: 300)

For those who saw the brief period of liberated homosexuality as a Greek phenomenon, a cult of male beauty and companionship in a new community of celebrants, the horror that followed seemed to have the quality of a Greek tragedy. One of the most compelling scenes in all of ancient tragedy is surely the opening scene of Aeschylus' *Eumenides*, when the ancient powers of retributive justice, the Erinyes, with their oozing sores and shriveled bodies, appear at Apollo's shrine at Delphi, center of light, to claim their victim, Orestes. The young hero, who has killed his own mother, is hounded by the ancient powers for his unnatural crime, a sin against the sacred bonds of family. Unlike most tragic heroes, Orestes survives, and his crime is exonerated, but not before we have experienced the terror of the chthonic Furies crowding around the youthful sinner and demanding his blood. The claim they make for their right to punish Orestes is one that had a familiar ring to many in the gay community:

> He'll long for death but we won't let him have it.
> We'll send him down to the underworld alive
> so the ghosts there can torment him even further.
> Forever and forever! What else have they got to do?
> Even the other sinners down there will shun him.
> Whoever has sinned against kinsman, parent, or guest
> will point to him as the bearer of greater guilt.
>   (*Eumenides* 243–249, trans. Slavitt)

As we have seen, not only did the majority of the population consider AIDS as appropriate punishment for an unnatural lifestyle, but gay men themselves often explicitly or implicitly invoked the myth of retribution. In his poem "Almost to Jesus," Michael Burkard makes his point clearly:

> & the sick are not to
> be touched for they

> are among us already
> for they have wronged
> and wronged us
>> (1989: 44)

And in "The Veteran," Edward Field seems relieved to put his guilt-ridden life away:

> How could it not have come, then, to this,
> the ultimate punishment of AIDS, an inner voice argues—
> even while good sense says it's just a disease,
> not a moral judgment.
>
> . . .
>
> it's with regret, but truthfully also relief,
> that this old veteran—masturbator, midnight stalker—
> fed up with it from a lifetime of guilt and worry,
> can at last put sex away, probably forever.
>> (1989: 76)

Searching for a Voice

Once gay artists and writers began to respond to AIDS, the outpouring of anger and grief was unstoppable. Much of the art proved more shocking to the public at large than the lifestyle that preceded the epidemic. How could anyone write about, photograph, choreograph, act a scenario as unglamorous and depressing as AIDS? But how could the gay artist avoid the subject? As Andrew Holleran put it in *Ground Zero:* "now the art of writing seemed of no help whatever, for a simple reason: writing could not produce a cure. That was all that mattered and all that anyone wanted. One couldn't, therefore, write about It—and yet one couldn't not" (1988: 16). But what form could one use, as a writer, that might be appropriate? "The novel is occasionally the way we bring some sort of order to the disorder of life. But *this* disorder seemed way beyond the writer's powers. Literature could not heal or explain this catastrophe" (ibid.).

For Holleran, like a number of prose writers, the truth of his life seemed stranger than fiction, and he wrote more or less autobiographically, confessionally, insisting on the need to distinguish this epidemic from all others. The war metaphor shifted from the disease, the cure, and society, to art itself:

writing about AIDS will appear, and in the short term will almost inevitably be judged as writing published in wartime is: by its effect on the people fighting—it must in some way be heartening—it must improve morale, for it to be allowed a place of honor. Otherwise it will be dismissed as useless, discouraging, immoral, like any art that accepts surrender during a war; even though the plague has produced a deep depression . . . (1988: 17)

In the short term, then, the writing was to be combative, but what would endure, Holleran realized, might be something quite different, something as traditional and familiar as grief itself: "I suspect the best writing will be nothing more or less than a lament" (1988: 18). Holleran's book itself, despite its sardonic humor and celebration of a carefree life vanished forever from its mecca (the discos, bars, moviehouses, and baths of Manhattan), is less of a morale-builder than a lament. The life he invites us to celebrate, unlike Monette's, was one of transient pleasures, of sexual encounters so brief and insubstantial that they left little behind them but a desire for more. As Holleran admits: "The Mayans left temples in the Yucatan; we seem to have left pornography" (23). Not much of this life was based on deep attachment, and yet there are inspiring accounts of caring gay men helping friends infected with the virus to bear their last illness. Counterpoised against this community solidarity is the phenomenon of the deliberate or simply careless spread of AIDS by infected men. The fear of being exposed to infection, according to Holleran, may have divided the gay community as much as it united them. "AIDS," in his view, "destroys trust" (189). "We cannot possibly investigate, much less be responsible for, what the man we are attracted to has done with the past five or seven years of his life . . . AIDS is a form of terrorism . . . We look at one another not merely as appetizing possibilities—we look at each other as lethal instruments" (ibid.).

The AIDS Elegy as Lament

As Holleran guessed, the form of writing that seems most likely to endure from all the angry outpourings of the bereaved gay community is the elegiac lament. There is already a literature growing up about the "AIDS elegy" as a new literary genre.[5] The elegy takes us back again to the world of ancient Greece. *Elegos* may ultimately derive from a verb meaning to wail or cry. The Greeks of the classical period took it to be derived from a combination of *e e* and *eu legein tous katoichoumenous* ("to say 'eh, eh,'" and "to speak well of the dead") (Alexiou 1974: 104). As a literary form, it seems to have begun with elegiac couplets traditionally accompanied by the *aulos*, a double-reed pipe that the Greeks associated with mourning. The elegy was also associated with the common meal or symposium. In this context it became a sort of afterdinner song, but one with a serious purpose, often broadened to include political or social themes (ibid.: 105).

As Gregory Woods has pointed out in his fine essay on the AIDS elegy (1992), the classic type of elegy is a poem describing a friendship cut short by death, a friendship that is frequently homoerotic. Peter Sacks (1985) notes that the elegy is a genre favored by the apprentice, one in which the aspiring poet displays not only his grief at the departure of a master, but his own readiness to fill his shoes. In the English genre of pastoral elegy, as Woods has commented, there is frequently a movement from grief, through remembrance, to hope (160). This change of mood is effected, in part, by a change of tense from the present-tense realization of death, to the past-tense memory of love, the present reiteration of death, and a future in which the beloved will live again.[6]

Woods may be idealizing the English elegy here. The sense of revelation is partly a display of self-confidence on the part of the poet, a statement of his ability to *make* the subject of the poem live through his own poetic art. As a formal genre of mourning, the elegy had become, by the beginning of the twentieth century, a rhetorical convention, and long ago lost its ability to express the outrage and anger of grief. Dylan Thomas expressed its inadequacy perfectly in his poem "A Refusal to Mourn the Death, by Fire, of a Child in London":

> I shall not murder
> The mankind of her going with a grave truth
> Nor blaspheme down the stations of her breath
> With any further
> Elegy of innocence and youth.
> . . .
> After the first death, there is no other.[7]

For Thomas' angry grief, the elegy of innocent life cut off before its time and the consolation of hope are not merely inadequate but insulting. Like the laments of women in many traditional cultures, his own poem of loss is a cry of grief with all its anger and despair unmuted.

The poems written for people who have died of AIDS have more of Dylan Thomas than of the traditional English elegy about them. In their starkness, they come closer to the original sense of the Greek verb *elegein*. In the AIDS elegy, a genre that seemed to have lost its resonance in our culture has resurfaced, and in it, like the lamenting women of many societies, men and women call to their dead lovers and friends with anger and pity for their own condition.

In an introduction to the AIDS anthology *Poets for Life*, Carol Muske writes: "Perhaps the single positive contribution of AIDS to our culture is a politics of death" (1989: 6). A friend of Paul Monette and his lover and a poet who makes her own powerful contribution to the volume, Muske notes the newness of this politics and how "the dying have voices, finally: angry, intuitive, dreamy, fearful, eloquent, funny. Listening to them changes the way we write about death . . . It seems to me we have left behind the tradition of 'let the dead bury their dead.' *These* dead will not lie quiet in their graves" (ibid.).

Muske's words might equally be applied to the lament singers of Greece, Ireland, and many other cultures in which the dead are addressed directly by the poet go-betweens. As we have seen, in these societies it is usually women who are able to speak for the restless dead. Their songs may be a means to contain grief or, if the occasion demands, to inflame it.

The poets writing about AIDS are angry. Some rage in private grief, others rail against a hostile society. Some also see AIDS as part of a larger modern tragedy. In "The Brothers Grief," Paul Mariah links the plight of the homeless with the victims of AIDS, Martin Luther King, and Tennessee Williams in a chain of communal grief that requires a new public voice to politicize it (1989: 148–150):

> We've become
> a nation of
> Grieving Men
> and we say our silent prayers

> as the Death of
> Tennessee Williams is announced . . .
> Of Martin Luther King,
> or George Moscone
> or Harvey Milk . . .
> Whoever the latest
> Death-lists list.
> We've grown up
> With a large public
> knowledge and
> private sophistication.

Mariah's dirge is addressed principally to an audience of fellow sufferers. It is, like so many AIDS-inspired works of art, an exhortation to bear witness, to remember the dead

> as we assume
> their spirit in
> our passing
> the fleshly corners
> of our body politic.

The sick body is, in Mariah's lament, also the body politic, and the dirge a demand for a public reexamination of its ills.

Remembering is the age-old task of the survivor. Like the grief of the Vietnam survivors, the grief of the AIDS survivors is tainted by public indifference, by the absence of a united response to death. Hence the task of bearing witness, of naming the dead, becomes political and urgent, as Michael Klein makes clear in "Naming the Elements":

> The names of the dead
> are messages on black marble
> and plunge into the earth.
> They are the notes
> of a war
> we imagined forgetting.
> What remains is how

things began: the naming—a linear
code narrowing—"Vietnam Vietnam"
(1989: 130)

Terrible as memory is, most of the poets and prose writers who lament their dead recognize that they can resist death only by insisting on it. The Chicana writer Ana Castillo, in her elegy in memory of a gay friend, quotes him saying to her: "What is hardest for me to give up is memory":

I moved my seat closer to his. "Perhaps memory, too,
will be transformed," I said.
"Will I remember you?" he asked.
"In another way," I speculated,
as is all we can do
with the memory of greetings and partings, and love
that resist death.
(1995: 54–55)

Metaphors of Guilt

In its insistence on memory, the AIDS elegy is a conventional response to death. But the grief of the gay community and their friends was complicated by another issue: guilt. However liberated they were, gay men found it hard to ignore the fact that most of the population saw their behavior as abnormal or worse. When death seemed to single them out, the response of many of the community was to accept their fate as the inevitable consequence of their behavior. In the elegies written for their dying friends and lovers, the poets of AIDS consistently employ biblical metaphors of a lost paradise and of the disease as a plague of God.

Paradise Lost

Grieving for their friends and themselves, the gay community also mourned the loss of what seemed now a brilliant and doomed moment of sexual and social liberation. Many of the poems about AIDS refer directly or indirectly to a time before the "plague" or before the "war," a time that seems, in retrospect, a "golden age." The fact that the brief interlude between Stonewall and AIDS was never as carefree or innocent as it seems in retrospect did not prevent it from becoming a symbolic paradise.[8] On the contrary, guilt made the metaphors of fall and expulsion from paradise inevitable. David Groff's "A Scene of the Crime" begins in 1978, near dawn on Fire Island:

> Going home near dawn from the last great party
> Of the '78 season, where Miss Fire Island
> Got a long drugged kiss from a Perry Ellis model . . .

The observer listens to the sounds of sex with pleasure, drops his cigarette,

> And heads home to his rented bed
> Drunk with other people's sex,
> Aware in other rooms and other houses, in the wild,
> Of the salty come-togethers of some thousand men.
> This odd domestic life—greased by drugs and easy-come,
> Easy-go—goes on, so naturally, so left-alone.
> Elsewhere, Sadat and Begin make their peace.
> He falls asleep, glad for the flaming island.

As he sleeps a drugged sleep, arson and war are waiting to engulf the island and its charmed inhabitants. Revisiting the island the following spring,

> He considers then the usual comparison to AIDS
> That sweeps his island like a fire.
> An accident they seem to breathe.
> At that moment on the island, in a thousand cities,
> Another dozen soldiers in the fiercest war
> Drop and collapse like stars,
> Caught by the sniper.
> (1989: 82–83)

In the time before, it seemed always to be warm. On the beaches of Fire Island, the West Coast, in the sweaty discothèques of Manhattan,

the clear air of Delphi or Mykonos, men basked in an endless summer.
The color to wear was, of course, white:

> . . . White muslin, white pillows, white
> everything! It was the summer of, the
> year of, the decade-return of designed
> China-white! I wondered what my hair
> would look like gone white . . .

It is not long before "Tony" finds out:

> When it happened
> Peter was gone, Vinnie was sick. I only
> needed six days—never knew what hit me.
>   (Picano 1989b: 195)

In another of Picano's poems, "After the Funerals," the protagonist
looks back nostalgically to the endless summer before all the funerals
began (1989a: 197):

> Yet . . . after the hospital vigils, the memorials
> I sometimes recall August days gilded
> like forever when, stepping off the dance floor
> spilling rhythm, even our sweat was silver.

The poems of paradise are filled with days of gold and silver, with sun-
lit beaches and the glitter of sweat on well-muscled bodies, an age of
light before darkness descended. In retrospect it seemed bound to end,
brief as the sexual encounters that dazzled the senses for an hour and
dropped to earth. As in Monette's memoir, there is frequently a Greek
flavor to these nostalgic elegies, some of which echo the form and
content of *The Greek Anthology* with uncanny precision. Take Thom
Gunn's "To the Dead Owner of a Gym" (1989: 87):

> I will remember well
> The elegant decision
> To that red line of tile

As margin round the showers
Of your gym, Norm,
In which so dashing a physique
As yours for several years,
Gained muscle every week
With sharper definition.
Death, on the other hand,
Is rigid and,
Finally as it may define
An absence with its cutting line,
    Alas,
    Lacks class.

The model for "Norm" might well have been Automedon's "The Gymnastics Teacher" (12.34, my translation):

Yesterday I dined with Demetrius,
the gymnastics teacher, luckiest
of men. One boy lay on his lap,
another leaned against his shoulder.
One brought food, one drink: a feast
for the eyes, that quartet. So
I said as a joke: "My dear,
do you train them at night too?"

A common theme of the epigram in *The Greek Anthology* is, as in the AIDS elegy, a beautiful young man cut off in his prime:

Why do we wander, wretched men
placing our trust in empty hopes,
oblivious of painful death?
Here lies Seleukos, silver-tongued,
his manners perfect, but his prime lasted
a brief season in the wilds of Spain,
so far from Lesbos. A stranger,
he lies on those uncharted shores.
        (Krinagorus 7.376, my translation)

In Phillis Levin's "What the Intern Saw" (1989: 145),

> He saw a face swollen beyond ugliness
> Of one who just a year ago
> Was Adonis
> Practicing routines of rapture.
>
> A boy who could appear
> To dodge the touch of time . . .

The essential difference between the lovely young men of the Greek epigrams and the AIDS elegies is that death comes as an inevitable destiny to the Greeks and as the wages of sin to the men of Fire Island. Centuries of social stigma cannot be lightly cast aside. In their laments for their dead and dying, the gay community reveal themselves to be creatures of their own time and place, unsure if they were entitled to the hedonistic pleasures of an endless summer.

God's Plague

More than war, the language and imagery of the plague dominate the poetry of AIDS. Perhaps the most elaborate working out of the analogy can be found in Edward Hirsch's "And Who Will Look upon Our Testimony." The narrative of the bubonic plague brought by black rats and fleas first to Messina, whence it spread across Europe, seemed synonymous with the medieval universe. The "Dance of Death" became the symbol for a macabre era:

> Some people imagined a black giant striding
>   Across the land,
> Others saw the fourth horseman of the Apocalypse.
>   Some believed the plague had descended
> In a rain of serpents and scorpions
>   When sheets of fire fell on the earth.
>   . . .
> Some danced to the sound of drums and trumpets,
>   Fighting the ghost
> With the high jollity of a happy music.
>   Some kept carefully unto themselves,

> Barricaded into their homes,
> > Avoiding the grasp of the evil one.
> > > (Hirsch 1989: 102–104)

What was hard to grasp in the accounts of plague was the possibility that it could all have been true. "Oh happy posterity who will not experience / Such abysmal woe— / And will look upon our testimony as fable," Hirsch quotes from Defoe's plague chronicle. Then, in the first and only reference to the present, he concludes with his own exhortation (108):

> Oh happy posterity
> Who will die in its own time
> With its own wondering tales of woe.

In the contemporary chronicles of a modern epidemic, AIDS and the plague have established a grim reciprocity. AIDS has taken the plague from the world of fable and made its horrors comprehensible, while the metaphor of plague has lent AIDS its most powerful correlative. In David Black's *The Plague Years*, which chronicles the early years of AIDS and the official response to it, extracts from works about plague or leprosy serve as epigraphs to each chapter. Such juxtaposition provokes shock and fear. What is happening here and now, the author reminds us, has the capacity to annihilate whole communities, great cities, to lay waste swathes of the continent, just as the plague did. But in the AIDS poems, the plague is seldom used as a metaphor to provoke action. It is invoked as the only model that resonates with all the horror of disease as punishment. One after another the poems of AIDS reiterate the same theme:

> Now as I watch the progress of the plague
> The friends surrounding me fall sick, grow thin
> And drop away . . .
> > (Gunn 1989a: 86)

> My thoughts are crowded with death
> and it draws so oddly on the sexual
> that I am confused

confused to be attracted
by, in effect, my own annihilation.
(Gunn 1989b: 88)

Many are gone or going. We see the light
that comes from a cold star and know the outcome.
At last report there was more still to night
than stars, or yet to life than heaven or home.
(Bell 1988: 28)

When the world has become a pestilence,
a sullen, inexplicable contagion,

when men, women, children
die in no sense realized, in
no time for anything, a
painful rush inward, isolate
(Creeley 1989: 56)

Robert Creeley's "painful rush inward" is an ironic reversal for so many of the AIDS poets, of what they had only just learned to do: come out. For the plague distances as it spreads, causing doors to shut, barriers to be erected, communal life to be abandoned. The gay communities of the United States had experienced only a brief open season. The blooming and the blight were immediately perceived as causally related. Permissiveness was a Pandora's box. To open it was to invite disaster.

The Triple Burden

If the community of gay white males was threatened with extinction and expressed deep fear and guilt in its writings, what of the nonwhite gay community?

To be gay and dying of AIDS is to be doubly burdened, to be Latino, African American, or Haitian American, gay, and dying of AIDS is to be triply burdened. Carlos Rodríguez Matos' anthology of AIDS elegies by Latino, Latin American, and Spanish poets (1995) is a poignant testimony to the triply burdened. In an elegy for his brother, the Chicano poet Benjamín Sáenz writes (1995: 142):

We were all so normal,
the six later arrivals,
rivals to the first born,
the oldest male:
gay and Chicano,
nothing worse than that.
We, the normal
sons and daughters
with talked-about lives,
never went inside your clubhouses.
Instead we marched straight
into the New Mexican sky
like little rows of cotton . . .

As in the white gay community, artists are disproportionately represented among the Chicano AIDS sufferers. In "All the Poets Are Dying . . ." Ramon García writes (1995a: 92):

All the poets are dying,
and in their dreams and flesh,
their words transform our silence.

The Spanish voices of America were accustomed to not being heard. Those who broke with the strict ties of their own community and joined the new *communitas* of gay liberation had already climbed a mountain. Now, as they sickened and died, they were filled with a rage of grief that was both proud of its own sexual energy and bitter at a society that never admitted them on equal terms but forced them to live on its fringes. As Rane Arroyo reminds his readers in "Los Angeles: Two Chapters from The Book of Lamentations" (1995: 22),

Only sex can save us from
a heaven of eunuchs.

I've learned much from gang members
to whom life and death is not

an abstract, but is a poem written
in blood, in fire, the inside

of oneself out in the world, the streets.
Sometimes you have to be tough,

or become as dead as this leather coat
I'm wearing. In my tight jeans,

I keep my personal compass.
I don't wait for heaven.

I find it, night after night,
dream after dream,

dance after dance,
kiss after kiss.

There's an ache below my waist
that sends a message to my soul:

live, goddam it, live.

In her poem "A García Lorca más a algunas otros," Ana Castillo
points an accusing finger at the "they" who have always excluded "us"
(1995: 57):

Call *them* by name these "they."
Point fingers in turn—*You:*
who sent us to Panama and Saudi Arabia—
with a bribe of college tuition, a mortgage loan
and bad medical care,
so merciless and trigger happy—*try*
to be rid of us.

We rise out of the ground
like margaritas,
yerba buena,
blades of grass, we the poets,
painters, a merry band of dissonant musicians:
Too many of us and too many of you
to silence with the yanking of one pure voice
    that rose
from the ashes of butterflies and doves
to call you by name.

In their rage against society, Latino poets do not expect to be understood outside the double boundary of their chosen and imposed ghettos. Writes Roman García (1995b: 92):

> We carry loss as the most essential part of ourselves. Our
>   poetry is
> dialogue with those that are gone. This is the age of exile.
> Not even death can bring us back home.

And in another poem, "Life Does Not Belong to Me," he laments (1995c: 936):

> When I die, the enemy will invent his own image over my
>   memory.
> I will be delivered to a God I have no faith in. Whatever
> country claims my final name
> will be telling a lie.

Established writers like Paul Monette and Thom Gunn write for an audience. Their anger is directed outward to the larger society beyond the community of gay men. By publicizing and politicizing their grief, they have the satisfaction of knowing they will be heard. What audience is addressed in the Latino poems? Some will perhaps reach the mainstream; most will not. Written in a mixture of English and Spanish, they will perhaps be read by a small fraction of the Spanish-speaking population of the United States, and an even smaller fraction of the population at large. They may be eccentric voices, but they are conscious of a tradition shared with more conventional Latinos. The voices raised in sorrow and anger speak of a "we" in opposition to a hostile or indifferent "they." Faced with death, many of the poets become aware they were never at home in any culture. For them, only the dead offer a sense of community, and perhaps it is for them that many of the most moving laments are written:

> alien,
> no matter where I go
> the dead are my friends . . .
>   (García 1995b: 91)

AIDS Art and the "Critic"

> If we ask what a show does that no hospital, clinic, church, or
> other kind of relief agency has so far been able to do, I think the
> answer is obvious. If we consider that the experience, open to the
> public, as it is, may also be intolerably voyeuristic, the remedy is
> also obvious: Don't go. In not reviewing "Still/Here," I'm sparing
> myself and my readers a bad time, and yet I don't see that I really
> have much choice.
>
>   Croce (1994/1995)

> The story of this pain belongs to all of us . . . No matter how
> much I fortify . . . AIDS seems to demand that I suffer too.
>
>   Campo (1993: 93)

In the performance of laments, wakes, dances, and other forms that are
part of the process of burial and grieving across many diverse cultures,
what is striking is not the differences but the similarities. The response
to death and loss is almost universally expressed in some structured and
traditional form; most communities see this expression as a necessary
part of the grieving process. In our modern urban culture the responses
to death are more varied. There is no one form to express the community's sorrow, but each subgroup must invent its own way to express
loss, one that seems appropriate to its needs.

When the AIDS epidemic broke out, the gay community was one already acquainted with untimely death. The gay writer already had a
legacy of martyrs.[9] Gay men, too, were disproportionately represented
in the artistic world, especially in the theater and dance world, but also
in the visual arts and in poetry. It was impossible for them not to respond to the disaster going on around them in the artistic forms they
knew and practiced. For many of them it seemed the only way to salvage their sanity, to make something out of the chaos of their grief and
fear and to struggle against prejudice, hostility, and indifference. The
most unlikely forms to express grief in our culture—dance, photogra-
phy, the quilt, cartoons—were enlisted in the service of this new polit-
ico-artistic campaign. Within the community there was division about
the negative impact of showing people images of the disfigured and dying. Some sought to emphasize the positive side of "living with AIDS";
others wanted to display the horrors of the disease to an indifferent

public. None arrived at their artistic decisions lightly. All were driven by the same fears, rage, and helplessness, by the desire to memorialize the dead and in some way assuage their own grief. The public and critical response to AIDS art was as varied as the art itself; at its most negative, it reminded the sufferers that death and art are expected to keep a discreet distance from one another in our society: to present them in stark juxtaposition is a form of cultural pornography.

Arlene Croce's much discussed review of Bill T. Jones's "Still/Here" exemplifies this view of AIDS-inspired art as cultural pornography. It appeared in the *New Yorker*, generally thought of as a liberal, broad-minded magazine with an intelligent readership. The critic invited her readers to stay away from a show she didn't intend to see but knew about by reputation, thus "sparing myself and my readers a bad time." What she spared them was a dance performance in which images of people dying of AIDS were screened behind the dancers. "In theatre," wrote Croce, "one chooses what one will be . . . the sick people whom Jones has lined up—have no choice other than to be sick. They are there on videotape, the better to be seen and heard, especially heard. They are the prime exhibits of a director-choreographer who has crossed the line between theatre and reality—who thinks that victimhood in and of itself is sufficient to the creation of an art spectacle" (1994/1995: 54).

There is nothing new, of course, about political art that focuses on the suffering of the innocent. The art of Christian Europe is, after all, dominated by representations of a scantily clad man dying a barbaric death. What Croce and some other modern critics are calling "victimhood" or "the art of the victim" is not so different from the art we have accepted since Aristotle as being of value precisely because of its power to elicit pity and fear.[10] In communities accustomed to terrible suffering, the line between the real sufferer and the presenter of suffering may be less cleanly drawn. Blacks and homosexuals, like victims of political oppression in Argentina, China, Peru, or South Africa, have often presented themselves or characters drawn from their immediate acquaintance as the subject matter of their art. Distancing, in art, has, in these societies, been a means to avoid persecution or social criticism rather than an artistic device. If playwrights cannot talk about McCarthyism, they may talk about the Salem witch hunts; if they cannot talk about fifth-century B.C.E. Athens, they may talk about Bronze Age Thebes. The audience has been encouraged to read through such deliberate distancing to the underlying message directed at the artist's contemporaries. If the work has been artistically successful, it has survived and been thought to have a universal message. Much art that had a political message has disappeared, but much has also survived. Even the most arrogant of critics are seldom prepared to take bets on what the next century will choose to retain.

In a city like New York and in the world of the theater, it is hard to imagine how artists could have left the question of AIDS aside. Were they supposed to avoid it "like the plague"? When their friends were dying all around them in horrible ways and they themselves were sick with fear and anger, were they expected to write and choreograph "positive" pieces that would distract them and the audience from the reality they lived with? And if they were to deal with a disease that had laid waste their community, how were they to avoid being accused of "victimhood"? Croce argued that artists who concentrate on the victims of AIDS arouse not compassion but complicity. How can you be complicit in death? And even supposing she is correct that only the sick and the dying can bear to watch the dying, don't they have a right to make art for such an audience?

Croce's article reveals a set of common prejudices and beliefs in the public attitude to AIDS. As the century drew to a close, and gay men became the minority of AIDS sufferers, such an attitude may ironically have become more politically correct. The battle to keep AIDS in the news is losing ground. For those who have always thought AIDS victims brought the disease on themselves by a deviant lifestyle, it is a time to come out and say what many of them said at the beginning of the epidemic: AIDS is the disease of the other. It doesn't touch me, and I don't want to hear about the grief and suffering it causes because it is irrelevant, politically suspect, and just not good entertainment.

At the opposite pole from the attitude displayed in the *New Yorker* critic's nonreview is an article by the Cuban American physician and poet Raphael Campo (1993a). As a gay doctor who specializes in treating persons with AIDS, Campo was torn between the conventions of his profession, which demand that he maintain some emotional distance from his suffering patients, and a desire to empathize with, even allow himself to love, them. No matter how much he fortified himself against it, he felt that "the story of this pain belongs to all of us." So he wrote poems about treating AIDS patients and was grateful for the poetry written about AIDS in that it has helped me so generously to locate myself in a world irrevocably altered by the presence of a virus. In contrast, the place where I first went for guidance—my medical education—at times steered me away from dealing with AIDS, even working with AIDS patients . . . I was armed with toxic drugs, because there had not been enough research yet to equip me with safer, more effective alternatives. I was even given an alter ego—as a future physician, I could not, by definition, be gay, and only marginally, and hardly noticeably Latin—and therefore I was protected. (96)

In the poem "Distant Moon," Campo describes his dilemma:

> One day I drew his blood, and while I did
> He laughed, and said I was his girlfriend now,
> His blood-brother. "Vampire-slut," he cried,
> "You'll make me live forever!" Wrinkled brows
> Were all I managed in reply . . .
>
> (1993b: 104)

Campo's refuge from the conflicting demands of professional medical codes of behavior and his painful identification with his patients was to write poetry, most of it formal in structure, because

> in [formal poetry] are present the fundamental beating contents of the body at peace: the regularity of the resting brain-wave activity in contrast to the disorganized spiking of a seizure; the gentle ebb and flow of breathing, or sobbing, in contrast to the harsh, spasmodic cough; the single-voiced, ringing chant of a slogan at an ACT UP rally in contrast to the indecipherable rumblings of AIDS funding debate on the Senate floor. The poem is a physical process, is bodily exercise: rhymes become the mental resting places in the ascending rhythmic stairway of memory. The poem perhaps is an idealization, or a dream of the physical—the imagined healthy form. Yet it does not renounce illness; rather it reinterprets it as the beginning point for healing. (1993a: 97–98)

If a lament singer were to analyze her art in such terms, she might say much the same thing. This art that comes from deep grief is, as we have seen, perceived by the community to be a therapeutic ordering of the chaos of death. Sung poetry, usually quite traditional in form, is the most common artistic response to death, but dance, theater, paintings, even bawdy games may be a society's way of managing the emotions it induces. Campo's eloquent plea for the art that AIDS has engendered allows the value of such art as therapy and recognizes it as art in its own right, not as something for the self; on the contrary, as something that allows for the noblest of human capacities—the ability to share and try to communicate the pain of the other. Campo describes the poems he writes and reads as "ampules of the purest, clearest drug of all, the essence of the process of living itself" (1993a: 98). They may not all be of the same artistic standard, but what is extraordinary is how many works of art inspired by AIDS transcend the pain and fear of death and have the ability to uplift the reader or audience.

Perhaps what transforms at least some of the art inspired by AIDS is the very sense of community that critics like Croce react against. The idea of communal art or traditional art, in a society that values the individual above all, is unusual. The AIDS memorial quilt that Croce dismisses as a "pathetic lumping together" is an anachronism, the work of people who feel a sense of community in suffering. They have not produced the equivalent of a medieval cathedral, perhaps, but their communal ongoing art form is similarly dedicated to a higher purpose. Like the cathedral, it is a site for services that try to reach above the miseries of a disease that has shattered their community and to communicate with the dead. The liturgy of names that accompanies the unfolding of the quilt is the very opposite of an "arts bureaucracy." It is a timeless, shared art of memorializing the individual through a dialogue with the dead.

AIDS and the Art of Living

The poet Rachel Hadas, who taught a poetry workshop at the Gay Men's Health Crisis Recreation Center in New York, found that unlike her experience in other poetry workshops, the question of what to write about never arose. The men who came to read and write poetry with her came with a need to express what they were living through. What drew her to offer the workshop was also need, a need to help in the way she knew how to, through poetry. In an anthology titled *Unending Dialogue* (1991), Hadas includes not only the poems of the men she worked with, but her own poems inspired by the experience. There is nothing in the poems she produced as a result of the friendships she made with the men dying of AIDS that suggests an unhealthy fascination or complicity with "victimhood." Hadas and the men who wanted to write poems about AIDS are similarly driven to try to express what so often is left unsaid. In a poem called "AIDS and the Art of Living," one of the men in her workshop, Dan Connor, says:

> Everything's art. Everything is
> if you see it that way. Dying's
> no different, living as always
> the same issue: breath and
> breakfast . . .

But his poem belies him, structuring even the most basic of human functions into a formal construct:

> I'm afraid to leave this efficiency
> for fear I'll crap my pants: what
> American doesn't share in this
> same fear: bodily functions
> on the crosstown bus, something
> taboo at the banquet, incontinent,
> incapable, potentially senile, dying
> of embarrassment? We'll leave this
> party all together
>   confident someone
>   else will clean up . . .
>   (1991: 21)

Tony Giordano, another member of the workshop, writes about the process of dying in a poem that counters terror with the only weapon he has, the words and rhythms of a small work of art:

> death is abstract
> but the process of dying
> is terrifying
> and one can't shake off
> those moments of

subterranean living
when a shadow prevails
and panic seizes
one by the heart and throat
and will not let go
this comes at night
at the turning off of lights.
(1991: 83)

Those artists and critics brave enough to confront a tragedy of our time and place will find nothing new in the endeavor. Rather, as Hadas was able to teach her students, they will find the same sadness, fear, and chaos that art has always struggled to express. W. H. Auden's poem "September 1, 1939," as the participants in the workshop recognized, might have been written in their own loft:

The lights must never go out
The music must always play,
All the conventions conspire
To make this fort assume
The furniture of home
Lest we should see where we are,
Lost in a haunted wood,
Children afraid of the night
Who have never been happy or good.
(Auden 1979: 87)

If anything good can be said to have come out of the suffering caused by the AIDS epidemic, it is surely the way the community of homosexual artists have transformed their grief into art and used that art to draw attention to their plight. There may be arguments about the quality of some of the art produced, but it is hard to quarrel with its political effectiveness. In a society in which the management of sickness, dying, and grief is generally institutionalized, gay men have reclaimed the right to deal with their grief in ways that often shock and offend but seldom fail to gain attention. One result has been a disproportionate funding of research into the disease and a grudging public awareness of the fact that no section of society is immune from its grasp. A more lasting effect for the gay community and for the community at large may be the realization that it is possible to wrestle something of beauty and dignity out of this most wretched and debasing of diseases. A community that was largely invested in the cult of youth, beauty, and pleasure might have been expected to be the last to respond with dignity to sickness and death. Instead, with the inventiveness that had characterized their pleasure-seeking, the gay community made an art of their grief.

Only such a community—marginalized yet organized and visible—could have responded to its own imminent annihilation with such a storm of publicity. As we have seen in the case of the mothers of the disappeared, it is often the most unlikely of communities that comes together to confront grief. AIDS activists succeeded not only in drawing attention to their suffering; as Stephen Epstein (1996) has demonstrated, they have changed the way doctors and patients interact and challenged the medical and scientific institutions of the United States. The AIDS epidemic, which so many artists have likened to the plague, differed from that disease in being selective. Neither Thucydides' Athenians nor Defoe's Londoners could point at a single subgroup of the population and call its suffering the wages of sin. Gay activists, who had struggled during the preceding decades, to have homosexuality regarded as a legitimate preference rather than a psychiatric disease, were already engaged in a debate with the medical and scientific establishment. Unlike the mothers of Argentina, they were socially mobilized, and many were seasoned activists. Their success sometimes masks the grief that motivated gay men to "act up," but terrible as the suffering is that inspires a group of people to manage their own grief and use it as a weapon, a work of art, or both, the result may be a sense of solidarity that is strangely uplifting.

~ 6

Memorials

When you go, please vent all of your spite coming from
resentment, unfulfilled love, unrequited desire. Please do well,
taking away all entangled dark clouds covering your heart, all
lamentations which have been frozen on your twelve rib bones.
　　　　　From a shamanic rite performed on Cheju Island, Korea

The Demands of the Dead

We have seen that in many societies, if the dead are restless and unsat-
isfied, if they have met violent and untimely deaths, if the proper rituals
of burial have not been observed, they are thought likely to return to
haunt the living.[1] Among the dead, too, in popular imagination, there is
often an unhealthy melancholia. The demands of the dead are simple:
retribution for wrongs inflicted on them in life, rituals that will ensure
their passage to a separate realm from the living, and a place in the
memory of the living. The rites of mourning, both collective and individual, are performed in an attempt to satisfy the imagined demands of
the dead. The solid memorials at the gravesite may seem more static,
but they are still the site of private performance, a locus for the dialogue between the living and the dead to continue.

When the dead are sufficiently important in the community or when
they are many and their deaths unnatural and premature, the problem
of ensuring them a place in the collective memory of the community
becomes acute. The performative arts of mourning seem insufficient to
the task. There is a desire to fix memory in a visible form. The monument to the fallen in wars, the battle site, the melted building left in
ruins, the huts that housed the prisoners of the concentration camps,
the museum of the martyred—all these are officially designated sites

of collective mourning. Such public memorials are always politically charged. They are expensive, large, visited by crowds. The crowds see themselves reflected in the monument (literally, in the case of the Vietnam memorial) just as the makers of monuments do, although both claim to be seeing an image of the desire of the dead for a place in the memory of the living.

The relationship of memory to memorial, of memorial to state and private mourning, of testimony and memoir to memory, of both to history are all issues that have been the focus of scholarly attention in the second half of the twentieth century. It has become difficult to speak of them without entering the twilight zone of postmodernist rhetoric, where meanings blur, words become slippery, mourning becomes a philosophical stance, the Holocaust an impossible subject to speak about. The debate and the questioning of traditional forms of remembering the dead have contributed to some of the most unusual memorials in history. To compare the Vietnam memorial or the AIDS Quilt to conventional monuments to the dead is to understand that a revolution in memorializing has taken place in our times. The Vietnam War and the AIDS epidemic are unusual events. The grief of the bereaved, as we have seen, was so politically charged, so equivocal in its relation to the abstract ideas of nation or patriotism that it inspired dramatic new forms to express its tangled threads.

The People's Princess

No event better illustrates the change that has occurred in public mourning than the funeral of Diana, Princess of Wales. The princess' death in a car crash provoked a crisis nobody could have predicted. The people interviewed in the streets of London seemed surprised by their outburst of emotion, as if the death of Diana had made them suddenly aware of the transformation of their own stereotype.

The British monarchy, that most conservative of institutions, was forced by an angry public to make a series of concessions not only to the formalities of royal mourning but to its own display of feeling.

The first concession was a public funeral on a royal scale. The second was the flying of the Union Jack at half-mast over Buckingham Palace. According to royal protocol, only the Queen's standard is ever flown over Buckingham Palace, and that only when she is in residence.

In deference to a storm of public protest, the Union Jack was left flying even after the Queen retired to Balmoral. The third was an un-
scheduled television speech, the most personal of her reign, in which
the Queen of England admitted there might be some lesson to be
learned from the life and death of her daughter-in-law Diana, Princess
of Wales.

It was not the first time that a monarch of the royal house of Windsor had been forced to modify her mourning behavior because of public pressure. Queen Victoria was so affected by the death of her husband, Prince Albert, that she withdrew from public life for ten years.
Her excessive mourning made her so unpopular that it took the serious illness of her son, the Prince of Wales, and the clever cajolery of
her prime minister, Benjamin Disraeli, to draw the Queen out of re-
tirement and restore her popularity. Queen Elizabeth II must have
thought of her great-great-grandmother as she was forced to modify
the way she mourned her daughter-in-law's death.

The heraldic funeral, that British invention which dignified the noble dead and marked them as a class apart, was not what the reigning
monarch would have wished for a young woman whom she regarded as
having publicly disgraced the heir to the throne and dragged the entire
royal family into the gutter press. But Diana got her heraldic funeral
despite the Queen. It was, to judge by the more than two billion people
who watched it, the most popular memorial service in history. And the
Queen, who had remained in Scotland and avoided even the mention
of Diana's name in the communiqués issued after her death, was forced
out of seclusion and into the funeral. She even showed signs of having
learned her first lesson from her daughter-in-law when she broke with
tradition by shaking some of the mourners' hands.

The funeral of Diana, like her married life, was a media event, a
soap-opera end to a soap-opera life. It was appropriately sentimental,
touching, and banal. It was also a demonstration of the politics of grief
in action. Like the flowers that spilled across the lawns of Kensington
Palace, the funeral was a spontaneous event, created by demand. The
crowds that gathered to pay tribute to the "People's Princess" had exercised their "flower power" to inform the royal house of Windsor that it
was out of touch with the times.[2] As the British people poured into central London and wept and hugged one another before the cameras,
they seemed to surprise even themselves by their frank display of emotion. When the royal marriage went wrong before their eyes, they had

taken sides with the photogenic princess against her not-so-charming prince. The outpouring of affection for Diana was an "upstairs-downstairs" affair in a country where the division between the aristocracy and the hoi polloi was no longer taken for granted. With their theatrical display of grief for the dead, disgraced princess, the downstairs people thumbed their noses at the upstairs folk. And in Westminster Abbey, a funeral took place as bizarre as any in history. Upstairs and downstairs Britain met in a ceremony designed for television, with a pop star belting out a sentimental song, the royal family starchily present, waves of applause interrupting the ceremony, the injured brother having his hour of triumph as he attacked the press, and the body of the princess carried out with all the pomp and splendor of a medieval queen.

The mourning for Diana may suggest that there has been a change in British behavior, or it may simply reflect a dissatisfaction with the way the unhappy princess was perceived to have been treated in life by her in-laws. If memory is, as Walter Benjamin put it, the "theater" of the past, its stage is frequently the funeral. The funeral is where the memory of the dead is ideally fashioned, either by women who weep and sing laments, by the makers of encomiums, or by all those who construct the rituals of mourning. The state designs the funerals of its leaders and heroes because it is aware of the theatrical opportunity afforded by the funeral and because it must control the memory of the past if it is to mold the future. Mark Antony knew what he was doing when he came to praise Caesar in the marketplace. He knew that if the dead have died an untimely or violent death there is nothing easier than to sway public sentiment in their favor before the body is cold. It is a lesson that the royal house of Windsor seems not to have learned but which Diana's brother took to heart. He may have been a philandering playboy for much of his life, but in his funeral speech he managed to transform his publicity-seeking sister into the victim of the very photographers whom she had so coyly courted through the years of her married life.

The unconventional mourning of Diana was not a unique event of our times. It is linked to what seems to be a change in public attitudes toward the expression and control of grief. The way we mourn and remember our dead is no longer taken for granted but debated in public. There have always been fashions in public mourning and monuments, but until the second half of the twentieth century, changes were made by the state rather than the public themselves. State or local officials were responsible for staging ceremonies and erecting monuments to the famous or to those who died in wars. In the last two decades of the century, in the developed world, we seem to have witnessed a desire by the public or groups of individuals to take the forms and style of mourning into their own hands. Memorials have become highly politicized; particular communities of people have chosen to design their own memorials in contrast to, sometimes in defiance of the state. Why should this have happened in our times? What do the funeral of Diana, the Vietnam Veterans Memorial, and the AIDS Memorial Quilt have in common? Why are we experiencing what has been referred to as a "monument glut" (*New York Times Magazine*, September 10, 1995: 48) in the capital of the United States?

Fallen Soldiers

In their various ways the memorials of the late twentieth century stand in deliberate contrast to the memorials of the past that nationalized death. George Mosse dates "the cult of the fallen soldier" to the era of the French Revolution (1990: 19). The cult depended on a change in the status of soldiers. Whatever the actual composition of the armies that fought in the French Revolution or the German Wars of Liberation against Napoleon, the presence of middle-class volunteers in the army's ranks altered the status of the common soldier and created what Mosse calls the "Myth of the War Experience" (15–20). The myth that only war could produce an ideal of personal and national regeneration encouraged a new, romantic view of death. Byron's death in the Greek War of Independence was one of the most celebrated and exotic manifestations of the adventurous soldier's death. His own letters from the field reveal that Byron was well aware of how little the realities of the Greek uprising corresponded to the myth of a reborn classical civilization (1972: 510–531), but he knew his own power to inspire recruits to the Greek cause. Between 1812 and 1821 "Childe Harold's Pilgrimage" went through at least twelve editions and was translated into the major European languages. Its rousing call to revolution attracted many followers (LXXXIV):

> Hereditary bondsmen! Know ye not
> Who would be free themselves must strike the blow?

When the thirty-six-year-old Byron died of a fever in Missolonghi, his fame as a poet, combined with the drama of his death, gave a new dimension to the cult of war: the myth of transcendent death. As Mosse notes, the Christian symbolism of resurrection, combined with heroic themes of ancient civilizations, was enshrined in the monuments to the dead: "military cemeteries and war monuments were often dominated by huge crosses or classical statues representing the heroic dead. They became the sacred spaces of a new religion . . . It was in these spaces that the Myth of the War Experience, as opposed to the reality of war, found its ultimate expression" (1990: 32–33).

The memorials and military cemeteries of the First World War extended the honor of a sacred death to the common soldier. For the first time, the graves of individual soldiers were marked with crosses, the names of the dead listed on monuments. As Mosse's study makes clear, the myths of the sacred nature of the conflict and the transcendence of death in war had been carefully prepared in Germany, France, and England during the nineteenth century, but the scale of the losses was something no country could have imagined. Across Europe the war deaths were confronted by a surge of "popular piety which saw hope in suffering according to the Christian tradition" (Mosse 1990: 74).[3] The belief that death in war imitated the Passion of Christ had a double benefit: it encouraged men to go to war, fearless of death (at least until they reached the front lines), and it helped fellow soldiers and families to accept the deaths of family members and friends. The fallen floated somewhere, ready to intervene in the affairs of the living, to redeem the future. In Germany, they were thought of as a golden chain, uniting the living and the dead in Germanic brotherhood (ibid.: 79). In all the countries that lost large numbers of men in the Great War, worship of the dead soldiers became a mass cult. As an inspiration to a new generation, it was important that the individual be subsumed into the vast army of the dead. Mourning for this ghostly army was not left to the bereaved, but taken over by the state as a national and civic duty.

Worship of the War Dead: The New Shrines

There were two sites where the war dead were worshipped: the war cemetery and the memorial. The nineteenth century had witnessed a revolution in the design of cemeteries. The garden cemetery, first developed in America, became popular in Europe. The new style of cemetery, removed from the center of cities and designed for contemplation and reflection rather than as a confrontation with the reality of death, was well suited to transforming the war cemeteries into shrines (Mosse 1990: 80). No sooner had the First World War begun than the French, English, and German authorities established official cemeteries whose design and upkeep were the business of the state. The British War Graves Commission was in charge of designing and maintaining war cemeteries not only for British dead but for Commonwealth soldiers (ibid.: 82). The president of the United States established the American Battle Monuments Commission to maintain cemeteries for the American soldiers who died in Europe. At the end of the war, care of the German and Austrian cemeteries was taken over by private organizations, but the design of all the war cemeteries was remarkably similar. A large "Cross of Sacrifice" and a stone were the central features of these burial grounds, which became sites of pilgrimage after the war. England and France subsidized tours to the cemeteries and provided free transportation for war widows and orphans (ibid.: 92). But the cemeteries abroad did not satisfy the needs of a national "cult of the fallen." For this, it was necessary to invent a new shrine and a new altar: the Tomb of the Unknown Soldier. This brilliantly effective idea seems to have arisen simultaneously in England and France. Bodies were exhumed from the battlefields and reburied with pomp and splendor in Paris at the Arc de Triomphe, in London at Westminster Abbey, and eventually in the other countries that fought in the war. Germany, where ambivalence surrounding the nation's defeat made representation problematic, was the only nation that did not opt for a symbolic corpse.

The image of a tomb, whether represented by the London Cenotaph, the hollow pyramids of the Australian memorials, the Neue Wache in Berlin, or the real tomb of an unknown soldier in France, provided the grieving nations of the interwar period with a state theater of mourning where war's tragedy could be periodically staged. The style of such ceremonies varied from country to country, and there was constant debate about their form and function. In Germany, the conservative Christian symbolism of the cult of the fallen inspired both the medieval and heroic imagery that dominated the design of monuments; it also provoked harsh criticism of modernist realistic monuments designed by German artists like Käthe Kollwitz and Ernst Barlach (Mosse 1990: 102–103).

What is remarkable about the monuments to the First World War, and to the ceremonies staged at them, is not their differences but their similarities. The Nazis may have used the "Myth of the War Experience" to enthuse another generation for war, but on the other side of the world a similar cult of martyrdom and resurrection shaped the myths of the nation. The place most visited in Australia is the Australian War Memorial in Canberra, but all state capitals have their vast memorials, temples, and cenotaphs that once dominated their skylines. In Australia as in Europe, the monuments and the dramas that were staged around them were carefully orchestrated to preserve the myth of war as a liberating, egalitarian experience, one that had ennobled the state. Private grief had no part in these grand ceremonies, certainly not the grief of women for sons, brothers, and husbands. If the "shrines of remembrance" or town monuments to the dead were devoted to keeping memory alive, it was a collective memory that subsumed the memory of individual suffering in a celebration of mass heroism. ANZAC Day was Australia's most important national holiday.[4] There were parades in the cities and towns, remembrance services at the shrines, wreaths placed on monuments, but mostly it was an excuse for men to get drunk together and reminisce about the war. The pubs were awash with beer,[5] brass bands played, men looked forward to seeing old comrades they had fought or trained with. The only touch of poignancy was an empty sleeve here or a wheelchair there.

The "heroic" attempt to gain a beachhead at Gallipoli on the Turkish coast in 1915 was a piece of military lunacy. Thousands of young Australians and New Zealanders were ordered by their British commanding officers to advance under heavy fire from the easily defended heights above the shore. For eight months the slaughter continued until 9,000 ANZACS, an equal number of French, and three times that number of British soldiers were dead. Perhaps because of its cussed foolishness it became a symbol of Australian heroism. Instead of causing revulsion, the debacle in the Dardanelles soon became an antipodean Thermopylae. The Anglican Synod of Melbourne declared the conflict to be a religious war; the voices of the Allies were being used by God to "maintain the moral order of the world" (Clark 1964: 205).

After the war came the need to glorify the war heroes. What actually happened at Gallipoli was of no interest to the builders of monuments and the choreographers of parades. Nor was the grief of individual families. The names of the dead were inscribed on "honor rolls" at their alma maters, chiseled into granite and marble on monuments, but the focus of the monuments was usually a bronze or marble figure, solid and square-jawed, bayonet at the ready.

In his memoir *Marching as to War,* Don Charlwood describes the atmosphere of a memorial service on ANZAC Day in the small seaside town of Frankston, near Melbourne, in 1924:

> Seventy returned soldiers marched there ahead of us, medals clinking and shining. They were not just Mr Ramsdale and Mr Pratt and Dr Maxwell of normal days; their eyes were fixed ahead, their arms swung, their feet fell together. Marching with them was the Prime Minister, Mr Bruce himself . . . After a biblical reading we sang "Nearer my God to Thee," then the "Captain Chaplain" spoke:
>
> "The men did their part and God did his part, Providence was fighting for the Allies and gave them the victory. A wonderful victory had been achieved, the fame and glory of which would continue as long as the Great God held the world in the hollow of his hand . . ."
>
> When his words ended we stood for one minute's silence. The war had receded by less than six years; there were several war widows present with orphaned children. In the silence a great wave of sorrow and pride built up; it intensified as the notes of the Last Post soared like a cry from the dead. It came near breaking as a piper played a lament. Our emotional outlet came with the *Recessional* . . . (1990: 63)

On the same day, Charlwood recalls, a new war memorial was unveiled in the town. The prime minister spoke to the crowd, reminding them that "during the war the torch of sacrifice and service was lighted in Australia and then the flame burnt bright. Now it is dim and at times flickering. It is necessary to keep that flame bright today as it was during the war." Then he pulled a cord, and the flag fell away, revealing the usual list of names cast in bronze with the customary inscription: "For God, King, and Empire" (Charlwood 1990: 64). The pomp and ceremony, the constant reminders of a higher purpose, not only enabled a country to call for further sacrifices in the future; they also enabled the personal grief of widows, siblings, orphans to be sublimated

and ultimately put to one side. The ceremonies called for a highly selective remembrance, one that had nothing to do with the gas-blinded
soldiers stumbling in agony through a sea of mud. They were elevated,
uplifting celebrations of war. And they were highly successful.

Charlwood's memoir was inspired by the question a child asked at his
school, where he had gone to talk about his days serving in a bomber
crew in the Second World War. "You were a navigator in a bomber
crew flying from England to bomb Germany?" the child asked. "Yes,"
said Charlwood. "Why were you there, when the war was here?" The
boy's second question referred to attacks by Japanese aircraft on northern Australia. The question prompted a book in which the author tries
to convey to younger readers, and perhaps to himself, why a generation
of young Australians could have been so gullible, so ready to die for
England, despite the loss of 60,000 men in the "war to end war." The
future airman and novelist had been one of the few, in his school years,
to question war. His English teacher (who happened to be my mother)
read W. B. Yeats, Francis Thomson, Rupert Brooke, and Walter de la
Mare to the class, but, as Charlwood remarks, "Wilfred Owen was not
known in Australia" (174).

When Britain declared war, the Australian prime minister, on hearing the news, followed suit without even consulting parliament; he
proclaimed: "where Britain stands, there stand the people of the entire British world" (Charlwood 1990: 193). Even the doubting young
writer was quick to enlist. First he went home: "I knew my mother expected me to join up; after all I had said myself that I must" (194). The
young volunteers swore on their Bibles to serve the King and resist
his enemies. Heady with the intensified patriotism of colonials, they
marched off to die. Mothers "expected" their sons to march to war, and
set to work, as they had done in the First World War, knitting warm
socks and gloves. What enabled them to face the deaths of their sons
with equanimity was not a sympathy for the fate of Poland or Czecho-
slovakia, but the success of the romantic myth of sacrifice followed by
resurrection. The religious symbolism of the monuments, the ceremonies, the poetry, the art of the interwar period gave a common, familiar
language to the bereaved, one that was pan-European and could be
shared. Just as Priam and Achilles could sit and weep for their dead together because they understood and respected each other's codes of
war, so the people of the nations who had fought in the Great War

mourned their dead in common, shored up by the symbols of an older world, confident that the sacrifice of their dead was in the service of a better world.

The dead of the First World War became symbolic dead. So widespread was the loss that scarcely a family was left untouched. To indulge too deeply in personal grief was to deny your neighbor's loss; to doubt the value of such widespread slaughter was to risk personal and civic collapse. The state and its religious institutions catered for mass grieving, giving the bereaved a sanctioned outlet for solemn contemplation but not for tears. The sacral character of the monuments encouraged self-control; the inspiration of heroic sacrifice made even wives and mothers dab fiercely at their tears with linen handkerchiefs. The memory of the individual dead soldier was erased, wiped away as carefully as a tear, and subsumed in the celebration of the "glorious dead."

The Secret War

The First World War was, it might be argued, the last of the secret wars in the West. War reports and photographs from the front lines took a long time to reach the press in each country, and the press was rigidly censored. It was still believed that women should be spared the gory details of battle. If a soldier dared to write the truth, it was censored by company officers. The lag and reticence in reporting from the front lines made the idealization of war easier. Coverage of the war in the home press was unabashed propaganda. Lord Northcliffe, for example, publisher of the London *Times*, reported after the first day's attack on the Somme: "We have elected to fight out our quarrel with the Germans and to give them as much battle as they want . . . Everything has gone well" (July 3, 1916). This was a précis of a battle in which, of the 110,000 British soldiers who began the attack at dawn, 60,000 were dead by nightfall. Such flagrant misreporting helped divide the countries at war into two mutually uncomprehending populations: those who had experienced war and knew its real nature, and those who stayed behind and encouraged the myth that the soldier in the front line was fighting and dying for the glory of his country.

After the war was over and almost any returning soldier could have dispelled the myth of heroic death on the battlefield, the shrines of remembrance and civic war memorials became the official sites of national mourning. The honor of the nation was invested in its war dead. Memory had nothing to do with it. On the contrary, war memorials were sites of politically orchestrated forgetting. "The old Lie" that the most impassioned of all the antiwar poets, Wilfred Owen, rejected so eloquently in his poem "Dulce et Decorum Est" was a lie that not only served a national function; it may also have had a beneficial effect on the mourners. It was Rupert Brooke, not Owen, after all, who was read with fervor by the nation that survived, that invested in memorials, that took comfort in the notion that the sons, husbands, and lovers it had lost had died in a good cause, still colonizing baser lands with their corpses (1979: 81):

> If I should die, think only this of me:
> That there's some corner of a foreign field
> That is forever England. There shall be
> In that rich earth a richer dust concealed;
> A dust that England bore, shaped, made aware.

One of the most popular poems of the interwar period, "The Soldier" anticipated Brooke's own death on the battlefield with the heroic spirit of imperialism bred in upper-class English schoolrooms.[6] The poet asks to be remembered without grief, not because he has brought glory back to his country, but because his remains have brought a touch of English civilization to a "foreign field."[7] Brooke managed to overcome, in the pride of his aristocratic patriotism, even that element of death in battle most dreaded by the fighters and their families: the absence of the corpse. Wherever it was spilled, English blood would, it seemed, ennoble and enrich.[8] The young poet about to die is quite explicit in his directions to those who will mourn him. They are to think of his death only in a single, griefless dimension, fixing their thoughts on that patch of sanctified ground.

The generation of young Englishmen like Brooke, who fought in the Great War, had been educated to face war in the spirit of the past. The poems they left behind them "illustrate the hypnotic power of a long cultural tradition; the tragic outcome of educating a generation to face not the future but the past" (Stallworthy 1984: xxvii–xxviii). As Jay Winter has noted, not only in England but in France and Germany,

"The soldier-poet was in the end a romantic figure" (1995: 221). Whether he spoke of war with fury or resignation, he spoke from a position of danger to a world unaware of the horrors of a soldier's life. Like the women who lament the dead in many traditional cultures, he acted as a go-between, a spokesman for the dead, interpreting their death for the survivors and almost always affirming their bravery. However untraditional their language, the "modernist" poets of the war and postwar era are generally romantic and traditional in sentiment; they "walk backwards into the future" (ibid.: 222–223).[9]

The Orchestration of National Memory

The Great War, so costly in lives, so appalling in its new weaponry, was so terrible that it required a careful orchestration of national mourning. Otherwise how could the nation-states responsible for unleashing such horror regain self-respect or regather their citizens to fight another war? How was the wanton waste of young lives so quickly erased from the public memory? By a process of what, in another context, Milan Kundera has called "organized forgetting" (1980: 235). Vernon Scannell's poem "The Great War" is a perfect illustration of the success of the process (1984: 223–224):

> Whenever war is spoken of
> I find
> The war that was called Great invades the mind.

It is not that the poet forgets the corpses and the fear, but that something else is at work:

> These things I see,
> But they are only part
> Of what it is that slyly probes the heart:
> Less vivid images and words excite
> The sensuous memory . . .

"Sensuous memory" seduces the poet, slyly peddling its version of events:

> And now,
> Whenever the November sky
> Quivers with a bugle's hoarse, sweet cry,
> The reason darkens; in its evening gleam
> Crosses and flares, tormented wire, grey earth
> Splattered with crimson flowers,
> And I remember,
> Not the war I fought in
> But the one called Great
> Which ended in a sepia November
> Four years before my birth.

The bugle's cry is "sweet," so inviting that it "darkens" reason. This is the war that has been preserved in sepia like the photographs of a generation of deluded young men who died in it. The poet has no memory of it at all, we discover, having been born after it ended, but he "remembers" it better than the war he fought in. Its memory was, for the most part, enshrined in still images. Its distant rumble did not invade the kitchens and living rooms of London, Berlin, or Sydney. It was, like the rugby matches at Eton, a man's business, played, with the exception of poison gas, according to the old rules and directed by aristocrats for the glory of the British and German empires.

As Paul Fussell notes, the sepia dream of the Great War cast its spell on American literature as it did on British. In Norman Mailer's *The Naked and the Dead*, Cummings steps up on a parapet and "peers cautiously into the gloom of No Man's Land" (quoted in Fussell 1975: 320). There were no parapets in the Second World War, nor any real no-man's-land, but "such anachronisms anchor Cummings' action within the mythical trench landscape of the Great War rather than his own and imply a powerful imaginative continuity between that war and the one he is fighting" (ibid.: 321). Skipping past the Second World War, writers of the 1960s and 1970s returned to the Great War as a source of inspiration. British novelists like John Harris and Derek Robinson and poets like Ted Hughes, who was too young to serve even in the Second World War, looked back at the Great War for a model. Was it because it was further back in time? Or was it because the myth of a meaningful death was so diligently pursued by the young soldiers themselves, by the men who trained them, and by the powers that squandered their lives? Christian sacrifice was the metaphor that made the squandering possible, and even those who understood it for what it was, like Wilfred Owen, were forced to employ it:

> For 14 hours yesterday I was at work—teaching Christ to lift his cross by numbers, and how to adjust his crown; and not to imagine he thirst until after the last halt. I attended his Supper to see that there were no complaints; and inspected his feet that they should be worthy of the nails. I see to it that he is dumb, and stands at attention before his accusers. With a piece of silver I buy him every day, and with maps I make him familiar with the topography of Golgotha.[10]

For a time, metaphors kept the slaughter going and the grief contained. But eventually grief entered the kitchens, the empty bedrooms, the hospitals and madhouses. For many families, the missing bodies made grief harder to bear. Most of the bodies lay somewhere on the Western Front, impossible to find, let alone to identify and return. In the end all the warring parties agreed to let them rest where most of them fell, in Flanders and France, and to satisfy the need for remains by a symbolic gesture of burial (Winter 1995: 27).

Even before the war was over, the creation of its memory began. Remembrance was a national preoccupation: selective remembrance, selectively commemorated. No expense was spared in constructing memorials of stone, museums, shrines. For both winners and losers the creation of these memorials was an act of patriotism. Lists of names of men who signed up were engraved in stone during the war years and completed at the end of the war.[11] They stood in town squares and parks, forming the centerpiece of ceremonies of remembrance. Reflecting community pride, they also formed a focal point for grieving families to place wreaths and to share their bereavement with others who had lost relatives.

The Memorial and the Mourner

How did the monument or memorial satisfy the needs of the huge numbers of bereaved? As Winter observes, despite their political and nationalistic character, the war memorials were "places where people could mourn. And be seen to mourn" (1995: 93). Mosse's characterization of them as places where the nation worshipped itself and which paved the way for fascism (1990: 70–80) does not contradict the part such monuments played in assuaging private and public grief. There was nothing ambiguous, at least on the Allied side, about the feelings of pride, patriotism, and sadness the mourners brought with them to these shrines. Despite or because of the modern weapons that had caused unprecedented suffering and slaughter, memorials to the Great War looked, for their models, to an age in which duty, sacrifice, and masculine honor still offered the bereaved a sense of proud involvement in the cause of war. In the English-speaking world, the words from Kipling's "Recessional" were the most frequently invoked, words written in 1897, before the horrors of trench warfare and gas, the dumping of thousands of bodies into unmarked graves on the battle site (1996: 1077–78):

> The tumult and the shouting dies—
> The captains and the kings depart—
> Still stands Thine ancient Sacrifice,
> An humble and a contrite heart.
> Lord God of Hosts, be with us yet,
> lest we forget—lest we forget!

The motto "Lest we forget!" inscribed in stone, recited at every occasion that remembered the fallen, insisted on memory as a Christian and patriotic duty. Under the "awful hand" of God, subjects of the empire were reminded that they held "Dominion over palm and pine." If Kipling's "we" were in danger of forgetting, then they were reminded, by memorial services, processions, monuments that dominated the streets and squares of every town, that they had a duty toward the collective dead.

The Breaking of the Covenant

Many of the men who fought in the First World War also fought in the Second. They marched off in the same spirit, confident in their belief, prepared to die and sure their sacrifice would be recognized with the same unequivocal national pride as the sacrifices of the previous war. In some cases they were right. In England, Australia, Canada, and the United States there was little ambivalence about the returning heroes or the dead soldiers left behind. Goodness had triumphed over unequivocal evil, the tablets of the dead could be expanded, new statues added to old monuments. In England civilians joined the ranks of heroes, and the two young princesses, jaunty in ambulance uniforms, had cheered bombed-out Londoners while their mother launched new battleships with champagne. But on the continent of Europe, in Japan, in the Jewish communities of the diaspora, feelings of guilt, paralysis, and incomprehension made traditional symbols of mourning seem hopelessly inadequate.

In his study of the Great War and its relation to memory, Paul Fussell states that "one notices what one has been 'coded'—usually by literature or its popular equivalent—to notice and remember" (1975: 247). When the codes no longer seem to fit, when nothing in the literary, spiritual, or national tradition supports memory, does collective amnesia set in? The first war of the twentieth century could still draw on the symbolism of the past to remember its dead, most of whom were men and soldiers. The Second World War was the first war in which civilians were the majority of the victims. It was also the first war in which the image became as dominant as the word. Photographs of the dead, the dying, the emaciated, of terrified children and ravaged cities no longer fitted the codes of noble sacrifice, of soldiers keeping a homeland safe.

The countries that fought in the Second World War experienced it so differently that it was difficult to speak of a common response. For the members of the British Commonwealth, it was still possible to add a list of names to the First World War memorials and to pretend that the war experience had not changed.[12] Under the sign of the ANZACs, the Australians mourned the dead of two wars without apparently noticing any incongruities. Nations, as Benedict Anderson has wisely remarked (1991: 205), fashion their biographies not according to the formula of a biblical chain of begettings, but "up time." National biographies, marked by deaths, begin at the present and move backward so that "World War II begets World War I." The Australian and New Zealand dead could drift back to join the ANZACs in the national memory, but in Europe the war had left almost no country untainted.

European Jewry had been all but obliterated. The beginnings of the Cold War merged with the end of the hostilities, carving the map of Europe in two, igniting new wars. The terrible losses sustained by the Soviet Union during the war went unrecognized for decades in the West. The deliberate incineration of German civilians and the dropping of the two atomic bombs on Japan left even the "good" soldiers tainted. A numbing sense of horror complicated grief and delayed the construction of new memorials. Even in Washington, a projected Second World War memorial, after the style of the Arc de Triomphe, has still to be built. In Germany, where new memorials had been built immediately after the defeat of 1918, the Allies did not permit the construction of memorials to the war dead until 1952. They also demanded the demolition of all monuments constructed by the Nazis and all other monuments thought likely to glorify the military tradition (Mosse 1990: 212). Monuments to the First World War dead were not in fact destroyed, although offending inscriptions were removed. The horrors of war rather than its glory were memorialized by the ruined buildings left standing in the middle of cities. The memory of the Second World War was one of universally experienced grieving, of victims rather than of heroes.

Memorials without Glory

The codes of war, codes that allowed the dead of the Great War to become the inspiration for a new generation of soldiers, had been broken. If the dead soldier was no longer a hero, how was grief to be assuaged, where was there solace for the survivors? How should memorials to the victims of Nazi genocide be categorized? How would they be related to the traditional war memorial, the symbolically traditional structures and iconography of the First World War? And how could they activate, suppress, or distort memory of something so "unspeakable"? Today there are thousands of Holocaust memorials in Europe, America, and Israel.[13] More than a hundred museums are devoted to the Nazi destruction, the most recent being the Holocaust Museum in Washington, D.C. The camps themselves have been turned into memorials. Yearly visitors to Auschwitz are estimated at 750,000, those to Dachau at 900,000. The Holocaust museum of Yad Vashem, in Israel, is visited by as many as 1.25 million people a year. In his memoir of the two years he spent in Mauthausen concentration camp, the Greek writer Iakovos Kambanellis describes climbing up to a former gun tower with a woman ex-prisoner after the liberation, and looking down on the camp. The woman asks him what will happen to the camp and its installations after they leave. Kambanellis replies:

> Who knows? Maybe they'll preserve it as a sight worth seeing. Entrance one mark. The entry fee to go to the widows and orphans of the S.S. . . . . Refreshments to the right . . . Postcards of executions, hangings, etc. . . . . Brief history of the camp, beautifully illustrated. "Ladies and gentlemen, the Mauthausen concentration camp is a work of the fourth decade of the twentieth century and one of many similar camps founded by the Germans under Adolf Hitler. Mauthausen is not one of the best known, but thanks to its very characteristic architecture it is regarded as among the best examples of the style. Unfortunately the name of the architect is not known . . . however all the buildings were erected by the personal labor of the prisoners under the supervision of the S.S. Let us proceed to the gas chambers . . ." (1995: 112–113)

With chilling foresight, the author envisages what seemed impossible: the site of the Nazi atrocities turned into a tourist attraction. Kambanellis' imagined resurrection of the camp is bitterly ironic. He understood that if it were to become a museum, it would benefit the country where it stood. Fifty years later, at the anniversary ceremony for the liberation of the camp by the Americans, his worst fears would be borne out.[14] All but one of the speeches at the ceremony—a brief statement by the American army officer who had been in charge of the troops who entered the camp in May 1945—were in German; and not a single speech was made by a survivor of the camp. Delegations from all over the world, holding flags of their home countries, marched into the central square of the camp, many placing wreaths to commemorate the dead. Mauthausen is now a state museum, as clean and beautifully maintained as any other in Austria. The fiftieth anniversary of its liberation was an opportunity for Austrian political officials to refute any charges of national amnesia. The thousands of survivors and descendants of survivors who came to the event were, after all, a valuable asset. The hotels of Linz were all filled to capacity, its restaurants crowded. For the Austrians, the visitors were a welcome boost to trade. For the survivors, their families, and thousands of others who had come to witness the ceremony, it was a curious and equivocal experience.

On the pristine site of Mauthausen, with its twenty memorial sculptures, one for each national group (a separate one for the Jews), the only feature that can never be cleaned or robbed of its power to provoke memory is the infamous staircase of 186 steep stone steps leading to the pit of the quarry. On it, thousands of prisoners lost their lives, crushed under the great stones they carried, pushed to their deaths, shot, or driven beyond the capacity of their malnourished bodies to endure. Even the tourist buses parked at the bottom of the stairs, the brightly clad teenagers chattering and photographing each other as they leap up the stairs unburdened, do nothing to lessen the impact of the stairs. I knew these stairs from the precise descriptions of a survivor, forced to haul great blocks of stone up them. It was his testimony I carried with me as I counted them. How does the staircase become anything other than a staircase when the people who walk on it have forgotten its ghosts? Weeks after the liberation of Mauthausen, before the surviving inhabitants had been repatriated, Kambanellis described the reactions of an Italian visitor to a stairway that the survivors had already turned into a site of pilgrimage:

> He stopped to read a sign written on a plank of wood propped above a heap of "impossible to carry" stones: "In this pit tens of thousands were martyred. *May their blood be remembered by us and by our children.*"
>
> He went towards the stairway and began to ascend. At this hour it was deserted, just as the pit was deserted. The pilgrims arrived in the afternoon. But on the steps he found, every so often, pieces of bread, the wicks of melted candles, a pair of glasses tied to a stone. And the names written on the rise of the steps . . .
>
> Benjamin Cohen
> because he was a Jew.
> Jaros Kovarik,
> a brave man from Straskov.

Each afternoon, the stairway became the site of communal grieving, each mourner paying homage in his own way:

> On one step someone had placed flowers and a piece of paper with strawberries on it. On another a name had been written in black paint. Near the middle of the stairway a man was busily rubbing the step with his hand as if he wanted to get a good hold on it . . . Further down, a man and a woman were kneeling and prostrating themselves, resting their foreheads on the step above. (Kambanellis 1995: 82)

Again, the voice of the Greek survivor is prescient. He revisits the places in the camp where he and his new girlfriend have witnessed terrible atrocities. Both are conscious of the need to "exorcise" the sites of their nightmarish visions, but these places have already been transformed. In the sunny afternoon light the stairway, despite its pilgrims, looks strangely altered: "Thousands of innocent men had been unspeakably tortured and murdered in this 'place of skulls.' How did it happen that this place could suddenly appear so 'innocent' itself? But I was doing the same thing. It was, thank God, afternoon, and I was so in love with the Lithuanian girl, that I avoided telling her we were passing through hell" (ibid.: 83).

The desire to forget and the need to remember great suffering are inextricably intertwined. The survivors' memorials were transient— a candle, some strawberries. They were the gestures, like Antigone's handful of dust, that represented rites denied to the dead. By obeying another set of laws, and performing their rituals of mourning for those who died by the inhuman laws of the camps, the survivors carried out what Gillian Rose calls "that intense work of the soul, that gradual arrangement of its boundaries, which must occur when a loved one is lost—so as to let go, to allow the other fully to depart, and hence fully to be regained beyond sorrow" (1996: 35). The survivors who stayed behind in the camps seemed to know instinctively what they had to do. Traumatized and ill though most of them were, they obeyed some unwritten law that prompted them to perform the rites they remembered from an age before the camps. They needed no props to memory, and so no solid memorial. But when the survivors die, what will be left of memory? Does the concentration-camp-as-museum fulfill a function?

Why do we come here? What do we want to understand when we come?

Gillian Rose has considered these questions more carefully than most. She and other consultants to the Polish Commission for the Future of Auschwitz (established in 1990, soon after the Polish government had taken over the running of the museum from the Soviet Union) were asked to advise the museum staff on restructuring Auschwitz 1 and on the organization of visits to Auschwitz 2 Birkenau. The work she was engaged in raised awkward questions. "Are our attempts at independent critical reflection merely another stage in the culture industry which Auschwitz has become?" she asked herself (1996: 30). The advisers were chosen on an individual, international basis, but they realized they were working in a context of conflicting interests; American Holocaust museums, for example, were in a bidding war to acquire the last remaining wooden barrack from the original camp. Rose's experience caused her to conclude: "The Holocaust has become a civil religion in the United States, with Auschwitz as the anti-city of the American political community" (ibid.).

The construction of Auschwitz or Mauthausen as an "anti-city" is a concomitant of what Rose calls "holocaust piety." There is a tradition, beginning with Theodor Adorno and continuing with Jean-François Lyotard, Jürgen Habermas, and others, that the Holocaust is a unique, ineffable event. But, as Rose points out, "To argue for silence, prayer, the banishment equally of poetry and knowledge, in short, the witness of 'ineffability,' that is non-representability, is *to mystify something we dare not understand*, because we fear that it may be all too understandable, all too continuous with what we are—human, all too human" (1996: 43).

The mystification of the Nazi camps lifts them out of human history and makes healthy mourning impossible. It makes the task of bearing witness, one that survivors themselves have considered to be urgent, suspect. It also makes all aesthetic representation inadequate. In a way, the creation of the survivor as an inevitably traumatized and hence unreliable witness to his own suffering may be as dangerous as the cult of the fallen soldier. On the other hand, if the Holocaust is not seen as a unique event, if it is approached historically as a genocidal phenomenon comparable to Stalin's gulags, as some contemporary German historians have viewed it, it may become "normalized" and so make the task of mourning the victims equally difficult. As historian Dominick LaCapra remarked: "To the extent to which this normalizing fade-out effect was successful, it would mitigate or obliterate the trauma caused by the Shoah and obviate the need to come to terms with it and to mourn victims of the Holocaust; indeed it would deny that need and foreclose the possibility for mourning" (1998: 50).

As we have seen, monuments and memorials to the Great War were sites of selective remembering, of deliberate forgetting. In a spirit of old-fashioned, nationalist, Christian idealism, the sacred dead became the focus of a cult that allowed relatives to mourn publicly as members of the nation. But this mourning was distinct from personal grief. It was an uplifting, shared experience that encouraged further sacrifice. The British, French, Australians, Americans, even the defeated Germans could mourn their dead together with only minor variations on a theme and with very few dissenters. In hindsight we may say that those who refused the state's version of death as sacrifice, those who were unable to join in the communal mourning, were wiser, that they faced their grief and worked through it. But state mourning has never been concerned with private grief. At its most successful it has been able to harness grief to its own ends. When there is no state or when the state has an ambiguous relationship to the dead, then the idea that it might successfully "mourn" them seems a paradox. For the victims of the Holocaust, most states made no attempt to create national memorials. The famous Rapaport memorial to the dead of the Warsaw Ghetto, erected in 1948, is an exception. Here, at least, there was a possibility for heroic representation, and the artist has reverted to the conventional tropes for such monuments. A bare-chested Mordecai Anielwitcz, Molotov cocktail in hand, strides resolutely forward, his heroic figure backed by a woman holding a baby, who, as David Roskies notes, seems to have stepped straight out of Delacroix's *Liberty Leading the People* (1984: 297). The heroic side of the monument is in complete contrast to the bas relief on the eastern wall. Here the procession of figures under guard bears a close resemblance to the bas relief on the Arch of Titus, where Roman soldiers carry booty from the Temple. Taken together the two sides of the monument remind the viewer that the extraordinary gesture of heroic defiance stands in contrast to an endless history of exile.[15]

Literature, Testimony, and Memory

It is not surprising that it should be the non-survivor who insists on the impossibility of the task of bearing witness, either in factual accounts or in works of art. Problematic and painful as it was, the survivors of the camps felt the task to be a necessity. Through the literature on the Holocaust runs the constant reiteration of the need to remember, to bear witness, not to allow such suffering to be forgotten. The process of testifying to traumatic experiences was always painful. It began in the camps immediately after the liberation and is still going on half a century later. It is a process that asks a great deal of the listener as well as the teller. When the officers of the military tribunal arrived at the camps after the liberation to take testimonies from the inmates, they found themselves caught up in a nightmare world that affected them mentally and physically:

> They worked late into the night, and we, who watched the lighted window, worked through our thoughts as much as we could so as to testify. The appearance of the investigators, who had arrived fresh and lively, began to change. Their eyes lost their lively look; they became heavy, thoughtful; they stared at the ground for long periods. What they were hearing every day from our mouths had shocked them. The depositions were a series of explosions which tore the ground from under their feet. They were two innocent doctors of law, hanging over an abyss, obliged to compile the brief of chaos. (Kambanellis 1995: 121)

The experience of testifying affected the survivors themselves even more violently: "Those who went to testify came back to the huts almost crazy. Many of them had seen the S.S. [prisoners]; they had been brought in for cross-examination" (ibid.: 121).

The depositions interrupted the urgent need of the former prisoners to put their experiences behind them. They made their painful statements because they were sure their stories would be believed. Shoshana Felman states: "As a relation to events, testimony seems to be composed of bits and pieces of a memory that has been overwhelmed by occurrences that have not settled into understanding or remembrance, acts that cannot be constructed as knowledge, nor assimilated into full cognition, events in excess of our frames of reference" (Felman and Laub 1992: 5). But is Felman making a false distinction between testimony about the experience of the Nazi camps and any other remembered experience from the past? Memory is always selective. The bereaved, the tortured, the traumatized are obsessed by the need to recover as much as they can from the past if they feel it serves a purpose. In the case of the Mauthausen prisoners, testifying before the representatives of the military tribunal gave them the satisfaction of possible revenge and the incentive to try to prevent a recurrence of atrocities. The more sophisticated prisoners testified knowing that their tale might never be listened to.

During the time he spent in Auschwitz the Italian writer and chemist Primo Levi had a recurrent nightmare that he would tell of his experiences in the camp and not be listened to: "My dream stands in front of me, still warm, and although awake I am still full of its anguish: and then I remember that it is not a haphazard dream, but that I have dreamed it not once but many times since I arrived here, with hardly any variations of environment or details" (1961: 54).

When he tells another prisoner about his dreams Levi is amazed to find that the prisoner and many others have the same recurrent dream. He asks why the pain of the prisoners' everyday life should be translated into "the ever-repeated scene of the unlistened-to story" (1961: 54). In a conversation with Ferdinando Camon he compared his dream to that of Tantalus, a dream of "'eating-almost,' of being able to bring the food to one's mouth but not succeed in biting into it. It's the dream of a primary need, the need to eat and drink. So was the need to talk about it . . . Later I chose to write about it as the equivalent of talking about it" (Camon 1989: 42).

Levi devoted the remainder of his life to his need to remember and testify to his memory of death and horror. The argument that the survivors were too shocked, too traumatized, that the task of representing the events that took place in the death camps was so difficult as to be impossible, has become common currency in post-Holocaust theory.[16] There is, however, persuasive evidence to suggest that it was not inevitable that the survivors themselves were too traumatized to recall their experiences, or to mourn their losses. Despite Adorno's dictum that poetry is impossible after Auschwitz, poetry, often in the form of laments for the dead, was written inside the camps and after the liberation. Novelists wrote novels, playwrights plays, artists produced paintings. Most survivors were, like Levi, driven by a compulsion to bear witness, but they did not limit themselves to factual accounts of their experience. The Israeli novelist Aharon Appelfeld went so far as to deny the value of the so-called objective testimony in the form of the memoir. The survivor, he wrote, "in the weakness of his own hand and the denial of his own experiences, [creates] the strange plural voice of the memoirist, which is nothing but externalization upon externalization, so that what is within will never be revealed" (1994: 14). Details, on the other hand, were important. What Appelfeld saw as the place of art, specifically of literature, as a response to the Holocaust, was not to make grand statements, to judge, or to preach, but rather to restore the importance of the individual:

> the Holocaust challenged the existence of the self, and I do not refer to the biological self which seeks to further its own existence. On the contrary, that self did everything it could, sometimes the impossible, and, if you will, even the inhuman, in order to stay alive. But the self as a spiritual essence, the self as an existing entity with obligations, that self, the essence of the human spirit, was endangered. (Ibid.: 22)

After the camps, in Appelfeld's view, the artist's task was not to try to memorialize the mass and general horror, not to call on memory to encompass the totality of the experience of Auschwitz or Birkenau. The important thing was to bring individual experience out of the obscurity that had denied its existence. When he was challenged about the place of art in response to such destruction, the novelist responded: "Who will take that great mass which everyone simply calls the 'dreadful horror' and break it up into those precious parcels?" (ibid.: 23). For that to happen, in Appelfeld's view, time had to elapse. The immediate aftermath of the Holocaust was so shattering that for most survivors, especially the Jewish survivors, any response seemed inadequate. Moral expression depends on the existence of some commonly held beliefs about the value of life, the place of the individual, a sense of duty. Even the mindless mass destruction of the First World War did not destroy that.

The survivors did not experience the horrors of the camps in the same way. As Levi and others have pointed out, there were differences in the way individuals and national groups (Greek Jews, for example) dealt with their experiences. The attempt to eliminate individuality in the camps was resisted; survivors emerged and quickly became nationals, often divided into groups by the liberating forces according to language. Before or after leaving the camp they mourned the dead in their own fashion. Those who chose to represent their experience in artistic form did so in unique ways, reaffirming their individuality. To deny them this would be to turn them back into a faceless mass.

Even when all artistic metaphors seemed to fail, even when language seemed exhausted by death, the individual poet found ways to say just that:

> Where are there other analogies to this
> This monstrous thing we suffered at their hands?
> There are none—no other analogies! (All words are shadows
>   of shadows)—
> That is the horror: no other analogies!
>
> (Greenberg 1994: 445)

The writers who emerged from the Holocaust, like the empty camps themselves, or the half-ruined buildings of Hiroshima or Berlin, do not refuse to remember. They refuse to accept the conventional myths of public monuments that focus attention on anonymous heroism. Instead, individuals and communities fashion their own memorials designed to keep the memory of each murdered person alive.

The Vietnam Wall and the AIDS Quilt

The two memorials of the late twentieth century that have most consciously broken with tradition are the Vietnam Veterans Memorial, designed by Maya Lin, and the AIDS Quilt, assembled by friends and relatives of those who have died of AIDS. The coincidence of these two memorials (the Quilt has been displayed in its entirety only on the Mall in Washington, laid out in view of the Vietnam Wall) and the implicit political criticism underlying their unusual designs reinforces the claim that there has been a shift in attitudes to war, death, and grieving in our

times. It is impossible not to see these two memorials as linked responses to events that tore America apart and complicated grief. They
have been characterized as "antimemorials," but it is important to recognize that they are not self-effacing creations. The Vietnam Wall,
however much it was contested, is a work of art, a winning entry in a
competition that brought instant fame to its designer because of the
boldness of its conception. The Quilt, although it is a collective project, was the inspiration of a single gay activist, Cleve Jones, who saw it
as "a national memorial of epic proportions" (Sturken 1997: 186). Both
memorials are simultaneously vast and modest, although Maya Lin's
pair of 500-foot-long walls is finite while the Quilt's dimensions continue to grow. Neither is monumental, in the sense of the First World
War memorials that towered above the landscape, but both force their
intimate perspectives on the viewer. They cannot be looked up to, only
read from close at hand.

How do these strange new memorials function? Does their refusal to
obey the conventions of monument design simply reflect a society's
profound unease in the face of an unpopular war and an epidemic associated in the public mind with anomalous sexuality and drugs? The
nearly simultaneous appearance and periodic physical juxtaposition of
the two memorials reinforce the political issues involved in their construction, but the insistence on similarity may blur some of the most
distinctive features of the two giant projects.

The Wall

By insisting on the importance of individual death and on the naming
of the dead without reference to their military rank, the Vietnam Veterans Memorial defies the convention of the unknown soldier who represented the glory of anonymous sacrifice for the fatherland. The naming of names on memorials is not new, but on Lin's wall the 58,196
names are what draw the eye to read and tempt the fingers to trace. No
figurative sculpture, vertical column, or triumphal arch distracts the
eye. Like many of the laments for the dead in traditional societies, the
vast list of names is both an accusation and an accounting. "Look how
many died day after day!" it seems to say, "and for what?" As if to emphasize what Sturken (1997: 58) calls "the expanse of cultural memory," all the names of the dead were read out as a roll-call of the dead

when the memorial was dedicated, and on the tenth anniversary of its dedication. The recital of large numbers of names became a theatrical gesture of remembrance, a refusal of anonymity. For many "The Wall" goes beyond this, becoming an accusation against the state for the sacrifice of young lives in an unpopular war and a failure to grant the dead their traditional place among the heroes of other wars.

As we have seen in relation to the Australian memorials to the dead at Gallipoli, there is also nothing new about constructing a monument to a military defeat. There are no outward signs to distinguish most monuments to defeat from monuments to victory. The monuments to the dead in the American Civil War are surprisingly similar in the North and South, although the economic devastation of the South meant that there was a time lag in the construction of such monuments (Mayo 1988: 171).[17] The type of commemoration depended less on victory or defeat than on the particular state's degree of involvement in the conflict, with New York and Pennsylvania building monuments at Gettysburg before the other Union states, and Mississippi building a memorial at Vicksburg ahead of other Confederate states (ibid.: 174). The monuments vary in style, from classical to romantic to modern, according to the fashions of the times, with the early sculptors creating realistic portraits of the casualties of war from the models they saw all around them. Even these soldiers with their tattered uniforms or marks of injury are presented in dignified poses. The Mississippi Memorial at Gettysburg shows a bareheaded Confederate soldier trampling Death underfoot and swinging the butt of his rifle furiously across his shoulder. As one observer notes: "The visitor unaware of history could just as easily perceive that the South had won these major battles. If defeat is meant to be seen here, it is defeat represented by communal loss rather than the defeat of a humiliated Confederacy by a righteous Union" (ibid.: 176).

What is distinct, in the remembrance of the Civil War dead, is the treatment of physical remains. Monuments and war memorials have historically been civic structures, decided on by committees and constructed at public expense. It is illogical to expect them to undermine public morale. The burial of the dead is another matter. The national military parks are where ambiguity and divisiveness about the war are expressed. The war cemeteries that border the major battlefields have become national military parks that tend to include only Union soldiers. The Confederate dead are buried elsewhere, or their bodies remain unidentified in makeshift graves in the battlefield itself. For example, there is no explicit graveyard for Confederates at Gettysburg, and at Vicksburg the Confederate cemetery is totally separated from the military park . . . Immediately after the battle, Union troops made graveyards by the battlefields, and after the war Union soldiers were recognized first when these graveyards were made national cemeteries. (Ibid.: 177–178)

In James Mayo's view, national military parks have become symbolic landscapes that honor the Union but reinforce the guilt of the Confederacy, but he acknowledges that although the cemeteries may apportion guilt selectively, the battlefields of the Civil War have become sites of communal guilt. Visitors leave them with a sense of the profligate expenditure of American lives.

In many ways the Vietnam Veterans Memorial is also a testament to communal guilt and to pointless slaughter. On the other hand the decision to erect it was made by the veterans themselves. Its purpose was to commemorate the Americans who died in an unpopular war that most members of the society would have preferred to forget. It is significant that the first efforts to commemorate the soldiers who died were made not by the government but by the armed forces. In 1969, with the war still going on, the U.S. Army's Special Forces, or "Green Berets," dedicated a monument to themselves at Fort Bragg, North Carolina. The statue of a sergeant in combat fatigues of the type worn in Vietnam and resting an M-16 rifle on one hip is not explicitly dedicated to the war but is placed next to a memorial inscribed with the names of soldiers killed in Vietnam.[18]

The Green Beret memorial was the first of a series of defensive, unofficial, and unorthodox monuments to the American dead in Vietnam. It was erected by those who believed in the war, but even those who didn't believe in it wanted their dead remembered and thought that they could use such a memorial to bring about reconciliation— even to end the war. The Disabled American Veterans' National Memorial in Eagle Nest, New Mexico, was the inspiration of Dr. Victor Westphall, whose son died in Vietnam. What began as a private memorial became a communal project: a chapel to peace dedicated in 1972.

The chapel appealed to many veterans and to families who provided photographs of their dead sons to place on one wall. Although it was given the title of a national memorial, it was an antiwar memorial created by a father for a son who opposed war in general and this war in particular. It did not satisfy the desire of many veterans for a large-scale memorial that would give the Vietnam War dead the public prominence they felt they deserved.

The veterans had come home from a horrible war to a country half-ashamed of its own behavior and still more ashamed of its failure to defeat a diminutive enemy. The veterans knew they could not expect a divided, chagrined administration to erect a national monument, so they raised money for their own memorial. They raised approximately seven million dollars and decided that the design should be selected through an open competition judged not by veterans but by designers. Contestants were informed that "the memorial will make no political statement regarding the war or its conduct. It will transcend these issues. The hope is that the memorial will begin a healing process, a reconciliation of the grievous division wrought by the war" (Vietnam Veterans Memorial Design 1980: 5).

Of course it was impossible for the memorial to make no political statement. Its very existence was a political statement, and whatever the outcome it could never have transcended the divisions that made it necessary for veterans to erect their own monument. The suggestion that the memorial itself could facilitate healing seems equally far-fetched. However imaginative its design, no single monument could have satisfied the grief of a nation so divided on the issue of the war. The angry Veterans who had raised the money for their memorial handed over all decisions about the design to a jury of "experts"—architects, landscape architects, sculptors, and a critic. These were the people who judged the design of a young Chinese American Yale architecture student as the winning entry. Everything about Maya Lin's design was self-conscious, symbolic, and conceived in opposition to the familiar monuments and memorials around it. The V-shaped walls are black granite (the traditional Western color of mourning), in contrast to the white stone memorials that dominate the Washington Mall. The end of one wall points to the Washington Monument, the other end to the Lincoln Memorial. It does not stand up against the skyline but can be seen only when one is close to it. The walls cut into the earth in what would be described by its detractors as a "black gash of shame and sorrow" (Sturken 1997: 51). The memorial is about as unheroic as a tribute to fallen soldiers could be.

With its endless names that force themselves on the viewer, demanding to be read, Lin's memorial is the iconographic reversal of the Tomb of the Unknowns. Its vast polished surface is the tombstone of the known. Unlike the conventional war memorials that often included an "honor roll" of the dead, Lin has deliberately listed the 58,196 dead men and women chronologically, by the date on which they died or were declared missing. Within each day of casualties, the names are listed alphabetically, with no military rank, no mention of which branch of the armed forces they belonged to. There is nothing so revolutionary about this leveling in death. The small white crosses of the military cemeteries of Europe and America had already established a tradition of such mass memorialization. What is new is the emphasis on the names that invite the eye and the hand to interact with the memorial. Just as we are tempted to read and trace the names on the tombstones in a village churchyard, visitors to the memorial read, touch, and make rubbings of the names, especially of those they knew. They come to identify, to commune with their dead, to leave offerings of flowers, beer cans, boots.

The black wall has become a public site of grief and the most visited memorial in the United States. Despite the opposition to Lin's design that began before construction and has continued ever since, "The Wall" is a shrine, a "Wailing Wall," a tourist mecca. It is not easy to explain why. Controversy itself may have played a part. Some of the better-known funders of the memorial, like Ross Perot, were critical of the design, and conservative critics saw it as another attempt to foist modernist art on an unwilling public.[19] In an attempt to placate the critics and minimize the effect of Lin's memorial, a second artist was commissioned to design a more conventional statue, which was to stand, together with a flag, at the apex of the walls. Lin hired a law firm to oppose what she saw as the desecration of her design. Frederick Hart's eight-foot-high sculpture of three soldiers, one white, one black, and one Hispanic, was eventually placed at some distance from the wall. Hart's design is thoroughly conventional and masculine, despite the expressions of uncertainty on the faces of the three men, but its conventional nature made it, too, the focus of some controversy. Women veterans, who had not objected to Maya Lin's design, found the male trio that excluded them offensive. Only 8 of the 11,500 women who served in Vietnam as civilians or nurses were killed, but they argued that their experience of the war was as traumatic as that of their male counterparts and Hart's statue inspired them to raise funds for a memorial of their own. The result was yet another realistic memorial, this time depicting two nurses, one holding a wounded soldier on her lap in the attitude of a Pietà, the other looking skyward as if waiting for a helicopter to arrive.

Neither Hart's doubting heroes nor Glen Goodacre's caring women have deflected much attention from the Wall. Judged on aesthetic grounds, they may appear sentimental and incongruous, rather like the ornamental sculpture in a cemetery. Just as in a cemetery, it is the grave with its inscription that we focus on. The giant tombstone remains the focus of the visitors' attention partly because it offers them a site for communal grieving. Side by side, relatives can scan the names for their dead. Massed together, the names represent a solidarity in death that was absent in life. For all their criticism of the design of the memorial, the Wall has become, for some veterans, a way to preserve their military honor. Like the black MIA flags that fly above public buildings across the country, the Wall has been adopted by such groups as the Veterans' Vigil for Honor as a solid banner to be guarded from harm, especially on Memorial Day. For these veterans, "The Wall is more than a sacred depository of memory; the Wall *is* Vietnam" (Haines 1986: 10).

The success of the Wall for the veterans is its very abstraction. By deliberately denying difference while insisting on the importance of names, the memorial constitutes a roll call of the dead, a parade ground where the dead still serve their country as symbols of a unified struggle. Not a single Vietnamese name appears on the list. The Vietnamese, even as allies, are invisible, erased. This is a war of "us" against "them," and if families weep, they do so proudly, in the heart of the nation's capital, at a memorial that, whatever its designer intended, has come to serve the function of most war memorials: to further the national myth by celebrating the soldiers who died in its service.

Vietnam's "Unknown" Soldier

Memorials are "sites of memory," but each person brings his or her own memories to them. As we saw, the memorials to the dead of the

Great War could be said to have "worked" because they honored an abstract belief in death as sacrifice rather than focusing on individual death. Private grief and personal memories were not what these memorials encouraged. Rather, they promoted pride and emphasized the commonality of suffering. The Tombs of the Unknown Soldier exemplified the symbolic solidarity of the dead. One soldier could stand for many because in life they were united in their willingness to die for their country. But the memorials that satisfied a more idealistic, confident America did not necessarily suit an age of individuality in which there was unprecedented access to information. The Reagan administration realized the political importance of adding a Vietnam War soldier's body to the Tomb of the Unknowns in Washington. Treating the body as another set of anonymous bones and interring it with the bones of soldiers from the First and Second World Wars and from the Korean War would placate the veterans and persuade the public that the Vietnam War was, like other wars their country had fought in, an honorable one.

On Memorial Day 1984 the remains of an American pilot, one of several who crashed near An Loc in 1972, were given an elaborate state funeral led by the president himself. But even that attempt to create a traditional memorial to the dead in Vietnam was to prove a failure. On May 7, 1998, the secretary of defense ordered the reopening of the Tomb of the Unknowns in Arlington National Cemetery so that the remains of the soldier who died in Vietnam could be removed for testing and identification (Meyers 1998b: A1). And at a time when there were major crises in international affairs, including India's testing of nuclear weapons, the secretary of defense himself presided at the ceremony where the tomb was reopened.

It was an ironic reversal of the tradition of putting the dead to rest. The decision to uncover the tomb of the nation's symbolic dead was made at the request of a family who believed the remains to be those of their son. It appears that in their haste to find an unknown soldier from the Vietnam War, the Pentagon reclassified as "unidentified" bones formerly identified as those of Air Force pilot Lieutenant Michael J. Blassie. Pentagon officials claimed that the tests they carried out made the original identification suspect, but Lieutenant Blassie's family and their supporters doubted their story. The need for a neutral set of bones was urgent. The Vietnam War and its aftermath of division and distrust of the administration required an orchestration of national grief that would link the war and its veterans with other, less ambiguous wars. Republican Senator Robert C. Smith claimed that the Pentagon had ignored evidence over the years that cast doubt on the anonymity of the "Unknown Soldier." He added: "If the Tomb of the Unknowns is going to remain sacred . . . the remains should be unknown" (Meyers 1998a: 15). The political exploitation of grief through costly attempts to recover and identify remains seems to have backfired. In an age in which all remains are potentially identifiable through testing, can a Vietnam Unknown Soldier ever be found? And if there are no symbolic remains, on what can the nation focus its collective grief?

The Wall seems to have provided a substitute of sorts. In the age of information, the relatives of the dead don't want a nameless body. They want the fragments scrutinized. They want answers and "closure." Even those who realize it will change nothing feel (or have been encouraged to feel by the new experts in grief) that identification will help them put their restless dead to sleep. The Wall keeps this desire for answers alive by marking the names of the identified dead with a diamond, those of MIAs with a cross. The cross is changed to a diamond if the remains that belong to the name are found and identified. There is also the teasing possibility of having the cross transformed into a circle if an American soldier were to turn up alive in the Laotian jungle. Needless to say there are no circles, but when the Wall was dedicated there were many who believed in the possibility. To them the Wall is still an information bulletin, a place where the dead and missing are not anonymous but posted for all to see and where hope is still held out, even on the vast, mirrored surface of a symbolic tombstone.

The Quilt: A Refusal of Mourning

At first glance, the AIDS Memorial Quilt is the mirror image of the Wall: an infinite, soft flag designed by no one, made up of more than 45,000 three-by-six-foot panels. The panels, sewn by lovers, families, and friends of the dead, include all sorts of memorabilia. To many of the activists who wished to bring attention to the epidemic, there seemed no solution but rage. The idea of the quilt came from the gay district of San Francisco on a night of protest and mourning for the mayor of San Francisco, George Moscone, and gay supervisor Harvey Milk, both of whom had been assassinated. On that night in 1985, many of the marchers carried placards with the names of people who had died of AIDS. They placed them on the Old Federal Building, covering its walls. The panels of names reminded AIDS activist Cleve Jones of a quilt. Two years later he and Michael Smith began the NAMES project, which maintains the Quilt (Sturken 1997: 185–186).

The Quilt may be the most unusual memorial ever made, at least in the West. From its genesis to its refusal to end, it is a powerful demonstration of the new attitude to mourning. Like the Mothers of Argentina, the community that initially suffered the most deaths took the homeliest of domestic articles, in this case a quilt, and turned it into a symbol of domestic grief. It is the individual who is commemorated on the AIDS Quilt, and not for a life lost in the service of a country or a cause but in a battle against a disease. The private and family life of the individual is remembered in each square, but the sum of all these lives, laid out on the Washington Mall, becomes a giant carpet that demands attention by its very extent. On each panel of the Quilt a pictorial and verbal drama is presented. Each panel is a work of love; it took time and effort to complete, but the sum is greater than the parts. The joining together of the panels is an act of solidarity, the seaming together of a community of bereaved who would not normally grieve together.

For a community that had been stigmatized, for families afraid to speak of the terrible disease that had carried off their relatives, the Quilt offered a social cohesiveness and solidarity in grief. Quilting is a homey art, American as apple pie. The home-sewn squares counteracted the image of AIDS as an unnatural disease of the modern era. The Quilt also crossed the barriers of gender, reuniting the gay male dead with their mothers and families. In this respect the Quilt and the Wall could not be more different. One is a contemporary design, the vision of an individual artist; the other, even if inspired by a single activist, is self-consciously traditional, anonymous, and collective. Its harking back to an earlier age is itself a form of retrieval of memory. The ceremonies in which the Quilt is laid out become rituals of mourning where anger about the government's response or the broader community's response is mediated by the familiar and comforting activity of unfolding an enormous bedcover.

The symbolism could not be more appropriate. The bed is, after all,

where most of the dead contracted their disease, and where they suffered and died. Most of the stories told in the panels are, as Cindy
Ruskin noted, "stories of love" (1988: 13), and not just of love but
of erotic love, most of it homosexual. The panel made by David
Kemmeries for his lover Jac Wall is one of the most explicit: "Jac Wall
is great in bed. Jac Wall is intelligent. I love Jac Wall. Jac Wall is with
me. Jac Wall turns me on. I miss Jac Wall. Jac Wall is faithful. Jac Wall
is a natural Indian. Jac Wall is young at heart. Jac Wall looks good naked. I love Jac Wall. I will be with you soon" (Sturken 1997: 203).

This celebration of sex in the face of death reminds us of the wake
games that were once an indispensable part of the funerals of Ireland
and other parts of Europe. The juxtaposition of frank eroticism and
grief is rare and provocative in our times. The Quilt is, despite the
humble nature of its materials, the most daring of memorials. It flouts
the clichés of modern memorials constructed by men to honor patriotism. Fathers and brothers of gay men have contributed very few of
the panels; most were made by gay men or by women. Cleve Jones
stated that he and his friends who conceived the idea of the Quilt deliberately tried to undermine stereotypes of masculinity. By making their
memorial a form of giant sewing bee, the gay community involved
many mothers, sisters, and women friends of the dead who shared experiences with bereaved gay lovers. The decision to choose a domestic,
nonthreatening symbol was part of a conscious desire on the part of
Jones and others in the gay community to reach out to a broader population. Jones offended many gay activists when he announced that the
NAMES Project was "not a gay organization" (Sturken 1997: 207).

Whether or not the AIDS Memorial Quilt, with its idealistic rhetoric of healing and preserving memory, is representative of the broader
population that has lost friends and relatives to the AIDS epidemic, it is
a memorial well suited to the gay community. It has all the deter-
minedly unconventional charm and flair that marked the lives of many
gay men who died of AIDS. Privileged as some of them were, they died
the same unglamorous death as the black, the straight, or the poor victims of the epidemic. Their friends mourned them knowing that their
grief was a way to "act up"—to politicize grief and draw attention to
the cause. The Quilt was conceived as both a form of therapy and a
theatrical gesture. As such, it was an immediate success; it appeared on
television programs; a documentary film was made about it; it was even
nominated, in 1989, for the Nobel Peace Prize.

State-sponsored grief requires the submerging of the individual in the collective, whereas private grief or communal grief, especially of a group that has suffered persecution and stigmatization, demands a recognition that no person is like another in life or in death. To remember the dead is not an act of "closure." For the families and lovers of those who died of AIDS, the Quilt is as diverse as its individual panels, and its point is to keep communication with the dead alive. Unlike the resentful Vietnam veterans' sponsorship of the Wall, the Quiltmakers' memorial is the work of the mourners' own hands. Within the specifications of size they can improvise their expressions of love, outrage, anger.

The fact that the Quilt is also an article of public display and political protest may have placed some constraints on the expression of private emotion. Richard Mohr writes: "sex is bleached right out of The Quilt, although sex was what was most distinctive of so many of the dead" (1992: 121). But however toned down, sex is there, all over the Quilt, for those who have eyes to see. If it is "bleached," it is because the community that made the Quilt needs no reminders of what they all know, and no help reading the messages of others. There are limits to what many may wish to make public, even for their friends to read. In many ways the joining up of the panels of the cloth into a single quilt is a stitching together of the individual's private life and suffering into a national monument or, as some observers have claimed, "a national guilt trip" (Hawkins 1993: 777). But the fact that the monument can be rolled up and taken away is as much a refusal of conventional mourning as Dylan Thomas' poem about a child dying in a London fire. The general effect of the Quilt is one of gaiety, in the old-fashioned sense of the word. Its bizarre patchwork is a celebration of life and love that cannot be neatly pigeonholed as just another national symbol of mourning.

The Wall rejects a stereotype of the war memorial but reduces the dead to a community of faceless names. Its message is of a vast and pointless expenditure of young lives. The Quilt, representing the lives lost to a sickness that has frequently been characterized as another war, is also a kind of unconventional war memorial (Sturken 1997: 218). At the end of the twentieth century, these two unusual memorials suggest that there has been a rejection, at least by certain communities in the United States, of the state's traditional role as chief mourner. Perhaps it is partly a question of scale. Vastness can be comprehended if the eye can still take it in at a glance. The numbers of dead in Vietnam or in the AIDS epidemic are still small enough not to be entirely meaningless. As observers have pointed out, a wall containing the names of the American dead from the Second World War would have to be one hundred times larger than the Vietnam Wall. Both the Quilt and the Wall are the expressions of a community of sufferers. It may be that the sense of community is finite. A relatively small group of sufferers can, it seems, come together to express their grief in new and original ways, ways that challenge the role of the state in determining how mass death will be memorialized.

There is, about the Vietnam Memorial, as there was, at least until the mid-1990s, about the Quilt, the feeling that these memorials were overdue tributes to the stigmatized and neglected dead. In the anger and grief of the bereaved there was a sense of purpose that gave both memorials a positive charge. They represented a population of dead, one finite, the other open-ended, that could be counted and accounted for. Culturally there was a need to fold these dead into the nation's community of honored dead. On the other hand there were feelings of resentment and anger that cast them as outsiders. Like Homer's restless dead and the unquiet dead of any culture, the Vietnam veterans and the men and women who have died of AIDS need to be placated if life is to go forward. Both monuments are ambivalent gestures of politicized grief that force the dead into the nation's memory while insisting on their individual deaths.

A Return to Tradition?

The Quilt and the Wall are memorials commissioned, created, and used by particular grieving communities to serve their needs. In choosing to create their own memorials or to mourn in a way that does not conform to established norms, the gay community and the Vietnam veterans may be reverting to an older tradition in which communities mourned their own dead. What links the mothers of Argentina's disappeared, the elegists and artists of the gay community, the survivors of the camps, and the veterans who erect their own monument is a desire to take control of the forms of mourning, and a sense of community that allows them to do so. The rituals of mourning are, as we have seen, generally believed to be beneficial both to the bereaved and to the community. They have evolved slowly, and, as their persistence in the face of state and church opposition suggests, they are not easily changed. That they do change is often as much a result of changes in the overall behavior of society as of any conscious desire for novelty. The exception would seem to be when grief is thwarted, derailed, or unusual. Then, if a community puts it to some use, it may draw on resources it is only dimly aware of to recreate its own memorials and rituals. The forms it chooses will be those that seem to offer what the conventions lack: a sense that the memorials and rituals of mourning are appropriate to the grieving community and their dead.

Afterthoughts

*H*AMLET AND *Electra* are doubles. *Hamlet* is a play about
a man grieving the death of his father. He cannot share his grief with
his mother, who has hastily remarried his father's brother and murderer. All three versions of the Electra story (Aeschylus' *Libation Bearers*, Sophocles' and Euripides' *Electra*) tell the tale of a daughter who
mourns her father's death, but cannot share her grief with her mother
because Clytemnestra and her lover Aegisthus murdered her father and
now rule the city of Mycenae. Electra waits, nursing her grief, until her
exiled brother, Orestes, arrives. Together they avenge the death of their
father, killing their mother and Aegisthus. However the three playwrights vary the telling, Electra stands at the center of the tale. The
passion of her grief is a potential threat to the new order of the city.
Temporarily she may appear helpless and humiliated, but she nurses
her pain carefully, confident of its ability to be translated into action on
her brother's return. Electra's drama is sandwiched between one violent murder and another; her grief feeds off the first death to plan the
next. The question the audience must consider is whether the deaths
are symmetrical. Does one death balance another, canceling out guilt?
Or is matricide a crime more heinous than slaying one's husband?
Since the story is preserved in three versions, we must presume that
these questions continued to fascinate ancient audiences.

Hamlet is the most perennially intriguing of Shakespeare's plays. The reasons for its popularity are, I think, rather different. Whereas the drama of Electra turns on her carefully nurtured grief and its inevitable translation into action, Hamlet's is focused on uncertainty. What is it about this drama of an indecisive prince that we find so attractive? "To be or not to be: that is the question" is hardly the most beautiful line in English verse, but it is the best known. What we respond to in Hamlet is precisely his vacillation. It makes him seem so modern—perhaps the first modern character in literature. The prince of Denmark has no peers; he grieves alone. He cannot even display his grief, let alone act on it. There is no coterie of sympathizers, of loyal followers of his father ready to join Hamlet's cause. The grieving women of Greek tragedy and of Shakespeare's own early history plays have none of Hamlet's scruples. In their grief they have an implacable energy that Hamlet struggles to fire in himself. The act he must commit to satisfy his father's ghost is repugnant to his nature. He has the cue for passion, but it fails to prompt him. Like an actor frozen on the stage, he can hear the words whispered from the wings but speech will not come.

Hamlet's grief, like our own, lacks the structure of traditional mourning or a community to shape a new response. In our world, grief overwhelms us, and we face it, for the most part, without a language of lament and laughter. We have been taught that grief and passion are two very different emotions. The Victorians articulated the separation for us. "I tell you," said Elizabeth Barrett Browning with perfect confidence, "hopeless grief is passionless" ("Grief," 1844). The long history of opposition to lament and wake games suggests that grief has not always been perceived in this way. Grief has been recognized as a violent emotion, capable of arousing such strong passions that it has been deliberately contained and managed, either by the community or by outside powers. Silence and composure, the "manly" responses to grief, are later impositions. Already, by Shakespeare's day, the conventions of measured grief are in place. The King can chide Hamlet for his continued mourning as a sign of "unmanly grief" that "shows a will most incorrect to heaven" (I.ii.92). In the King's nervous reprimand, we see that such conventions are imposed precisely because of the passionate nature of grief. There is a recognition that emotions must be reined in, controlled by the self, as the established religion demands. Hamlet's refusal to give up either the clothing of mourning or his eccentric behavior is a deliberate flouting of convention.

What Hamlet wants is to keep the pain of his grief alive so that he can use it. This is a notion we have seen in a number of different contexts. In a well-known Greek lament, a mother says that she will take her pain to the goldsmith to have it made into an amulet so she can wear it forever. The mothers of the "disappeared" in Argentina refuse to accept the bones of their dead children so that they can "keep their wounds open." Gay artists in New York film, photograph, and elegize the dying to keep them in the public view. The Vietnam veterans cooperate with their former enemies to recover the bodies of the dead on both sides of an unpopular war. The monument they commission for their comrades is not designed to put grief away, but stands like an angry gash in the heart of the U.S. capital. These displays of mourning have in common the desire to keep grief alive. We might say they are responses to unusual grief, to grief that is mixed with violent anger and frustration. But they remind us that grief is not a "passionless" state. In many ways, it is the opposite of depression, although the bereaved in our society are expected to be depressed and often treated as though they were. The grief-stricken are intensely alive.

Grief is probably the most powerful emotion we ever feel. It carries us to the edge of madness. Once, this madness was a shared and valued experience. It was indulged, performed, shaped into song, used as an amulet to flout death. Not surprisingly, grief's excesses have always been feared. Figures of authority observing the behavior of mourners at a funeral have recognized that this is the site where emotions can be fired and revolutions sparked. They have taken over from the chorus of lamenting women and the bawdy jesters and made mourning a dull business. Sometimes, though, the manipulators of mourning have been beaten at their own game. The men in paper tiaras at a funeral of an AIDS victim, the silent women wearing the diapers of their dead children, the lists of names without rank on a black wall, the piles of shoes and spectacles—these are displays of grief that defy the clichés of mourning.

Notes

References

Index

Notes

Introduction

1. As Lorraine Helms (1997: 122) notes, the silent heralds at Henry V's funeral are no mere silent props. They "wore long mourning robes and over them, elaborately embroidered tabards, symbolizing the authority that the crown delegated to them for ordering the ceremony . . . the heraldic funeral was individualistic, its raison d'être the extravagant display of status."

2. Ibid.: 123.

3. The widespread practice of lamenting the dead is documented in Rosenblatt, Walsh, and Jackson (1976). Anthropologists studying cultures as diverse as those of New Guinea, China, Russia, and the Balkans have noted that women are generally those who weep for the dead and compose laments. See, e.g., Feld (1982) on New Guinea, Tolbert (1990a, 1990b) on the Finno-Ingrian peoples of the former Soviet Union, Briggs (1990) on the Warao people of Venezuela, Bourke (1988, 1993) on Ireland, and Alexiou (1974), Caraveli-Chaves (1980), Danforth (1982), Holst-Warhaft (1992), and Seremetakis (1991) on Greece.

4. Solon's laws restricting laments and elaborate displays of grief at funerals are examined in Holst-Warhaft (1992) and Alexiou (1974).

5. Among the more influential studies in this area are Ariès (1974), Cannandine (1981), Glazer and Strauss (1965a, 1965b, 1968, 1971), Gorer (1965), Illich (1977), Kastenbaum (1975), and Kübler-Ross (1969).

6. Kai Erikson (1976: 137) argued that following a disastrous flood that devastated the small Appalachian community of Buffalo Creek, West Virginia, in 1972, an intervention program in which people were separated from other grieving families by being placed randomly in caravan parks worked against any resolution of grief.

7. See, e.g., Gorer (1965) and Marris (1986). Cannandine (1981) and R. Rich-

ardson (1988) challenge these arguments and what they see as the idealization of Victorian rituals of mourning.

8. Reported in the Binghamton, N.Y., *Press and Sun-Bulletin*, March 4, 1996. The stages of grieving are based on the theories of Kübler-Ross (1969), whose studies have become the basis of much of the popular rhetoric about grief.

9. Among the illuminating anthropological studies of grief, mourning, and anger are Abu-Lughod (1986), Behar (1993), Schieffelin (1976), and Seremetakis (1991).

10. The anthropology of emotions has, as Leavitt (1996) notes, become a burgeoning field since the 1980s. Among the more influential articles and books in the field are Abu-Lughod and Lutz (1990), Bedford (1986), Briggs (1970), Cohen (1994), D'Andrade and Strauss (1992), Desjarlais (1992), Harré (1986), Izard, Kagan, and Zajonc (1984), Kitayama and Markus (1994), R. Levy (1983), Lutz (1988, 1990), Lutz and White (1986), Lynch (1990), and M. Rosaldo (1980, 1984).

11. One of the few anthropologists to have explored the issue of the relationship of AIDS to heterosexual marriage is John Borneman. In an article surveying the anthropological literature on marriage (1996), Borneman notes the reluctance of anthropologists to deal with AIDS. Observing that heterosexual marriage remains central to anthropology, Borneman conjectures that the avoidance of any discussion of AIDS in relation to marriage and death can be attributed to "the totemic nature of marriage in anthropological discourse" (230). In an article questioning the primacy of marriage in anthropological studies (1997), Borneman argues for an emerging view of human relationships based on the need to care and be cared for. Such a view becomes more urgent in an age of AIDS, where ties between the sick and those who care for them are frequently not sanctioned by society.

1. Tears

1. See Helms (1997: 201). I am indebted to her subtle account of lament in Shakespeare's historical plays.

2. Women who have had abortions in Japan frequently adopt a *mizuko jizo*, or babylike stone guardian of an unborn fetus. They pay a fee to a Buddhist temple for the small figure on which they inscribe their names and come regularly to dress the statues and mourn their unborn babies.

3. *New York Times*, April 17, 1995, p. A12. See Gorer (1965) and Hockey (1993).

4. Anthropologist John Andromedas observed a wake in Mani in the 1950s at which the sister of the deceased was wailing beside his body in such an abandoned manner that she was taken away from the bier and shut in her room for a time to collect herself (interview with the author, 1998). In his article on the management of time and gender at a Cretan funeral, Michael Herzfeld (1993) also documents the enjoinders to female mourners to restrain the excesses of their mourning, restrictions women did not necessarily obey.

5. In the large bibliography on lament, among the most interesting studies are Abu-Lughod (1986), Alexiou (1974), Briggs (1992, 1993), Caraveli (1986), Caraveli-Chaves (1980), Danforth (1982), Feld (1982), Herzfeld (1993), Johnson (1988), Kim (1989), Seremetakis (1991), and Tolbert (1990a, 1990b).

6. Translation by Mihail Miriou.

7. For a fuller discussion of Solon's laws see Holst-Warhaft (1992: chap. 4) and Alexiou (1974: chap. 1).

8. Unpublished transcription by Elizabeth Tolbert, August 15, 1985.

9. Seremetakis (1991: 119). Rodney Needham (1967) argues that percussive noises of varying types are a common feature not only of death rituals but of other *rites de passage*. Referring to the work of other scholars who have examined the use of drums, gongs, bells, and even firecrackers at funerals and in shamanistic ceremonies, he concludes that such percussive and explosive noises are universally associated with transitional states (613). In the case of female lamenters, perhaps one could say that the rhythmic beating of the breasts and the high volume of sound fulfills a similar need for aural stimulation. The chest is, after all, a kind of percussive instrument, producing a sound that is, like a loud explosion, both audible and experienced as a shock to the body.

10. Her small, wise book (1991) is salutary reading for the starry-eyed admirers of classical Athenian democracy.

2. Laughter

1. The song in the epigraph may not in fact be traditional. Like a number of such ballads, it may have been composed in England in the nineteenth century as a satire on the odd behavior of the Irish.

2. The laws passed by Solon at Athens in the sixth century B.C.E. "regulated women's appearance in public, as well as their festivals" (Plutarch, *Solon* 21).

3. For two differing views on the behavior of the women at the *Adonia*, see Detienne (1977) and Winkler (1990). For a view that incorporates the "fun" with mourning see Holst-Warhaft (1992: chap. 4) and Reed (1995). See also Stehle (1990).

4. The translation and references to this text are from Olender (1985: 88–89).

5. Iambe is the eponym for the iambic rhythm, originally used by Archilochus, which, as N. J. Richardson (1974: 213) points out, was the home both of an important Demeter cult and of Baubo herself. Iambic meter seems to have been used for the ritual jesting and abuse *(skommata, aischrologia)* related to the Eleusinian mysteries and other festivals (see Richardson 213–216 for a detailed account of the evidence).

6. Olender (1985: 91–97) summarizes this controversy and the various approaches to Baubo as a fertility figure.

7. Here it may be worth keeping in mind the observations of Turner (1967, 1969), Van Gennep (1960), and others on the temporary death in rites of passage, in which a symbolic death at circumcision, for example, may be accompanied by traditional mourning rites. Turner notes that among the Ndembu the color black symbolizes death but also sexual passion. During the seclusion of novice girls charred bark is used to blacken their vulvas in order to enhance their sexual attraction (1967: 73). See also Reed's (1995: 337) discussion of the symbolic death of initiation being mythopoeically transformed into actual death in the Greek myths of Dionysus, Hyacinthus, and Orion and followed by resurrection.

8. The earliest examination of the parallels between the Baubo figure and Egyptian and Japanese myths of a similar character is probably that of Salomon Reinach (1912: 109–129), who compares the Baubo story with Plutarch's and

Pausanias' accounts of the festival of Daedala at Plataea, in Boeotia. In Plutarch's account, Hera was angry with Zeus and hid herself in a mountain. A Boeotian prince suggested a trick to Zeus to lure his wife back. An oak tree was cut down, fashioned into a maiden, and covered with long veils. A mock wedding was celebrated, and Hera, hearing the wedding music, could not restrain her jealousy and came running from Cythera. When she discovered the hoax, she burst out laughing. Later her jealousy revived, and she burned the statue. Much the same story is told by Pausanias, except that Hera tears the wedding garments of the wooden bride to shreds. Reinach concludes that both ancient observers failed to understand that the story was based on an older myth of a Boeotian cult of Hera as a vegetation goddess like Demeter. The burning of a wooden statue, he notes, is a common feature of fertility rites. The story of Baubo was grafted onto the rites of the mysteries, in Reinach's opinion, in order to explain them (116). Reinach also relates the exposure of Baubo to the account in Plutarch of the Lycian women who, when menaced by Bellerophon and a tidal wave, chased the invaders while exposing themselves, causing the enemy and the waters to recede in terror (*On the Virtues of Women* 248). The precise parallel of the Baubo story with the Egyptian myth of Hathor was elaborated by Isidore Levy (1936), and the relationship of both stories to rituals in other countries was further explored by Meuli (1943). The most recent and thorough examination of the Baubo material is Maurice Olender's (1990). Olender's rejection of a cross-cultural anthropological approach to the subject in favor of a more local and linguistic one may cause him to neglect the association with death and the cessation of mourning that seems central to the Baubo/Demeter myth.

9. Although the question of the possible Egyptian origin of the Eleusinian mysteries does not concern me here, the Baubo/Hathor parallel appears to support those scholars who, like Martin Bernal (1987), favor the Egyptian case.

10. The earliest reference is Abel (1885: 289–91 = *PGM* iv.2714–83, 2759–60), quoted in Olender (1990: 101n.). See also his discussion of the connection between Baubo and toads in ancient comedy.

11. Philippi notes that the *kamï* that results from Izanagi's tears (Nakisawa-me) "undoubtedly reflects the practice of using female lamenters or professional mourners (*naki-me*, 'weeping woman') at funerals" (1989: 58).

12. Ebersole (1989) argues convincingly for the use and interpretation of this myth as a politically charged "charter myth" for the imperial succession. Whatever its political uses, the myth can be read on a number of levels. Ebersole elaborates on these in his excellent discussion (79–122).

13. Bakhtin's positive reading of the carnivalesque has been challenged by a number of critics, including Bernstein (1983: 283–385) and Carrière (1979), but I have located no attempt to refocus the genre around the funeral games.

14. On the opposition of the city-states of ancient Greece to women's behavior at funerals, particularly the performance of laments, see Holst-Warhaft (1992: chap. 4). See also Alexiou (1974) on the classical period and on the attitude of the early church fathers to women lamenters.

15. Antony's funeral oration in *Julius Caesar* is delivered in the marketplace. On the use of funeral laments to incite revenge, see Holst-Warhaft (1992: chaps. 3 and 4).

16. As Fiona Macintosh (1994: 36) points out, the notion of the corpse as host was also a feature of the *perideipnon*, or funeral banquet, in ancient Greece.

17. The games appear to have lasted until quite recent times in Romania. The French anthropologist Jean Cuisenier, observing death rituals in the Moldavian village of Sucevitsa, was told that during the three-day-long wake, funeral games had once been a part of the ceremonies but that these were "idiocies," "spectacles," "nothing but folly from beginning to end" (1986: 24). There was some disagreement among his sources about the attitude of the church and secular authorities to these games, but Cuisenier understood they had been forbidden by the police (26). Despite the fragmentary, dismissive, and perhaps deliberately misleading accounts given by his informants, Cuisenier pieced together some sort of scenario for the games, several of which involved violence.

After the elaborate laments were finished, Cuisenier's informants told him, came the games, which were harmless at first but turned serious and sometimes nasty. One of the popular games was the "Mill Game": "And to play the Mill Game, they placed a chair in the middle of the room, covering it with a blanket and placing a hot coal under it. The players would knock on the chair and then hammer on it, imitating the sound of marching feet . . . A boy dressed in the costume of an old miller's wife would go from one to another telling how many sacks of flour she had bought and how many she had sold, and she would approach the dead too, and say to him: 'I'm not crying because I'm miserable, it's so that someone will give me a carpet! It's not because you were dear to me that I'm crying, it's so that someone will give me some cows!'" (26).

As Cuisenier remarks, the contrast must have been striking between such games and the laments and solemn religious ceremonies that preceded them: "To the intimate, personal, moving relationship of the domestic ceremony, in which all the actors had a definite relationship with the dead person, responds the erratic, abstract relationship, unreal but no less anguished of the *Game of Death and the Devil*." In this game, his informant told him, "'they dressed up as death and the devil—Death had a face painted in white, the devil in black. And death tried to catch the girls to give them to the devil. Then everyone would cry out and run away'" (ibid.). All the games took place in full view of the open coffin and continued each night of the wake.

18. For a detailed discussion of ritual as a process see Victor Turner (1967, 1969).

19. O'Súilleabháin (1967: 157–158) gives examples of directives against wakes in Germany, France, Norway, and the British Isles in the medieval period.

20. On the relationship of the wake games to the laments and the reason for the condemnation of both see Angela Bourke (1993), which also includes a full bibliography of sources on the subject of laments in Irish.

21. See Morris (1938), who infers an unbroken tradition of wake games inextricably linked to lament from pagan times.

22. The origin of these athletic contests was probably the games held in honor of the dead kings of Ireland. Macintosh notes that in Synge's *Playboy of the Western World* the athletic contest at the wake gives Christy the opportunity "to confirm his 'heroic' status" (1994: 36n.).

23. See Bloch and Parry (1982), who also summarize much of the material on the subject.

24. Herzfeld argues that the use of the possessive pronoun with *epitafios* avoids any impugning of the village icon. His argument links the metaphor with the com-

mon Greek idiom "I copulate with your Virgin," in which the Virgin of one's enemies becomes, in effect, a "different" Virgin: "At the moment of conflict, it is 'as though' one's opponent were so utterly removed from one's own sphere of humanity that his very cosmology must be different also" (1979: 291–292).

25. Freud (1963: 345–366). One of the figurines is reproduced in the text.

26. Sutterlin (1988) links the Sheela-na-gig figure to a plethora of figures from geographically and historically varied traditions depicting males and females exposing their genitals. She concludes that their main purpose is one of apotropaic magic, the warding off of evil. In the case of the Sheela-na-gig, she quotes a nineteenth-century German traveler to Ireland who claimed he was informed by locals that a woman displaying her genitals, either in sculpture or in real life, was meant to ward off evil (67).

3. Bones

1. I have slightly altered the translation in the interests of clarity.

2. Sometimes accompanied by fuzzy photographs of prisoners ostensibly still being held in Vietnam or the jungles of Laos, reports continued to be printed in the 1990s, even in newspapers like the *New York Times*. A 1994 article in the *Times* talked of a "top secret report written by a North Vietnamese general" in September 1972 stating that North Vietnam was holding 1,205 American prisoners. The report was said to have been "authenticated by leading experts and . . . circulated among United States government officials." The report was given widespread media attention and described by the POW/MIA lobby as the "smoking gun" that proved the U.S. government had been lying about POWs. Subsequently it was discredited, but not before it had contributed to the myth of the coverup. For a full account of the hoax, see the *Far Eastern Economic Review*, May 6, 1993.

3. Alexiou (1974: 48). Trigger (1976: 85–90) notes that when the Huron Indians abandoned a large village, they held a feast of the dead in which they exhumed the bodies of their dead and invited neighboring tribes to join them in placing the remains of their relatives in a common ossuary. The female relatives stripped the bodies of any remaining flesh, and the clean bones were wrapped in a beaverskin bag. After a week of feasting, the bags were reopened and mourned over, then mingled in a pit with the bones of neighboring villagers to ensure peaceful relationships between communities.

4. Disappearance

1. "In Memory of W. B. Yeats" (1940), pt. 1.

2. The National Commission on the Disappeared in Argentina (CONADEP), which was formed after President Alfonsín came to power, published a number of 9,000 on the basis of testimony they had heard, but the Mothers of the Plaza de Mayo, who based their account on their own surveys and testimonies, and claimed that many families of the disappeared were too frightened to testify to officials of the government, have always insisted on the figure of 30,000 as a minimum.

3. The most famous of the junta's Jewish prisoners was Jacopo Timerman, whose account of his torture and imprisonment, titled *Prisoner without a Name, Cell*

without a Name, made international headlines and drew attention to the antisemitism of the regime.

4. Noemie de Álvarez Rojas, interview with Marguerite Bouvard, November 1990 (Bouvard 1994: 24–25).

5. See Bouvard (1994: 65–70) for accounts of women's mobilization.

6. See Ronald Dworkin's analysis in his introduction to the first U.S. edition of *Nunca Más* (1986: xi–xviii).

7. Laws 22.068 and 22.062. See Bouvard (1994: 139).

8. Noga Tarnopolsky, "Murdering Memory in Argentina," *New York Times,* December 12, 1994.

9. "In My Country," trans. Zoë Anglesey; in Partnoy (1988: 233–235).

10. See, e.g., Irigaray (1981), Kristeva (1983), and Butler (1993).

5. Plague

1. To quote Gilman again, "the appearance of the disease in the 1970s linked two (at that time) unrelated social concerns: first, the perception of the increase in sexually transmitted diseases in society . . . second, the growth of the public awareness of the homosexual emancipation movement, at least in large urban areas" (1988: 247).

2. Interview with Georgette King and Angel Sierra, Tomkins County AIDS-WORK office.

3. Susan Sontag's *Illness as Metaphor* (1978) is the most famous discussion of this rhetoric, but most commentators have noted the belligerence of the discussion about AIDS.

4. For a discussion of political AIDS funerals, see Watney (1994: chap. 28).

5. See, e.g., Woods (1992) and Muske (1989).

6. Spenser's "Astrophel," mourning the death of Sir Philip Sidney, Milton's "Lycidas," Shelley's "Adonais," lamenting the death of John Keats, and Tennyson's "In Memoriam" all contain what Woods describes as "the breathtaking revelation on which the change of mood from grief, through resignation, to hope is hinged" (1992: 160).

7. As David McCann has pointed out (1998), the poem distantly echoes Pericles' funeral oration in the mention of the parents, the city, and the first dead, though with a decidedly different emphasis.

8. On June 27, 1969, the police raided the Stonewall Inn in New York City, a gathering place for transvestites and drag queens. Amid shouts of "Gay Power," riots broke out. Most of the U.S. gay community saw "Stonewall" as the beginning of the movement for gay rights. Woods (1992: 156) comments on the sense of foreboding in the works of Larry Kramer and others during this period.

9. Woods (1992: 156) points to Lorca, Wilde, Crane, Rimbaud, and Pasolini as having died "pointless deaths" directly or indirectly because of their sexual orientation.

10. Hal Foster's op-ed piece in the *New York Times* (December 30, 1994), for example, criticized the contemporary United States as a "culture of abjection" in which victimhood is celebrated.

6. Memorials

1. The epigraph is quoted in Kim (1989: 263). In the 1948 Communist uprising, thousands of Cheju Island's population were massacred. Until recently, memory of the uprising had been erased from historical texts, and the massacre appeared to have been forgotten by the people of the island. According to Kim, the memory of the violent events of 1948 has been reconstituted through the people's belief in the spirits of the dead and in shamanic healing rituals (252).

2. Warren Hoge coined the term "People's Princess" in the *New York Times*, September 8, 1997, pp. 1, 10.

3. See Mosse (1990: 74–80) for examples of this Christian tradition in art, literature, and popular culture. See also Winter (1995: 85 ff.).

4. The term ANZACs was adopted during the campaign in the Dardanelles for the members of the Australian and New Zealand Army Corps.

5. Bruce Kapferer (1988: 155–161) notes the importance of the Australian ideology of drinking alcohol to the ANZAC ceremonies. As a source of potency, of the male egalitarian and individualist ethos that dominates Australia, drinking reinforces the symbolism of men marching in groups.

6. As Jon Stallworthy remarks (1984: xxiv–xxv), Henry Newbolt's poems, written at the turn of the century, reflected a new ethos of chivalry in England, one encouraged on the playing fields of Rugby and Eton:

> The river of death has brimmed his banks,
> And England's far, and Honour a name,
> But the voice of a schoolboy rallies the ranks:
> Play up! play up! and play the game!

7. It is not an original thought. As Silkin reminds us (1979: 30), Thomas Hardy used it effectively in his poem about the Boer War, "Drummer Hodge."

8. In the debate after the war, about whether bodies that had fallen on French soil should be brought home for burial or left where they lay, Lady Cecil wrote a letter of support to those who believed the war dead should remain in France. Her son had died in 1915, and she believed "he should remain with his men, asleep in the soil of France, which will become dearer to me because my son is buried there" (Winter 1995: 27).

9. Winter links his argument to Walter Benjamin's analysis of Paul Klee's *Angelus Novus*. Benjamin imagines the angel of history as looking toward the past, his body propelled backward toward the future by a violent storm.

10. Letter from Wilfred Owen to Osbert Sitwell, July 1918; quoted in Fussell (1975: 119).

11. This practice was particularly popular in Australia, where the lists were used to encourage enlistment and remained a permanent reminder to those who had failed to enlist, of their lack of patriotic fervor (Winter 1995: 80).

12. Although monuments to the First World War were often merely extended in England, there was a movement to commemorate individuals on the Second World War memorials and to include some warning about the dangers of war (Mosse 1990: 221). The National Land Fund, established in 1946, began acquiring country houses and tracts of land to be memorials to the war dead, open to the public.

13. Young (1993: xi). Young's thorough and illuminating study of the monuments and the issues raised by and during their construction is indispensable reading on the subject.

14. Having translated Kambanellis' memoir and worked with Theodorakis as a musician, I was invited to attend the ceremony. Kambanellis himself declined the invitation, warning me in a letter that "the Mauthausen you will see is not that Mauthausen."

15. Roskies compares the two sides of the monument with the two sides of popular writers like Isaac Bashevis Singer and Elie Wiesel, "who have allowed the tyranny of language and the politics of publishing to separate and dichotomize the knowledge of apocalypse and the statement of group survival" (1984: 302).

16. Rose (1996: 42) quotes a review of the film *Schindler's List* by Bryan Cheyette (*Times Literary Supplement*, February 18, 1994) in which he refers to "the difficulties inherent in representing the ineffable." The view of the Holocaust as "ineffable" is picked up in a response to the review which quotes Habermas in support. Rose objects to the rhetoric of Habermas' statement, which ends with the claim that "Auschwitz has changed the basis for the continuity of the conditions of life within history." In Rose's opinion, such claims of uniqueness and the inexpressible nature of the horror preclude knowledge and understanding, let alone mourning.

17. James Mayo (1988: 171) notes that the construction of Confederate monuments did not begin until the 1900s, when economic recovery allowed for expenditure on large-scale memorials.

18. As Mayo remarks, "The implicit message of the Green Beret memorial is that if the American people are unwilling to honor the Vietnam dead, then their comrades-in-arms will take up the cause. Until and unless another war adds the names of many other fallen Green Berets, this monument will be mainly regarded as a Vietnam War memorial" (1994: 199).

19. Tom Wolfe, for example, referred to it as "a perfect piece of sculptural orthodoxy for the early 1980s. The style of sculpture the mullahs today regard as most pure (most non-bourgeois) is minimal sculpture. The perfect minimal sculpture is an elemental, even banal form comprised solely of straight lines and flat planes" (1982).

References

Abel, Eugenius, ed. 1885. *Orphica*. Leipzig: G. Freytag.

Abu-Lughod, Lila. 1986. *Veiled Sentiments: Honor and Poetry in a Bedouin Society*. Berkeley: University of California Press.

Abu-Lughod, Lila, and Catherine A. Lutz. 1990. "Emotion, Discourse, and the Rhetoric of Emotions." In *Language and the Politics of Emotion*, ed. Catherine A. Lutz and Lila Abu-Lughod. Cambridge: Cambridge University Press, 1–23.

Aeschylus. 1993. *The Oresteia*. Trans. Richmond Lattimore. Chicago: University of Chicago Press.

Aggleton, Peter, Graham Hart, and Peter Davies, eds. 1989. *AIDS: Social Representations, Social Practices*. New York: Falmer Press.

Alexiou, Margaret. 1974. *The Ritual Lament in Greek Tradition*. Cambridge: Cambridge University Press.

Almond, Brenda, ed. 1990. *AIDS, a Moral Issue: The Ethical, Legal, and Social Aspects*. New York: St. Martin's Press.

Altman, Dennis. 1986. *AIDS in the Mind of America*. New York: Anchor Press/Doubleday.

Anderson, Benedict. 1991. *Imagined Communities*. London: Verso.

Appelfeld, Aharon. 1994. *Beyond Despair: Three Lectures and a Conversation with Philip Roth*. Trans. Jeffrey M. Green. New York: Fromm.

Apte, Mahadev L. 1985. *Humor and Laughter: An Anthropological Approach*. Ithaca: Cornell University Press.

Ariès, Philippe. 1974. *Western Attitudes to Death from the Middle Ages to the Present*. Trans. Patricia N. Ranum. Baltimore: Johns Hopkins Press.

——— 1977. *L'Homme devant la mort*. Paris: Editions du Seuil.

Arroyo, Rane. 1995. "Los Angeles: Two Chapters from the Book of Lamentations." In Rodríguez Matos, 18–19.

Astrada, Etelvina. 1988. "In My Country." In *You Can't Drown the Fire: Latin American Women Writing in Exile*, ed. Alicia P. Portnoy. Pittsburgh: Cleis, 233–235.

Auden, W. H. 1989. *Selected Poems*, ed. Edward Mendelson. New York: Vintage Books.

Automedon. Epigram (12.34). In *The Greek Anthology*. Vol. 4. Ed. W. R. Paton. Cambridge, Mass.: Harvard University Press, 297.

Bakhtin, Mikhail. 1981. *The Dialogic Imagination: Four Essays*. Trans. M. Holquist and C. Emerson. Austin: University of Texas Press.

——— 1984a. *Rabelais and His World*. Trans. Helene Iswolski. Bloomington: University of Indiana Press.

——— 1984b. *Problems of Dostoevsky's Poetics*. Trans. C. Emerson. Minneapolis: University of Minnesota Press.

Becker, Ernst. 1973. *The Denial of Death*. New York: Free Press.

Bedford, Errol. 1986. "Emotions and Statements about Them." In *The Social Construction of Emotions*, ed. Rom Harré. Oxford: Blackwell, 15–31.

Behar, Ruth. 1993. *Translated Woman: Crossing the Border with Esperanza's Story*. Boston: Beacon Press.

Bell, Marvin. 1989. "The Plague." In Klein.

Benjamin, Walter. 1968. *Illuminations*. Trans. H. Zohn. New York: Harcourt, Brace and World.

Bergman, David. 1992. "Larry Kramer and the Rhetoric of AIDS." In *AIDS: The Literary Response*, ed. Emmanuel S. Nelson. New York: Twayne, 175–186.

Bernal, Martin. 1987. *Black Athena: The Afro-Asiatic Roots of Classical Civilization*. Vol. 1: *The Fabrication of Ancient Greece, 1875–1985*. London: Free Association Books.

Bernstein, Michael André. 1983. "When the Carnival Turns Bitter: Preliminary Reflections upon the Abject Hero." *Critical Inquiry* 10: 283–385.

Black, David. 1985. *The Plague Years: A Chronicle of AIDS, the Epidemic of Our Time*. New York: Simon and Schuster.

Bloch, Maurice, and Jonathan Parry. 1982. *Death and the Regeneration of Life*. Cambridge: Cambridge University Press.

Borges, Jorge Luis. 1998. "Possession of Yesterday." Trans. N. S. Araus. In *World Poetry: An Anthology of Verse from Antiquity to Our Time*, ed. K. Washburn et al. New York: W. W. Norton, 1022.

Borneman, John. 1996. "Until Death Do Us Part: Marriage/Death in Anthropological Discourse." *American Ethnologist* 23: 215–235.

——— 1997. "Caring and Being Cared For: Displacing Marriage, Kinship, Gender, and Sexuality." *International Social Science Journal* 154: 573–584.

Bourke, Angela. 1988. "The Irish Traditional Lament and the Grieving Process." *Women's Studies International Forum* 11: 287–291.

——— 1993. "More in Anger than in Sorrow." In *Feminist Messages: Coding in Women's Folk Culture*, ed. J. N. Radner. Urbana: University of Illinois Press, 160–181.

Bouvard, Marguerite Guzman. 1994. *Revolutionizing Motherhood: The Mothers of the Plaza de Mayo*. Wilmington, Del.: Scholarly Resources.

Briggs, Charles. "Since I Am a Woman I Will Chastise My Relatives: Gender, Reported Speech, and the (Re)production of Social Relations in Warao Ritual Wailing." *American Ethnologist* 19: 337–361.

———— "Personal Sentiments and Polyphonic Voices in Warao Women's Ritual Wailing: Music and Poetics in a Critical and Collective Discourse." *American Anthropologist* 95: 929–957.

Briggs, Jean. 1970. *Never in Anger.* Cambridge, Mass.: Harvard University Press.

Brooke, Rupert. 1979. "The Soldier." In *The Penguin Book of First World War Poetry*, ed. Jon Silkin. Harmondsworth: Penguin.

Broumas, Olga. 1989. *Perpetua.* Port Townsend, Wash.: Copper Canyon Press.

Browning, Elizabeth Barrett. 1988. "Grief." In *Selected Poems of Elizabeth Barrett Browning*, ed. Margaret Forster. London: Chatto and Windus.

Burkard, Michael. 1989. "Almost to Jesus." In Klein.

Butler, Judith. 1993. *Bodies That Matter: On the Discursive Limits of Sex.* New York: Routledge.

Byron, George Gordon, Lord. 1957. "Childe Harold's Pilgrimage." In *The Poetical Works of Byron.* Oxford: Oxford University Press.

———— 1972. *Selected Prose.* Harmondsworth: Penguin.

Camon, Ferdinando. 1989. *Conversations with Primo Levi.* Trans. John Shepley. Marlboro, Vt.: Marlboro Press.

Cannandine, D. 1981. "War and Death: Grief and Mourning in Modern Britain." In *Mirrors of Mortality: Studies in the Social History of Death*, ed. J. Whaley. London: Bedford Square Press, 182–242.

Caraveli, Ana. 1986. "The Bitter Wounding: The Lament as Social Protest in Rural Greece." In *Gender and Power in Rural Greece*, ed. Jill Dubisch. Princeton: Princeton University Press, 169–194.

Caraveli-Chaves, Ana. 1980. "Bridge between Worlds: The Greek Woman's Lament as Communicative Event." *Journal of American Folklore* 93: 129–157.

Carrière, Jean-Claude. *Le Carnivale et la politique.* Paris: Centre des recherches d'histoire ancienne.

Carson, Anne. 1998. *Eros the Bittersweet: An Essay.* Princeton: Princeton University Press.

Carter, Eric, and Simon Watney. 1989. *Taking Liberties: AIDS and Cultural Politics.* London: Serpent's Tail.

Castillo, Ana. 1995a. "A García Lorca más a algunas otros." In Rodríguez Matos.

———— 1995b. "On the Meaning of Things." In Rodríguez Matos.

Charlwood, Don. 1990. *Marching as to War.* Hawthorn, Australia: Hudson.

Clark, David, ed. 1993. *The Sociology of Death: Theory, Culture, Practice.* Oxford: Blackwell.

Clark, Manning. 1969. *A Short History of Australia.* London: Heinemann.

Cohen, Anthony. 1994. *Self-Consciousness: An Alternative Anthropology of Identity.* London: Routledge.

Connor, Dan. 1991. "AIDS and the Art of Living." In Hadas, 21.

Cox, Harvey. 1969. *The Feast of Fools: A Theological Essay on Festivity and Fantasy.* Cambridge, Mass.: Harvard University Press.

Creeley, Robert. 1989. "Plague." In Klein, 56.

Croce, Arlene. 1994/1995. "Discussing the Undiscussable." *New Yorker*, December 28–January 4, 54–60.

Cuisenier, Jean. 1986. "Lamentations et rituels de deuil en Roumanie." In *Les Rites de passage aujourd'hui: Actes du colloque de Neuchatel 1981.* Lausanne: L'Age d'homme.

D'Andrade, Roy, and Claudia Strauss, eds. 1992. *Human Motives and Cultural Models.* Cambridge: Cambridge University Press.

Danforth, Loring. 1982. *The Death Rituals of Rural Greece.* Princeton: Princeton University Press.

Davis, Peter (director). 1974. *Hearts and Minds.* RBC Films.

Desjarlais, Robert R. 1992. *Body and Emotion: The Aesthetics of Illness and Healing in the Nepal Himalayas.* Philadelphia: University of Pennsylvania Press.

Detienne, Marcel. 1977. *The Gardens of Adonis: Spices in Greek Mythology.* Trans. Janet Lloyd. Atlantic Highlands, N.J.: Humanities Press.

Dhomhnaill, Nuala Ni. 1995. "Why I Choose to Write in Irish: The Corpse That Sits Up and Talks Back." *New York Times Book Review*, January 8.

Doty, Mark. 1989. "Tiara." In Klein.

Douglas, Mary. 1966. *Purity and Danger: An Analysis of Pollution and Taboo.* London: Routledge and Kegan Paul.

DuBois, Page. 1991. *Torture and Truth.* New York: Routledge.

Eassie, W. 1875. *The Cremation of the Dead: Its History and Bearings upon Public Health.* London: Smith, Elder.

Ebersole, Gary L. 1989. *Ritual Poetry and the Politics of Death in Early Japan.* Princeton: Princeton University Press.

Edwards, Anthony T. 1989. "Historicizing the Popular Grotesque." In *Theater and Society in the Classical World*, ed. R. Scodel. Ann Arbor: University of Michigan Press.

Ehrhart, W. D. 1993. "POW/MIA." In Franklin 1993, 199–200.

Elias, Norbert. 1985. *The Loneliness of the Dying.* Trans. Edmund Jeffcott. Oxford: Blackwell.

Epstein, Steven. 1996. *AIDS, Activism, and the Politics of Knowledge.* Berkeley: University of California Press.

Erikson, Kai. 1976. *Everything in Its Path.* New York: Simon and Schuster.

Evans, E. Estyn. 1957. *Irish Folk Ways.* London: Routledge and Kegan Paul.

Feld, Steven. 1982. *Sound and Sentiment: Birds, Weeping, Poetics, and Song in Kululi Expression.* Philadelphia: University of Pennsylvania Press.

Felman, Shoshana, and Dori Laub. 1992. *Testimony: Crises of Witnessing in Literature, Psychology, and History.* New York: Routledge.

Field, Edward. 1989. "The Veteran." In Klein.

Fisher, Josephine. 1989. *Mothers of the Disappeared.* Boston: South End Press.

Fletcher, James. 1984. "Homosexuality: Kick and Kickback." *Southern Medical Journal* 77: 149–150.

Foucault, Michel. 1980. *Power/Knowledge: Selected Interviews and Other Writings*, ed. and trans. Colin Gordon. New York: Pantheon.

Franklin, H. Bruce. 1991. "The POW/MIA Myth." *Atlantic Monthly*, December, 45–81.

——— 1993. *M.I.A., or Mythmaking in America.* New Brunswick, N.J.: Rutgers University Press.

French, Howard. 1996. "Among the Funeral Rites, a Lively Dating Game." *New York Times*, November 4, p. A4.

Freud, Sigmund. 1957. "Mourning and Melancholia" (1917). In *The Standard Edition of the Complete Psychological Works*, ed. and trans. James Strachey. Vol. 14. London: Hogarth Press.

——— 1960. "Jokes and Their Relation to the Unconscious" (1905). In *The Standard Edition of the Complete Psychological Works*, ed. and trans. James Strachey. Vol. 8. London: Hogarth Press.

——— 1963. "A Mythological Parallel to a Visual Obsession" (1916). In *Collected Papers*, ed. Philip Rieff. Vol. 4. New York: Collier Books.

Fussell, Paul. 1975. *The Great War and Modern Memory*. New York: Oxford University Press.

García, Ramon. 1995a. "All the Poets Are Dying." In Rodríguez Matos, 91.

——— 1995b. "Foreigner." In Rodríguez Matos, 93.

——— 1995c. "Life Does Not Belong to Me." In Rodríguez Matos, 92.

Garland, Robert. 1985. *The Greek Way of Death*. Ithaca: Cornell University Press.

Geertz, Clifford. 1960. *The Religion of Java*. New York: Free Press.

Gellman, Barton. 1995. "Israelis Split over Soldiers' Tears." *Guardian Weekly/Washington Post*, November 5, p. 16.

Gilman, Sander L. 1988. *Disease and Representation: Images of Illness from Madness to AIDS*. Ithaca: Cornell University Press.

Giordano, Tony. 1991. "Death Is Abstract." In Hadas.

Glaser, B. G., and A. L. Strauss. 1965a. *Awareness of Dying*. Chicago: Aldine.

——— 1965b. "Temporal Aspects of Dying as a Non-Scheduled Status Passage." *American Journal of Sociology* 71: 48–59.

——— 1968. *Time for Dying*. Chicago: Aldine.

——— 1971. *Status Passage*. London: Routledge and Kegan Paul.

Gorer, Geoffrey. 1965. *Death, Grief, and Mourning*. London: Cresset.

Greenberg, Uri Zvi. 1994. "We Were Not Like Dogs." Trans. Robert Mezey. In Teichman and Leder.

Groff, David. 1989. "A Scene of the Crime." In Klein.

Gunn, Thom. 1989a. "The Missing." In Klein.

——— 1989b. "To the Dead Owner of a Gym." In Klein.

Hadas, Rachel. 1991. *Unending Dialogue: Voices from an AIDS Poetry Workshop*. London: Faber and Faber.

Haines, Harry. 1986. "What Kind of War?" *Critical Studies in Mass Communication* 3, no. 1 (March): 10.

Halperin, David M., John Winkler, and Froma Zeitlin, eds. 1990. *Before Sexuality: The Construction of the Erotic Experience in the Ancient Greek World*. Princeton: Princeton University Press.

Harré, Rom, ed. 1986. *The Social Construction of Emotions*. Oxford: Blackwell.

Hawkins, Peter. 1993. "Naming Names: The Art of Memory and the NAMES Project AIDS Quilt." *Critical Inquiry* 19: 752–779.

Helms, Lorraine R. 1997. *Seneca by Candlelight and Other Stories of Renaissance Drama*. Philadelphia: University of Pennsylvania Press.

Hertz, R. 1960. *Death and the Right Hand*. Trans. R. Needham and C. Needham. Glencoe, Ill.: Free Press.

Herzfeld, Michael. 1979. "Exploring a Metaphor of Exposure." *Journal of American Folklore* 92: 285–301.

——— 1993. "In Defiance of Destiny: The Management of Time and Gender at a Cretan Funeral." *American Ethnologist* 20: 241–255.

Hirsch, Edward. 1989. "And Who Will Look upon Our Testimony?" In Klein.

Hockey, Jenny. 1993. "The Acceptable Face of Human Grieving." In *The Sociology of Death: Theory, Culture, Practice*, ed. David Clark. Oxford: Blackwell, 129–148.

Hoge, Warren. 1997. "Flower Power." *New York Times*, September 5.

Holleran, David. 1988. *Ground Zero*. New York: William Morrow.

Holst-Warhaft, Gail. 1992. *Dangerous Voices: Women's Laments and Greek Literature*. London: Routledge.

Homer. 1974. *The Iliad*. Trans. Robert Fitzgerald. Garden City, N.Y.: Doubleday/Anchor.

Huntington, Richard, and Peter Metcalf. 1979. *Celebrations of Death: The Anthropology of Mortuary Ritual*. Cambridge: Cambridge University Press.

Indochina Newsletter. 1993. No. 2.

Illich, Ivan. 1977. *Limits to Medicine: Medical Nemesis and the Expropriation of Health*. Harmondsworth: Penguin.

Irigaray, Luce. 1981. *Le Corps-à-corps avec la mère*. Montreal: Editions de la pleine lune.

Izard, Carol E., Jerome Kagan, and Robert B. Zajonc, eds. 1984. *Emotions, Cognition, and Behavior*. Cambridge: Cambridge University Press.

Johnson, Fenton. 1994. "Death into Life." *New York Times*, December 24, p. 25.

Kambanellis, Iakovos. 1995. *Mauthausen*. Trans. Gail Holst-Warhaft. Athens: Kedros.

Kane, Robert (director). 1991. *Lament of a Warrior's Wife*. Washington, D.C.: Asia Resource Center.

Kapferer, Bruce. 1988. *Legends of People, Myths of State: Violence, Intolerance, and Political Culture in Sri Lanka and Australia*. Washington, D.C.: Smithsonian Institution.

Karp, Ivan. 1987. "Laughter at Marriage: Subversion in Performance." In *Transformations of African Marriage*, ed. David Parkin and David Nyamwaya. Manchester: Manchester University Press, 137–154.

Kassis, Kyriakos. 1979–1981. *Mirologhia tis Mesa Manis* [Laments of Inner Mani]. 3 vols. Athens.

Kastenbaum, Robert J. 1975. "Is Death a Life Crisis? On the Confrontation with Death in Theory and Practice." In *Life-span Developmental Psychology*, ed. N. Datan and L. H. Ginsburg. New York: Academic Press, 19–50.

Kaufman, Nikolao, and Dimitrina Kaufman. 1988. *Pogrebalni i drugi opllakvariia v. Bulgariia* [Burial and other laments in Bulgaria]. Sofia: Izd-vo na Bulgarskaba akademiia na naukite.

Kaufmann, Walter. 1976. *Existentialism, Religion, and Death*. London: New English Library.

Khouri, Nagib. 1993. *Le Feu et la cendre: Travail de deuil et rites funéraires dans un village libanais*. Paris: L'Harmattan.

Kim, Seong Nae. 1989. "Lamentations of the Dead: The Historical Imagery of Violence on Cheju Island, South Korea." *Journal of Ritual Studies* 3: 252–317.

Kipling, Rudyard. 1996. "Recessional." In *The Norton Anthology of Poetry*, ed. M. Ferguson, M. J. Salter, and J. Stallworthy. New York: W. W. Norton.

Kiss, Lajos, and Benjamin Rajeczky, eds. 1966. *Corpus Musicae Popularis Hungaricae*. Vol. 5. Budapest: Akademiai Kiado.

Kitayama, Shinobu, and Hazel Rose Markus, eds. 1994. *Emotion and Culture: Empirical Studies of Mutual Influence*. Washington, D.C.: American Psychological Association.

Klein, Michael, ed. 1989. *Poets for Life: Seventy-six Poets Respond to AIDS.* New York: Crown.

Kramer, Larry. 1978. *Faggots.* New York: Random House.

——— 1985. *The Normal Heart.* New York: New American Library.

——— 1989. *Reports from the Holocaust: The Making of an AIDS Activist.* New York: St. Martin's.

Krinagorus. 1983. Epigram (7.376). In *The Greek Anthology,* ed. W. R. Paton. Vol. 2. Cambridge, Mass.: Harvard University Press, 200.

Kristeva, Julia. 1983. *Histoires d'amour.* Paris: Denoël.

Kübler-Ross, Elizabeth. 1969. *On Death and Dying.* New York: Macmillan.

——— 1981. *Living with Death and Dying.* New York: Macmillan.

Kundera, Milan. 1980. *The Book of Laughter and Forgetting.* Trans. Michael Henry Heim. New York: Penguin.

LaCapra, Dominick. 1998. *History and Memory after Auschwitz.* Ithaca: Cornell University Press.

Leavitt, John. 1996. "Meaning and Feeling in the Anthropology of Emotions." *American Ethnologist* 23: 514–539.

Levi, Primo. 1961. *Survival in Auschwitz.* New York: Collier.

Levin, Phillis. 1989. "What the Intern Saw." In Klein.

Levy, Isidore. 1936. "Autour d'un roman mythologique Egyptien." In *Mélanges Franz Cumont. Annuaire de l'Institut de philologie et d'histoire orientales et Slaves.* Vol. 4. Brussels: Secrétariat de l'Institut.

Levy, Robert 1983. "Introduction: Self and Emotion." *Ethos* 11: 128–134.

Littlewood, Jane. 1993. "The Denial of Death and Rites of Passage in Contemporary Societies." *Sociological Review* 41: 69–84.

Loraux, Nicole. 1998. *Mothers in Mourning.* Trans. Corinne Pache. Ithaca: Cornell University Press.

Lutz, Catherine A. 1988. *Unnatural Emotions: Everyday Sentiments on a Micronesian Atoll and Their Challenge to Western Theory.* Chicago: University of Chicago Press.

——— 1990. "Engendered Emotion: Gender, Power, and Rhetoric of Emotional Control in American Discourse." In *Language and the Politics of Emotion,* ed. Catherine A. Lutz and Lila Abu-Lughod. Cambridge: Cambridge University Press, 69–91.

Lutz, Catherine A., and Geoffrey M. White. 1986. "The Anthropology of Emotion." *Annual Reviews in Anthropology* 15: 405–436.

Lynch, Owen M., ed. 1990. *Divine Passions: The Social Construction of Emotion in India.* Berkeley: University of California Press.

Lynch, Thomas. 1994. "The Undertaking." *London Review of Books,* December 22.

Macintosh, Fiona. 1994. *Dying Acts: Death in Ancient Greece and Modern Irish Tragic Drama.* Cork: Cork University Press.

Mariah, Paul. 1989. "The Brothers Grief." In Klein.

Marris, P. 1986. *Loss and Change: A Sociology of Ageing and Dying.* Rev. ed. London: Routledge and Kegan Paul.

Martínez, Tomás Eloy. 1996. *Santa Evita.* Trans. Helen Lane. New York: Alfred A. Knopf.

Mayo, James. 1988. *War Memorials as Political Landscape: The American Experience and Beyond.* New York: Praeger.

McCann, David R. 1998. "The Korean War and American Popular Culture." In

America's Wars in Asia: A Cultural Approach to History and Memory, ed. Philip West, Steven Levine, and Jackie Hiltz. Armonk, N.Y.: M. E. Sharpe.

McConnell, Malcolm. 1995. *Inside Hanoi's Secret Archives: Solving the MIA Mystery.* New York: Simon and Schuster.

Mercier, Vivian. 1962. *The Irish Comic Tradition.* Oxford: Clarendon Press.

Meyers, Steven. 1998a. "Pentagon Seeks to Open Unknowns' Tomb." *New York Times*, April 28.

——— 1998b. "Remains of Vietnam Soldier Are Ordered Exhumed from Tomb of Unknowns." *New York Times*, May 8.

Miller, J. 1974. *Aberfan: A Disaster and Its Aftermath.* London: Constable.

Mohr, Richard D. 1992. "Text(ile): Reading the NAMES Project's AIDS Quilt." In *Gay Ideas: Outing and Other Controversies*, ed. Richard Mohr. Boston: Beacon Press, 105–128.

Monette, Paul. 1988. *Borrowed Time: An AIDS Memoir.* New York: Harcourt Brace Jovanovich.

——— 1989. "Your Sightless Days." In Klein.

Morris, Henry. 1938. "Irish Wake Games." *Béaloideas: The Journal of the Folklore of Ireland* 8: 123–141.

Mosse, George. 1990. *Fallen Soldiers: Reshaping the Memory of the World Wars.* Oxford: Oxford University Press.

Murphy, Timothy F., and Suzanne Porier, eds. 1993. *Writing AIDS: Gay Literature, Language, and Analysis.* New York: Columbia University Press.

Muske, Carol. 1989. "Re-writing the Elegy." In Klein.

Needham, Rodney. 1969. "Percussion and Transition." *Man*, n.s. 2: 606–614.

Nelson, Emmanuel S. 1992. *AIDS: The Literary Response.* New York: Twayne.

Nguyen Thi Vinh. 1959. "Exhumation." Trans. Le Van Hoan. Saigon: International P.E.N. Vietnam Centre.

Northcliffe, Lord. 1916. Editorial. *The Times* (London), July 3.

The Norton Anthology of Poetry. 1996. Edited by Margaret Ferguson, Mary Jo Salter, and Jon Stallworthy. 4th ed. New York: W. W. Norton.

Nunca Más: Report of the Argentine National Committee on the Disappeared. 1986. Edited by Ronald Dworkin. New York: Farrar, Straus and Giroux in association with the Index on Censorship (London).

Olender, Maurice. 1985. "Aspects de Baubo: Textes et contextes antiques." *Revue de l'histoire des religions* 202: 3–55.

O'Súilleabháin, Sean. 1967. *Irish Wake Amusements.* Cork: Mercier Press.

Padel, Ruth. 1995. *Whom the Gods Destroy: Elements of Greek and Tragic Madness.* Princeton: Princeton University Press.

Padgug, Robert A. 1989. "Gay Villain, Gay Hero: Homosexuality and the Social Construction of AIDS." In *Passion and Power: Sexuality in History*, ed. K. Peiss, C. Simmons, and R. Padgug. Philadelphia: Temple University Press.

Partnoy, Alicia P., ed. 1988. *You Can't Drown the Fire: Latin American Women Writing in Exile.* Pittsburgh: Cleis.

Partridge, Angela. 1980. "Wild Men and Wailing Women." *Eigse* 18: 25–37.

Pascal, Blaise. 1954. *Pensées.* In *Oeuvres complètes*, ed. J. Chevalier. Paris: Bibliothèque de la Pléiade.

Philippi, Donald, trans. 1969. *Kojiki.* Princeton: Princeton University Press.

Picano, Felice. 1989a. "After the Funeral." In Klein.

———— 1989b. "Three Men Speak to Me." In ibid.

Picard, C. 1927. "L'Épisode de Baubo dans les mystères d'Eleusis." *Revue de l'histoire des religions* 95: 220–255.

Plato. 1926. *Laws*, ed. and trans. R. G. Bury. London: Heinemann, Loeb Classical Library.

———— 1934. *Republic*, ed. and trans. Paul Shoney. London: Heinemann, Loeb Classical Library.

Prim, J. G. A. 1853. "Olden Popular Pastimes in Kilkenny." *Journal of the Royal Society of Antiquaries of Ireland* 2: 319–335.

Rank, Otto. 1945. *Will Therapy and Truth and Reality*. New York: Alfred A. Knopf.

Reed, Joseph D. 1995. "The Sexuality of Adonis." *Classical Antiquity* 14: 317–374.

Reinach, Salomon. 1912, 1923. *Cultes, mythes et religions*. Vols. 4 and 5. Paris: Ernest Leroux.

Reston, James, Jr. 1995. "The Monument Glut." *New York Times Magazine*, September 10.

Richardson, Nicholas James, ed. 1974. *Homeric Hymn to Demeter*. Oxford: Oxford University Press.

Richardson, R. 1988. *Death, Destitution, and the Destitute*. London: Routledge.

Rodríguez Matos, Carlos A., ed. *POESÍdA: An Anthology of AIDS Poetry from the United States, Latin America, and Spain*. Jackson Heights, N.Y.: Ollantay Press.

Rosaldo, Michelle Zimbalist. 1980. *Knowledge and Passion: Ilongot Notions of Self and Social Life*. Cambridge: Cambridge University Press.

———— 1984. "Toward an Anthropology of Self and Feeling." In *Culture Theory: Essays on Mind, Self, and Emotion*, ed. Richard A. Shweder and Robert A. Levine. Cambridge: Cambridge University Press, 137–158.

Rosaldo, Renato I. 1984. "Grief and a Headhunter's Rage: On the Cultural Force of Emotions." In *Text, Play, and Story: 1983 Proceedings of the American Ethnological Society*, ed. Edward M. Bruner. Washington, D.C.: American Ethnological Society, 178–195.

Rose, Gillian. 1996. *Mourning Becomes the Law: Philosophy and Representation*. Cambridge: Cambridge University Press.

Rosenblatt, Paul, R. Patricia Walsh, and Douglas Jackson. 1976. *Grief and Mourning in Cross-Cultural Perspective*. New Haven: Human Relations Area Files Press.

Roskies, David G. 1984. *Against the Apocalypse: Responses to Catastrophe in Modern Jewish Culture*. Cambridge, Mass.: Harvard University Press.

Sacks, Peter. 1985. *The English Elegy*. Baltimore: Johns Hopkins University Press.

Sáenz, Benjamín Alire. 1995. "Poem." In Rodríguez Matos.

Scarry, Elaine. 1985. *The Body in Pain: The Making and Unmaking of the World*. New York: Oxford University Press.

Schieffelin, Edward. 1976. *The Sorrow of the Lonely and the Burning of the Dancers*. New York: St. Martin's Press.

Seremetakis, C. Nadia. 1991. *The Last Word: Women, Death, and Divination in Inner Mani*. Chicago: University of Chicago Press.

Silkin, Jon, ed. 1979. *The Penguin Book of First World War Poetry*. Harmondsworth: Penguin.

Sontag, Susan. 1978. *Illness as Metaphor*. New York: Farrar, Straus and Giroux.

Spenser, Edmund. 1934. *A View of the Present State of Ireland*, ed. W. L. Renwick. London: E. Partridge, Scholastic Press.

Stallworthy, Jon, ed. 1984. *The Oxford Book of War Poetry*. Oxford: Oxford University Press.

—— 1986. *The Poems of Wilfred Owen*. New York: W. W. Norton.

Stanihurst, Richard. 1979. "A Plain and Perfect Description of Ireland." In *Holinshed's Irish Chronicle: The Historie of Irelande from the First Inhabitation Thereof unto the Yeare 1509/Collected by Raphaelle Holinshed & Continued till the Yeare 1547 by Richarde Stanyhurst*, ed. L. Miller and E. Power. Atlantic Highlands, N.J.: Humanities Press.

Stehle, E. 1990. "Sappho's Gaze: Fantasies of a Goddess and a Young Man." *Differences* 2: 88–125.

Sturken, Marita. 1997. *Tangled Memories: The Vietnam War, the AIDS Epidemic, and the Politics of Remembering*. Berkeley: University of California Press.

Sutterlin, Christa. 1989. "Universals in Apotropaic Symbolism: A Behavioral and Comparative Approach to Some Medieval Sculptures." *Leonardo* 22: 65–74.

Synge, J. M. 1911. *The Aran Islands*. Reprint, St. Paul: Blackstaff Press, 1988.

Teichman, Milton, and Sharon Leder, eds. 1994. *Truth and Lamentation: Stories and Poems on the Holocaust*. Urbana: University of Illinois Press.

Thomas, Dylan. 1996. "A Refusal to Mourn the Death, by Fire, of a Child in London." In *The Norton Antholology of Poetry*.

Thucydides. 1988. *History of the Peloponnesian War*. Trans. Rex Warner. London: Penguin Books.

Tolbert, Elizabeth. 1990a. "Magico-religious Power and Gender in the Karelian Lament." In *Music, Culture, and Gender*, ed. Marcia Herndon and Suzanne Ziegler. Berlin: Institute for Comparative Music Studies, 41–56.

—— 1990b. "Women Cry with Words: Symbolization of Affect in the Karelian Lament." *Yearbook for Traditional Music* 22: 80–105.

Trigger, Bruce G. 1976. *The Children of Aataentsic: A History of the Huron People to 1660*. Montreal: McGill–Queens University Press.

Tsouderou, Yiannis Efthyvoulos. 1976. *Kritika miroloyia* [Cretan laments]. Athens.

Turner, Victor. 1967. *The Forest of Symbols*. Ithaca: Cornell University Press.

—— 1969. *The Ritual Process*. Ithaca: Cornell University Press.

Van Gennep, Arnold. 1960. *The Rites of Passage*. Trans. Monika B. Vizendom and Gabrielle L. Caffee. Chicago: University of Chicago Press.

Virgil. 1983. *The Aeneid*. Trans. Robert Fitzgerald. New York: Random House.

Watney, Simon. 1994. *Practices of Freedom: Selected Writings on HIV/AIDS*. Durham, N.C.: Duke University Press.

Wellenkamp, Jane. 1988. "Notions of Grief and Catharsis among the Toraja." *American Ethnologist* 15: 486–500.

Whelan, Kevin. 1988. "The Regional Impact of Irish Catholicism, 1700–1850." In *Common Ground: Essays on the Historical Geography of Ireland*, ed. William J. Smyth and Kevin Whelan. Cork: Cork University Press.

White, Geoffrey. 1990. "Moral Discourse and the Rhetoric of Emotion." In *Language and the Politics of Emotion*, ed. Catherine A. Lutz and Lila Abu-Lughod. Cambridge: Cambridge University Press, 46–68.

Winkler, John J. 1990. *The Constraints of Desire: The Anthropology of Sex and Gender in Ancient Greece*. London: Routledge and Kegan Paul.

Winter, Jay. 1995. *Sites of Memory, Sites of Mourning*. Cambridge: Cambridge University Press.

Witoszek, Nina. 1987. "Ireland, a Funerary Culture?" *Studies* (Dublin) 76: 206–215.

Wolfe, Tom. 1982. "Art Disputes War: The Battle of the Vietnam Memorial." *Washington Post*, October 13.

Woods, Gregory. 1989. "AIDS to Remembrance: The Uses of Elegy." In *AIDS: The Literary Response*, ed. Emmanuel S. Nelson. New York: Twayne, 155–166.

Young, James E. 1993. *The Texture of Memory: Holocaust Memorials and Meaning*. New Haven: Yale University Press.

Index